IMAGES
of America

ANTIETAM NATIONAL
BATTLEFIELD

On the Cover: The 20th New York's second monument on the Antietam battlefield marks their position during an attack toward the West Woods on the afternoon of September 17. During the assault, the regiment lost 145 men killed, wounded, missing, or captured. Forty-eight veterans dedicated this monument in 1912 on the 50th anniversary of the Battle of Antietam. (Courtesy of the National Park Service.)

IMAGES of America
ANTIETAM NATIONAL BATTLEFIELD

Kevin R. Pawlak

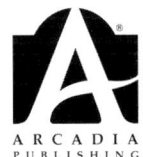

Copyright © 2019 by Kevin R. Pawlak
ISBN 978-1-4671-0348-0

Published by Arcadia Publishing
Charleston, South Carolina

Printed in the United States of America

Library of Congress Control Number: 2019930553

For all general information, please contact Arcadia Publishing:
Telephone 843-853-2070
Fax 843-853-0044
E-mail sales@arcadiapublishing.com
For customer service and orders:
Toll-Free 1-888-313-2665

Visit us on the Internet at www.arcadiapublishing.com

Contents

Acknowledgments		6
Introduction		7
1.	The Battle	11
2.	The Cemetery	37
3.	The Battlefield	49
4.	The Memorial	93
Bibliography		127

Acknowledgments

No book is possible without the support and help of many people.

My editor, Caroline Anderson, was a pleasure to work with and was always helpful and patient when it came to answering my questions.

Numerous people helped me locate enough photographs to complete this project. Lori Wheeler at the US Army Heritage and Education Center in Carlisle, Pennsylvania, provided me with high-quality images from the extensive Military Order of the Loyal Legion of the United States (MOLLUS) Collection housed there. Stephanie Gray and Keith Snyder at Antietam National Battlefield guided me through the park's extensive and valuable photograph collection. At the John F. Kennedy Presidential Library and Museum in Massachusetts, I want to thank Maryrose Grossman for sending me images of President Kennedy's 1963 visit to the Antietam battlefield. She also pointed me toward sources covering the president's trip. John Frye, the historian and curator at the Washington County Free Library's Western Maryland Room, gave me free rein with their photographs of Antietam National Battlefield, for which I am very grateful.

Dr. Richard Quest read the manuscript and provided guidance throughout the process, all of which was useful and helpful.

Lastly, I want to thank my wife, Kristen, for reading the manuscript and allowing me to take on this project, even though she knew it would mean time in front of my computer and away from her. She is always supportive, and I cannot thank her enough.

Introduction

On the evening of September 16, 1862, Union general Joseph Hooker rode among his men to conduct a personal reconnaissance of the enemy's lines in front of him. He was well aware of the clash of arms about to begin on the morrow. Satisfied with the situation at the front, Hooker rode to the rear to a barn he called his headquarters. The general dismounted from his horse, stepped into the barn, and before bedding down for a few hours, turned to his staff officers and said, "We are through for to-night, but to-morrow we fight the battle that will decide the fate of the Republic."

By the summer of 1862, the United States of America was losing the Civil War. Earlier that year, it came close to achieving the opposite outcome. Federal forces under Maj. Gen. George B. McClellan's command took position less than 10 miles from the gates of Richmond, Virginia, the Confederacy's capital. Some northern newspapers predicted that the rebellion would be crushed by the Fourth of July. Then suddenly, a Confederate army under the command of Gen. Robert E. Lee ferociously attacked the threatening enemy army, forcing it away from Richmond. This campaign cheered the Confederacy's population and propelled a major Confederate offensive in Virginia.

About that time, a second Union army led by John Pope began approaching Richmond on the overland route between the Confederate capital and Washington, DC. Pope brought a different and harder style of war against Virginians, a philosophy falling more in line with Abraham Lincoln's view of the conflict. From the mainstream Northern perspective, the war was about bringing the rebellious Southern states back into the Union. But from its outset, an ever-louder group of radicals in the Republican Party—Lincoln's party—called for the abolition of slavery as not only a means to end the war, but also as a prerequisite for peace. Lincoln, thanks to pressure from members of his party, newly escaped slaves, and his personal antislavery views began to consider taking the Federal war effort a step further.

While Pope's army snaked its way into central Virginia, on July 22, 1862, Abraham Lincoln met with his cabinet and showed them a preliminary draft of a proclamation emancipating the Confederacy's slaves. Lincoln stood firm on the issue, telling his cabinet members that he "had not called them together to ask their advice." The president's advisors voiced both approval and dissatisfaction, but Lincoln did not budge from his decision. However, when Secretary of State William Seward chimed in, Lincoln listened. Seward supported the proclamation, but believed to announce it now to the country from a position of weakness with the war going against them would do no good. Instead, Seward suggested, wait "until the eagle of victory takes his flight," then follow the good news with the Emancipation Proclamation. Lincoln concurred and agreed to wait for a victory.

Lincoln's wait was longer than he anticipated. John Pope and Robert E. Lee came to grips in central Virginia. Weeks of maneuvering for position—all of which served the Confederates well as Pope withdrew farther north—ended in late August along the banks of Bull Run, a stream approximately 25 miles from the front door of the Executive Mansion. For three days, August 28, 29, and 30, 1862, Pope's and Lee's soldiers battled. On August 30, Confederates unexpectedly slammed into a weakened portion of the Federal line and drove Pope's soldiers to the ring of fortifications surrounding Washington.

Blessed with another resounding victory, Lee decided to keep the pressure on the Union. Attacking Washington and its strong defenses was out of the question, so Lee turned his gaze north to Maryland, a state that had not left the Union but allowed slavery within its borders. Doing so would not give the two battered Federal armies—Pope's and McClellan's—time to refit and reorganize, Lee hoped. It would also carry the war out of ravaged Virginia. The Confederate government expected that the presence of their army in Maryland might drive that state's men to join them while it might also bring the state into the Confederacy. Such a move could equally impact the approaching midterm elections in the United States. Great Britain and France seemed on the verge of recognizing the Confederate States of America, and one more victory, especially north of the Potomac River, could force their hand. Or perhaps one more victory alone might bring the war to a close, leaving the Confederacy to be its own nation. If Lee could achieve just one more victory, all of this could fall into place. "There is a general feeling that the Southern Confederacy will be recognized & that they deserve to be recognized," concluded dejected Union general Marsena Patrick on the eve of the campaign. He shared that sentiment with other Northerners.

As Lee's jubilant soldiers of the Army of Northern Virginia waded across the Potomac River and moved through Maryland while other Confederate offensives moved north through western Virginia and Kentucky toward the Ohio River, panic and fear spread within Washington. Disappointed by the setbacks, President Lincoln told his cabinet "he felt almost ready to hang himself." He turned to the out-of-favor George B. McClellan to make some sense of the beaten Union forces, lead them from Washington, and push Lee's force out of Maryland and back into Virginia. McClellan immediately set to work preparing a field army for the task.

After several days allowing his army to rest around Frederick, Maryland, Lee devised a plan to quickly divide his army, secure the town of Harpers Ferry, Virginia (now West Virginia), capture or drive off the Federal garrison stationed there, and then springboard his command into Pennsylvania. Unfortunately for Lee, his strategy lapsed behind schedule. McClellan's army leaped on Lee's divided command and won a striking victory against the Confederate defenders fighting for time atop the South Mountain range on September 14, 1862. Lee initially believed his foray into Maryland was done but changed course once the surrender of Harpers Ferry allowed his disparate commands to reunite on the heights of Sharpsburg, Maryland, behind Antietam Creek.

On September 17, 1862, the two armies fought one another outside the western Maryland town from dawn to dusk. They struggled with one another through a cornfield owned by the Miller family, around a simple whitewashed church used by the Dunkers—a pacifist religious sect—through a sunken farm lane on a property line that farmers used as a shortcut, and across a stone bridge carrying one of western Maryland's roads across Antietam Creek. This battle, the bloodiest single-day action in American military history, was called "Antietam" by the Federals and "Sharpsburg" by the Confederates.

Though his gains were slight, McClellan declared victory. Lee, not willing to give up the campaign just yet, recrossed the Potomac into Virginia with intentions to be back in Maryland within a few days. Smaller actions along the river snuffed out his hopes. Thus, five days after the Battle of Antietam, Abraham Lincoln had his victory. On September 22, he called his cabinet together two months to the day from his July meeting and said that now he had the victory with which he could publicly announce the Emancipation Proclamation. Over three months later, on New Year's Day 1863, Lincoln's proclamation became official, transforming the Federal war effort from one of simple restoration into one of reformation, as well.

The Union victory at Antietam, followed by the announcement of the Emancipation Proclamation, advanced Antietam's status as a crucial turning point in the American Civil War. Maj. Gen. James Longstreet, Lee's second in command during the Maryland Campaign, peered back years later and wrote, "At Sharpsburg was sprung the keystone of the arch upon which the Confederate cause rested." However, neither the Battle of Antietam nor the end of the Civil War stopped the change and differences that played out on the battlefield's landscape.

National attention focused on the Antietam battlefield once more shortly after the war's termination. A movement commenced creating a cemetery on the old battleground. The cemetery's location in Maryland, a state with contentious memories of the war, continued the political footballing of the site.

In 1890, Antietam, alongside Gettysburg, Chickamauga and Chattanooga, Shiloh, and Vicksburg, became one of America's first five national military parks. Though a federal government presence at the battlefield grew, the US War Department and the Antietam Battlefield Board originally preserved little of the battlefield itself. Still, monuments and markers sprouted across the landscape as veterans sought to craft a collective public memory of their deeds from 1861 to 1865. Doing so did not come without new clashes at Antietam.

While the battlefield came to be thought of as a quiet place of remembrance, it was also actively used in its early days for other purposes, and it still is today. Military groups visited the site as part of their lesson plans and training or to stage large mock battles for their own use and the edification of the public. Postwar buildings popped up throughout the battlefield and on the fringes of its boundaries, threatening the 1862 landscape.

Antietam National Battlefield is currently considered one of the most pristine battlefields in the United States, though the fight to achieve that title was never easy. It is hoped that the images and accompanying text contained within this book will present a sliver of Antietam's vast history and how the convergence of two armies who fought a battle there forever—and permanently—altered its features. Along the way, people trying to make a living, both commercially and privately, transformed the battlefield. But through it all, Antietam has become a place forever linked with horror and freedom, death and liberty. It has a tremendous story to tell, from 1862 to the present.

One

THE BATTLE

In the Civil War's second summer, a Confederate army led by Robert E. Lee—spurred by recent victories—crossed into Maryland in an attempt to achieve Southern independence. It was one of several Confederate offensive thrusts rolling north that summer. One more Confederate victory might be enough to end the war. For Abraham Lincoln and the United States, the stakes were perhaps never higher. Something had to be done to drive Lee's Confederates back into Virginia.

Lee's forces clashed in the climactic battle of the campaign with US soldiers under George B. McClellan's command along the banks of Antietam Creek. The farming community of Sharpsburg in western Maryland played host to over 100,000 soldiers, who clashed on September 17, 1862. By the end of the day, approximately 23,110 soldiers were casualties of war—killed, wounded, captured, or missing. "From sunrise to sunset the waves of battle ebbed and flowed. Men wrestled with each other in lines of regiment, brigade, and division while regiment, brigade, and division faded away under a terrible fire, leaving long lines of dead to mark where stood the living. Fields of corn were trampled into shreds, forests were battered and scathed, huge limbs sent crashing to the earth, rent by shell or round shot. Grape and canister mingled their hissing scream in this hellish carnival," wrote Union general George Gordon. The woodlots, cornfields, orchards, and homes that served as the backdrop for America's bloodiest day forever became intertwined with Antietam's carnage.

Before all the dead were buried, sketch artists and, most significantly, two photographers, Alexander Gardner and James Gibson, arrived on the battlefield recently vacated by the Confederates on their way back to Virginia. Gardner and Gibson captured Antietam in all its raw horror for the public to see—bloated corpses, shot-strewn trees and structures, and the charred ruins of a once stately home. Their work brought the war home to Americans like never before.

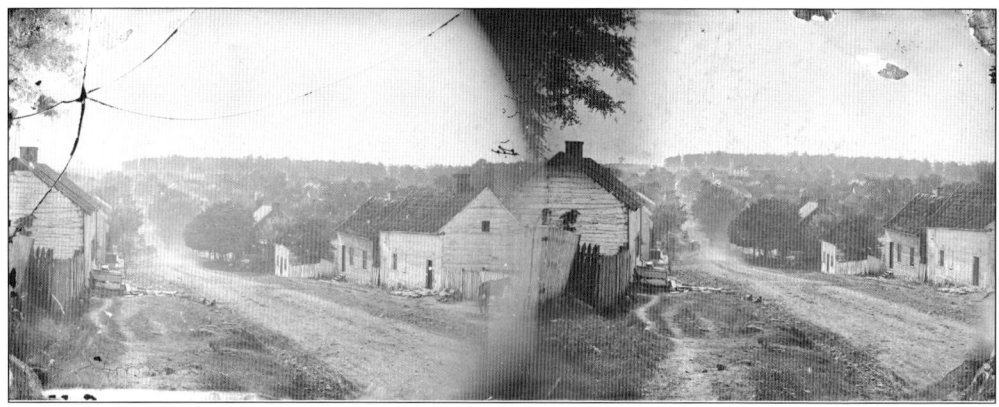

In 1862, Sharpsburg was on the verge of celebrating the centennial anniversary of its founding in 1763. Approximately 1,300 people called the town home in 1860. Many German farmers settled the area. A total of 150 slaves and 203 free blacks lived there in the year prior to the beginning of the Civil War. Sharpsburg suffered extensive damage during the Battle of Antietam as the two armies battled through the fields adjoining the town. "The streets were filled with wreckage," recalled Massachusetts soldier Robert Goldthwaite Carter. "Here and there a wagon, a wheel, a dead mule, or a defunct caisson were keeled up as though in their death agonies." (Both, courtesy of the Library of Congress.)

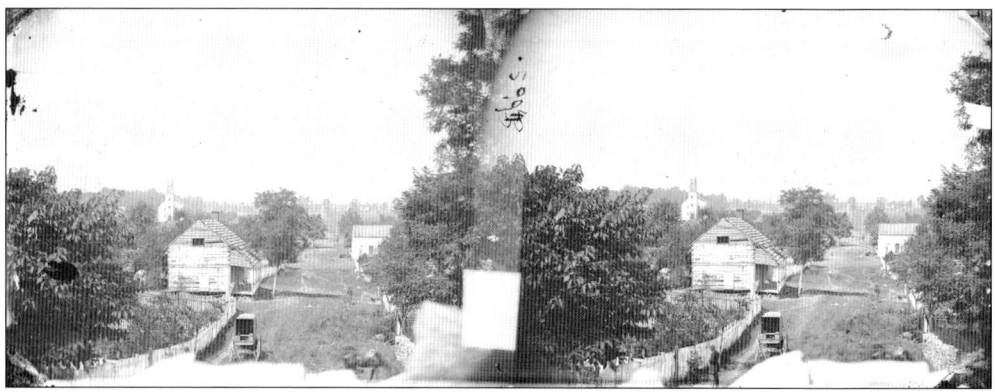

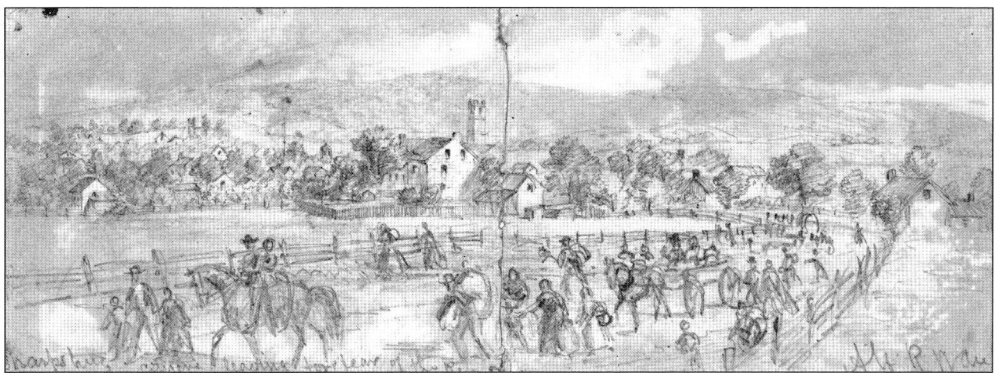

Warned of an impending battle, the civilians of Sharpsburg fled the town in droves. "Many of the inhabitants . . . terror stricken fled from the town to the country, carrying with them a few articles of clothing," recalled young resident John P. Smith. Some sought shelter at Killiansburg Cave along the Potomac River, while others escaped to neighboring communities. (Courtesy of the Library of Congress.)

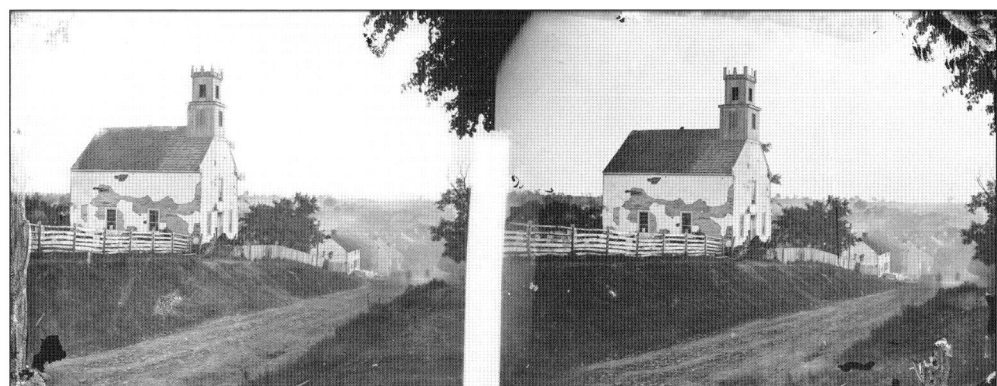

Sharpsburg's Lutheran Church, constructed in 1768, suffered heavily during the battle. Confederate signalmen used its steeple as an observation point, which attracted Union artillery. In the battle's aftermath, the Federal army filled the building with sick and wounded soldiers. The church was so heavily damaged, as evidenced in the photograph, that its parishioners tore it down and built a new sanctuary. (Courtesy of the Library of Congress.)

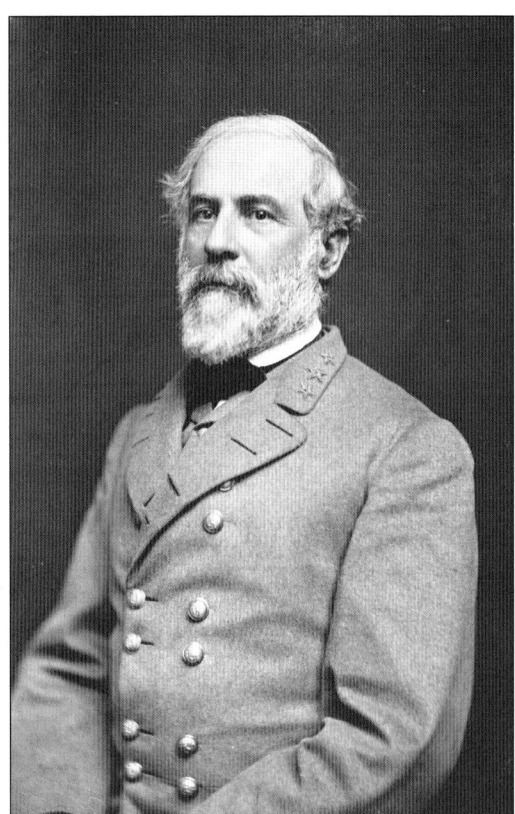

Robert E. Lee was 55 years old at the time of the Maryland Campaign. Throughout most of the campaign, Lee rode in an ambulance, unable to ride a horse due to injuries to his hands. He still commanded his army well at Antietam. Of 37,351 Confederates engaged, the Confederate army had 10,316 casualties—men killed, wounded, missing, or captured. (Courtesy of the Library of Congress.)

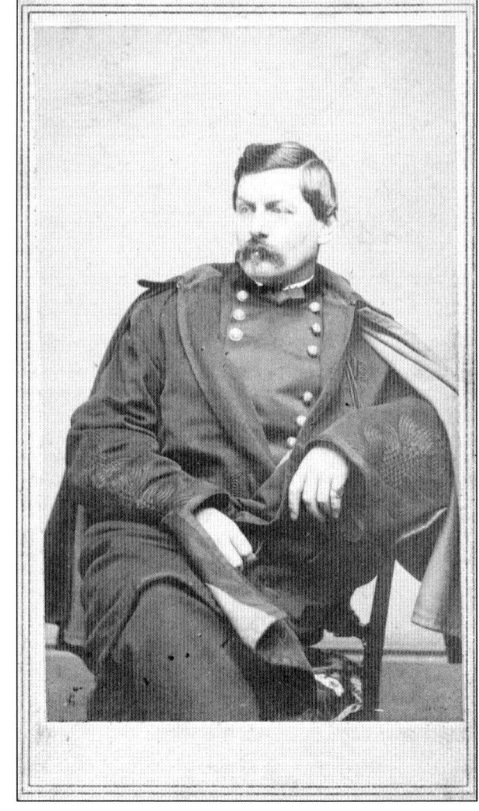

George B. McClellan was 20 years Lee's junior in September 1862. He commanded an amalgamation of several Union armies formed under the title the Army of the Potomac. McClellan engaged 55,956 men on September 17, and 12,401 became casualties. His campaign stopped the first Confederate invasion north of the Potomac River. (Courtesy of the Library of Congress.)

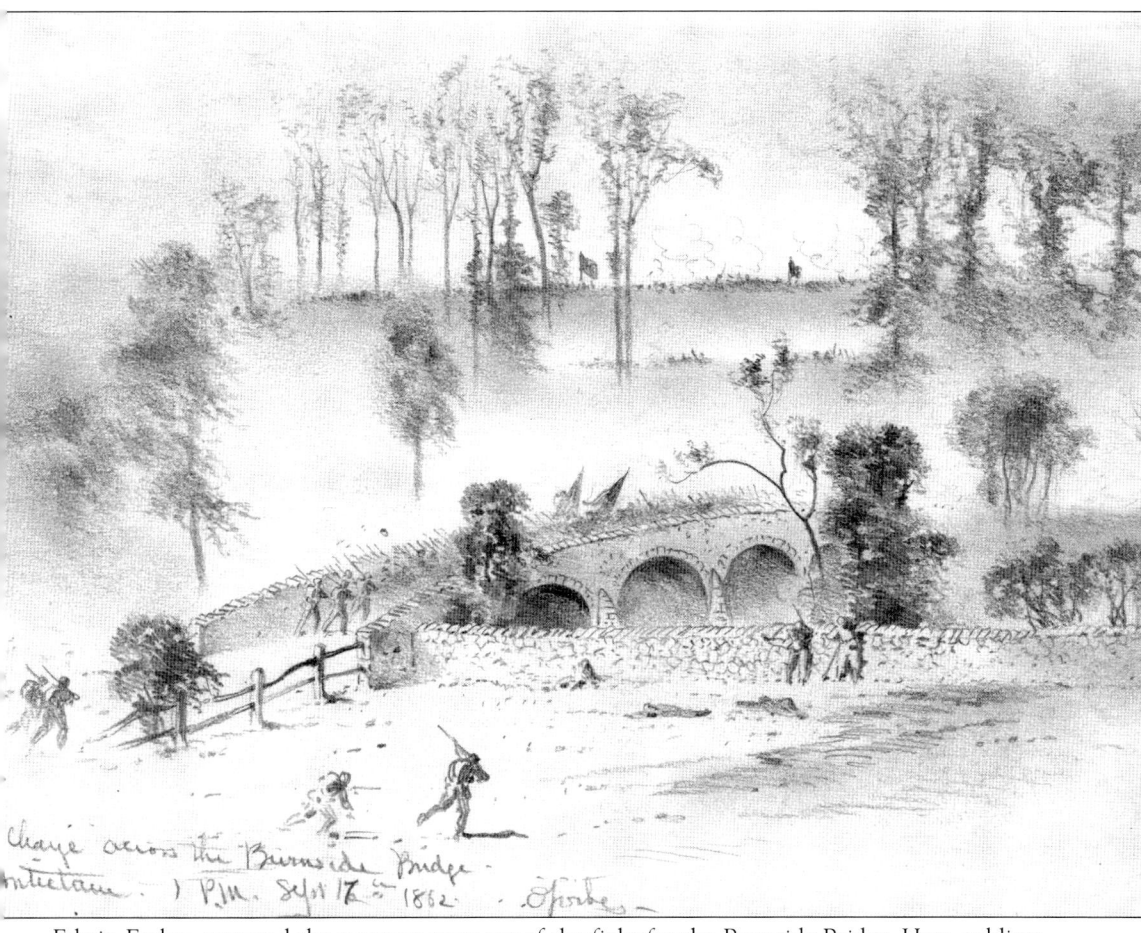

Edwin Forbes captured the supreme moment of the fight for the Burnside Bridge. Here, soldiers of the 51st New York and 51st Pennsylvania are shown charging across the span and driving the Confederate defenders away. The two regiments had about 670 men total and collectively lost 207 men in the day's fight. Union general Samuel Sturgis wrote of the charge in his after-action report, "[I] directed them to charge with the bayonet. They started on their mission of death full of enthusiasm, and taking a route less exposed than the regiments which had made the effort before them, rushed at a double-quick over the slope leading to the bridge and over the bridge itself with an impetuosity which the enemy could not resist, and the Stars and Stripes were planted on the opposite bank at 1 o'clock p.m., amid the most enthusiastic cheering from every part of the field from where they could be seen." (Courtesy of the Library of Congress.)

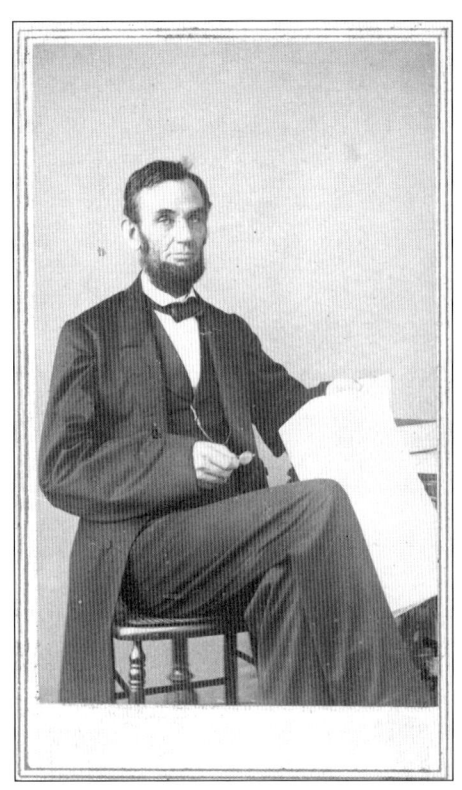

Abraham Lincoln vowed not to renege on signing the Emancipation Proclamation on January 1, 1863, after announcing his intention to do so following the Battle of Antietam. However, reactions were split, even among Northern citizens. Capt. Robert Gould Shaw, famous for leading an all-black regiment in the Civil War, wrote of it, "I can't see what practical good it can do now." The Confederacy vowed to fight on after Lincoln penned his name to the celebrated document, which was reproduced in many forms and iterations. Ultimately, Secretary of War Edwin Stanton claimed the measure "shook each day more and more the fabric built on human slavery" and helped end the war in favor of the Union. (Both, courtesy of the Library of Congress.)

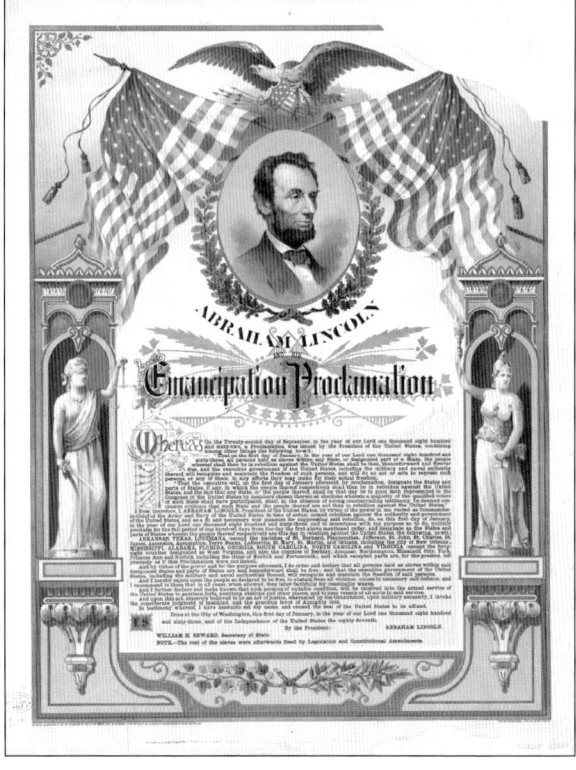

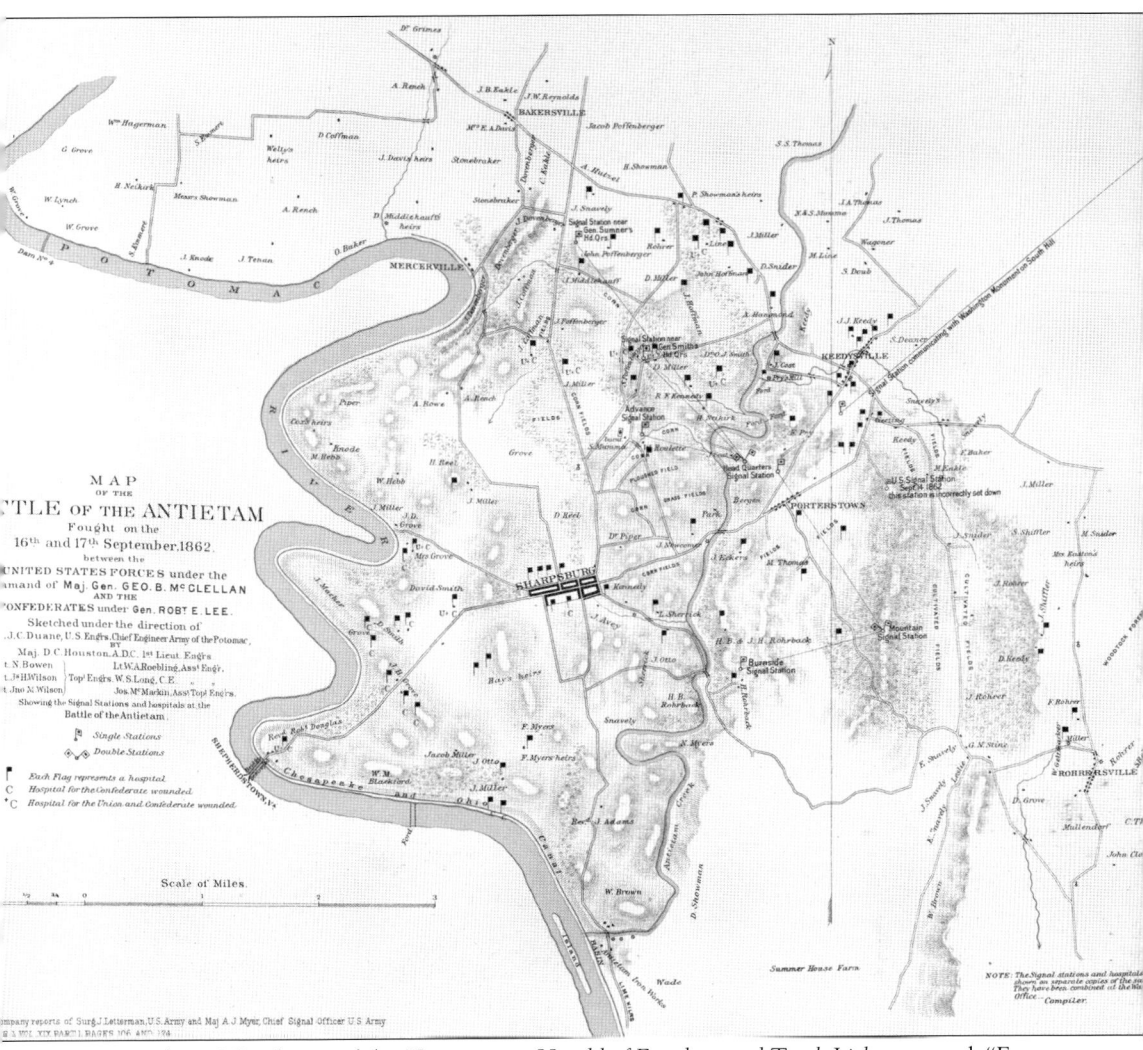

A September 1862 edition of the Hagerstown *Herald of Freedom and Torch Light* reported, "From Hagerstown to the Southern limits of [Washington] county wounded and dying soldiers are to be found in every neighborhood and in nearly every house. The whole region of country between Boonsboro and Sharpsburg is one vast Hospital. Houses and Barns are filled with them, and nearly the whole population is engaged in waiting on and ministering to their wants." Each of the flags in this contemporary map marks the position of a hospital following the Battle of Antietam. Besides houses and barns, churches were also prominently used, particularly in nearby Frederick, Maryland, and Shepherdstown, West Virginia, which became a haven for approximately 6,000 wounded Confederates. Some of the hospitals formed as a result of the battle did not disband until the next spring. (Courtesy of the Library of Congress.)

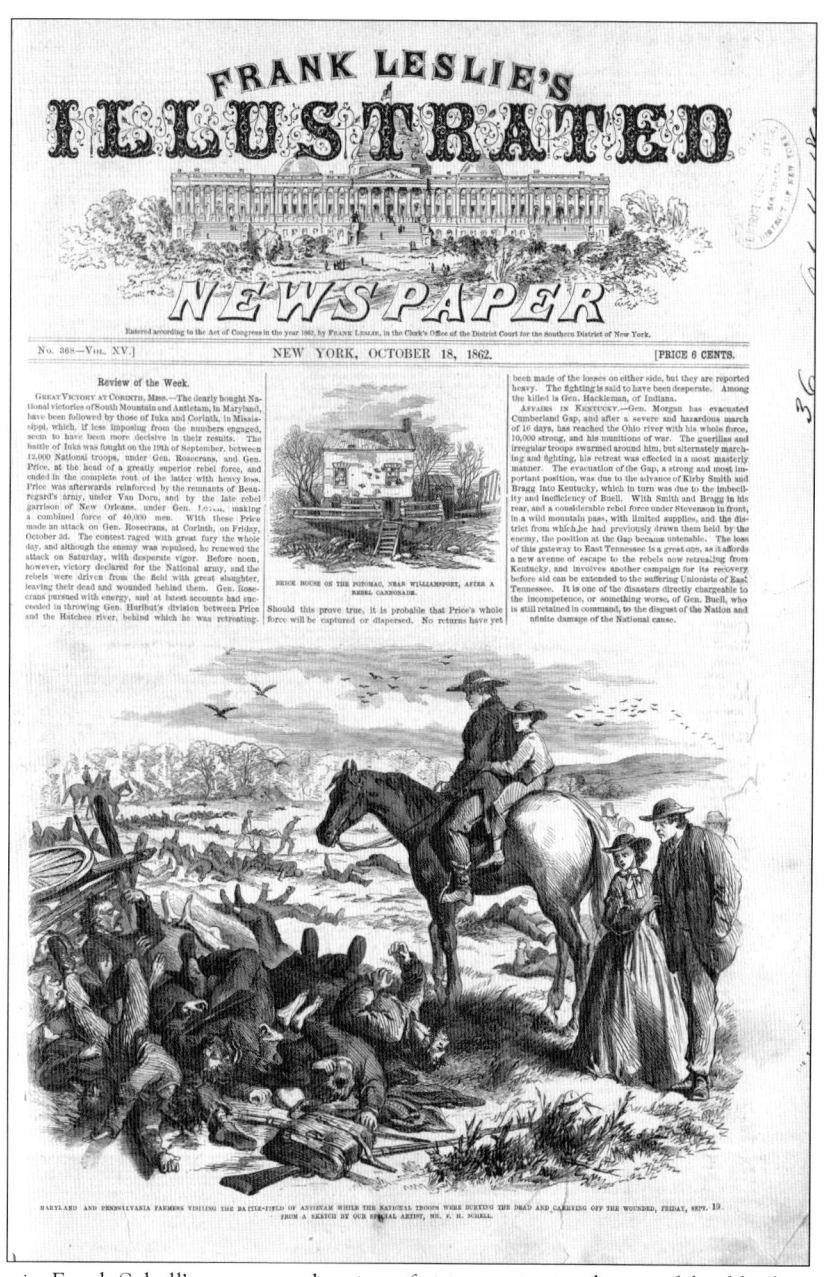

Sketch artist Frank Schell's gruesome drawing of citizens viewing heaps of dead bodies ready for burial reached a wide viewership in *Frank Leslie's Illustrated Newspaper*. Schell also published his reminiscences of Antietam after the war ended, recalling "the terrible evidences of the struggle lay around me plentifully." Schell's harrowing account continued, "On the west side of the pike were Miller's barn, haystacks, and mowing and threshing machines, in close communion with the open-mouthed cannon and other implements of destruction. Could peace and war in juxtaposition be more impressively illustrated? The wheat was gathered in, the corn destroyed, and the crop of corpses and one with a fresh 'plug,' that left him a horribly mangled corpse." Similar descriptions, illustrations, and photographs brought the war home to a public that never experienced or saw anything like this before. (Courtesy of the Library of Congress.)

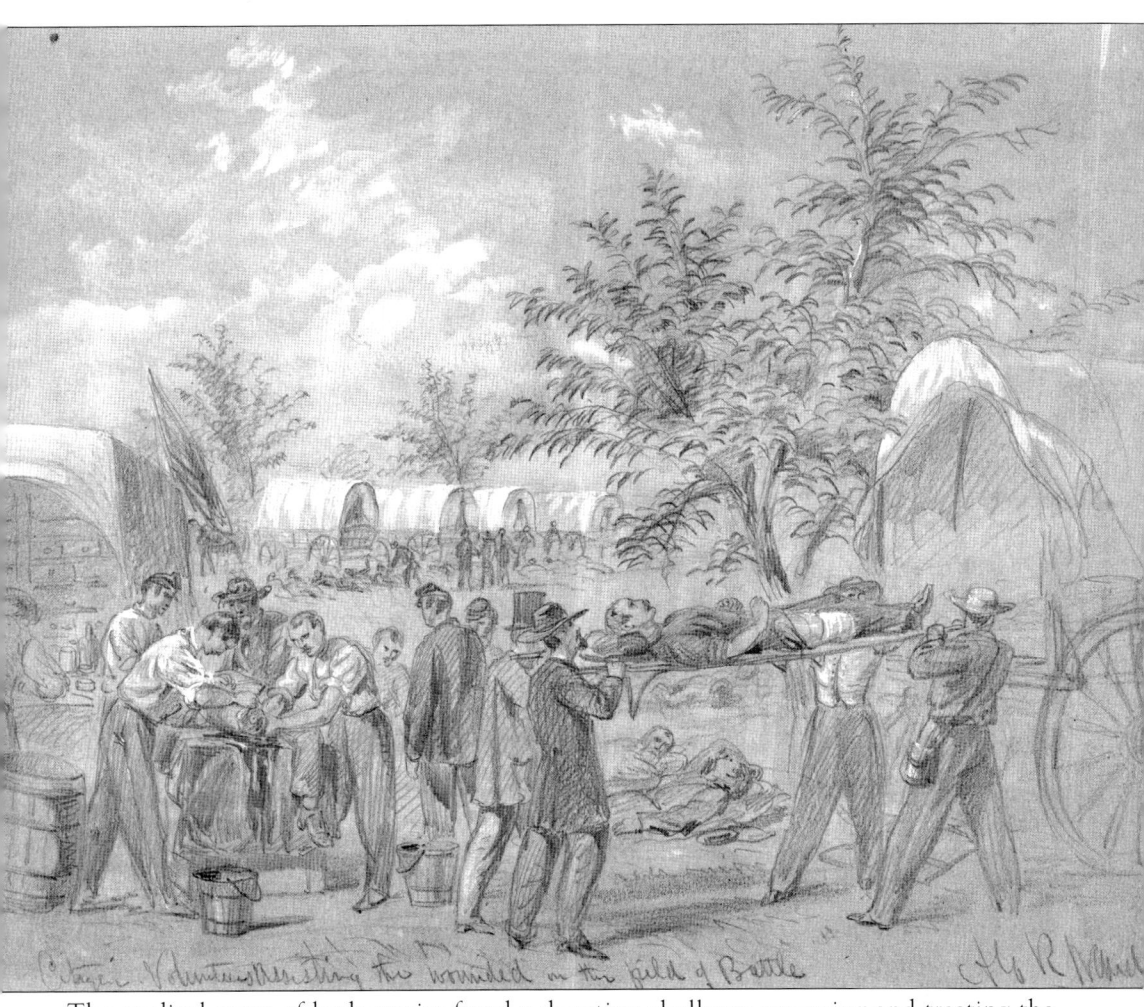

The medical corps of both armies faced a daunting challenge removing and treating the approximately 17,000 wounded soldiers. Army of the Potomac medical director Jonathan Letterman implemented a sophisticated plan, known as the triage system, to accomplish the job. This system, first used on the Antietam battlefield, is still in use today by the US armed forces to care for and remove wounded from a battlefield. The Army of Northern Virginia's Medical Corps, under the command of Lafayette Guild, had to remove its wounded from the field of battle in the face of the enemy twice in the campaign—at South Mountain and Antietam. Letterman recorded that approximately 2,500 Confederate sick and wounded were left behind, meaning his surgeons had to look after them as well. He believed his surgeons cared for the wounded enemy as best as they could, for "Humanity teaches us that a wounded and prostrate foe is not then our enemy." (Courtesy of the Library of Congress.)

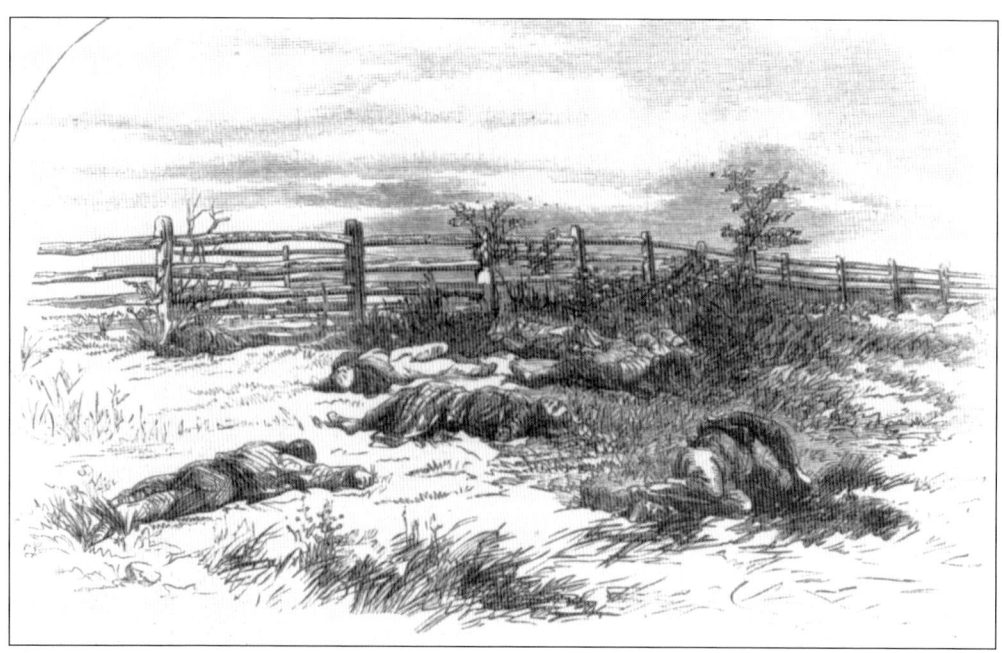

Photographic historian William Frassanito theorizes that the Confederate dead lying along the fences bordering the Hagerstown Pike were the first scenes that Alexander Gardner and James Gibson photographed on the Antietam battlefield. Images like this were shocking to America's citizens, as it was the first time the public had been exposed to images of dead soldiers on a field of battle and the horrors of war. Besides being shown in Mathew Brady's New York City studio, *Harper's Weekly* published woodcut sketches of these scenes, likely drawing from Gardner's images. "Mr. Brady has done something to bring home to us the terrible reality and earnestness of war," said one *New York Times* review. "If he has not brought bodies and laid them in our door-yards and along streets, he has done something very like it." (Both, courtesy of the Library of Congress.)

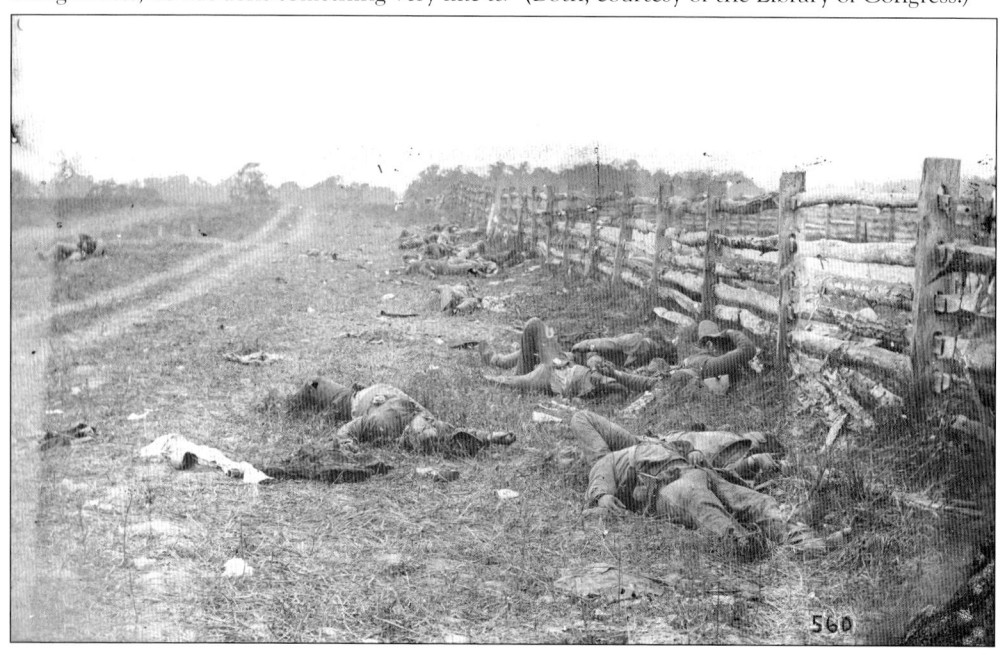

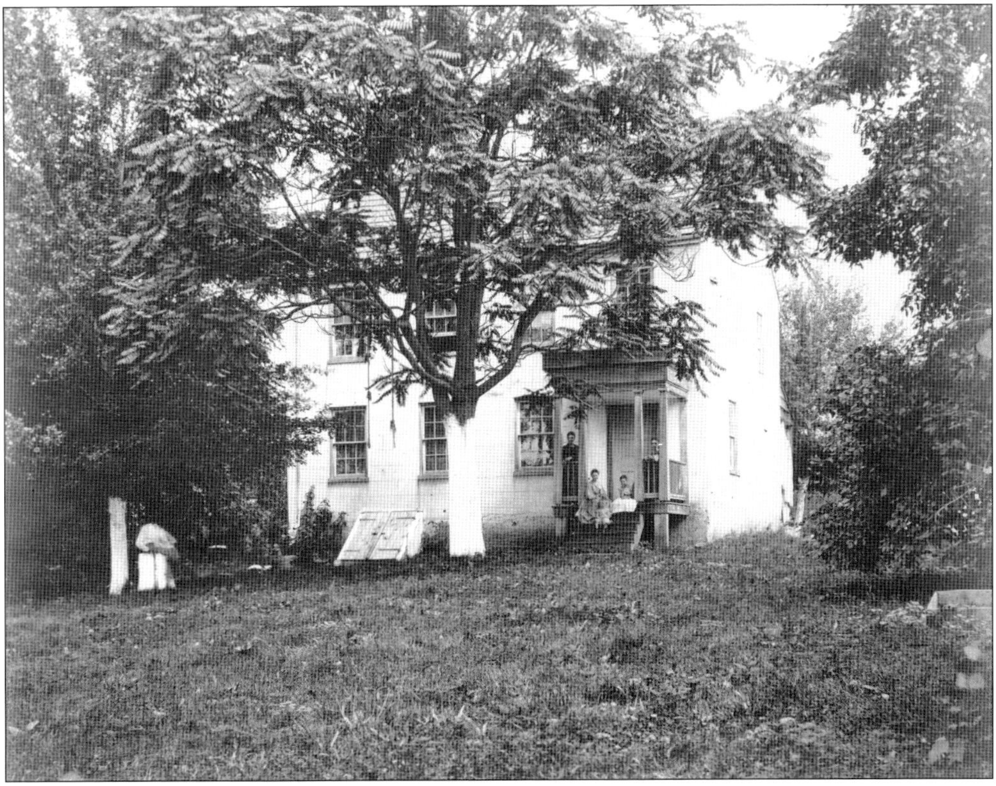

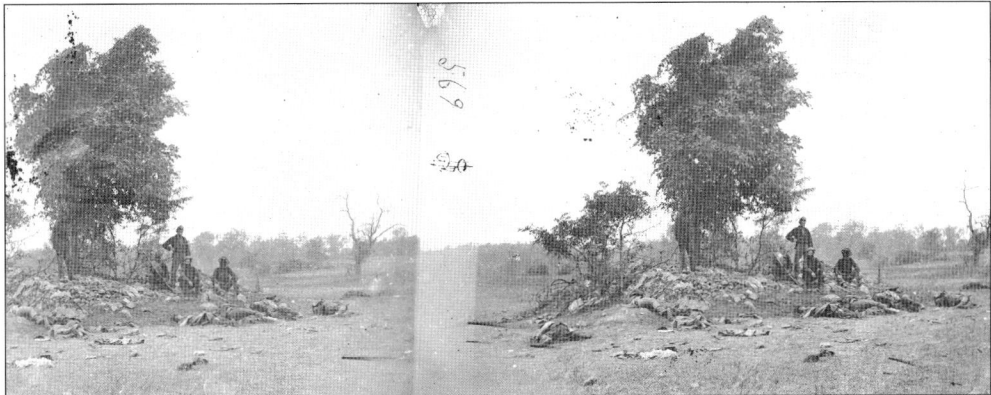

David R. Miller and his family, including their pet parrot, escaped from their home prior to the battle, seeking shelter at Miller's father's house nearer to Sharpsburg. Fighting swirled around their house and barn and, most famously, through David Miller's cornfield. After the battle, the family received $995 for the damage their property suffered during the fighting. (Courtesy of the Library of Congress.)

Alexander Gardner captured this scene of Union soldiers looking over the remains of their dead enemies just south of the Miller Cornfield. The rock ledge the Federal soldiers are seated on was occupied by several Union regiments in the early hours of the battle. It can still be found today along modern Cornfield Avenue. (Courtesy of the Library of Congress.)

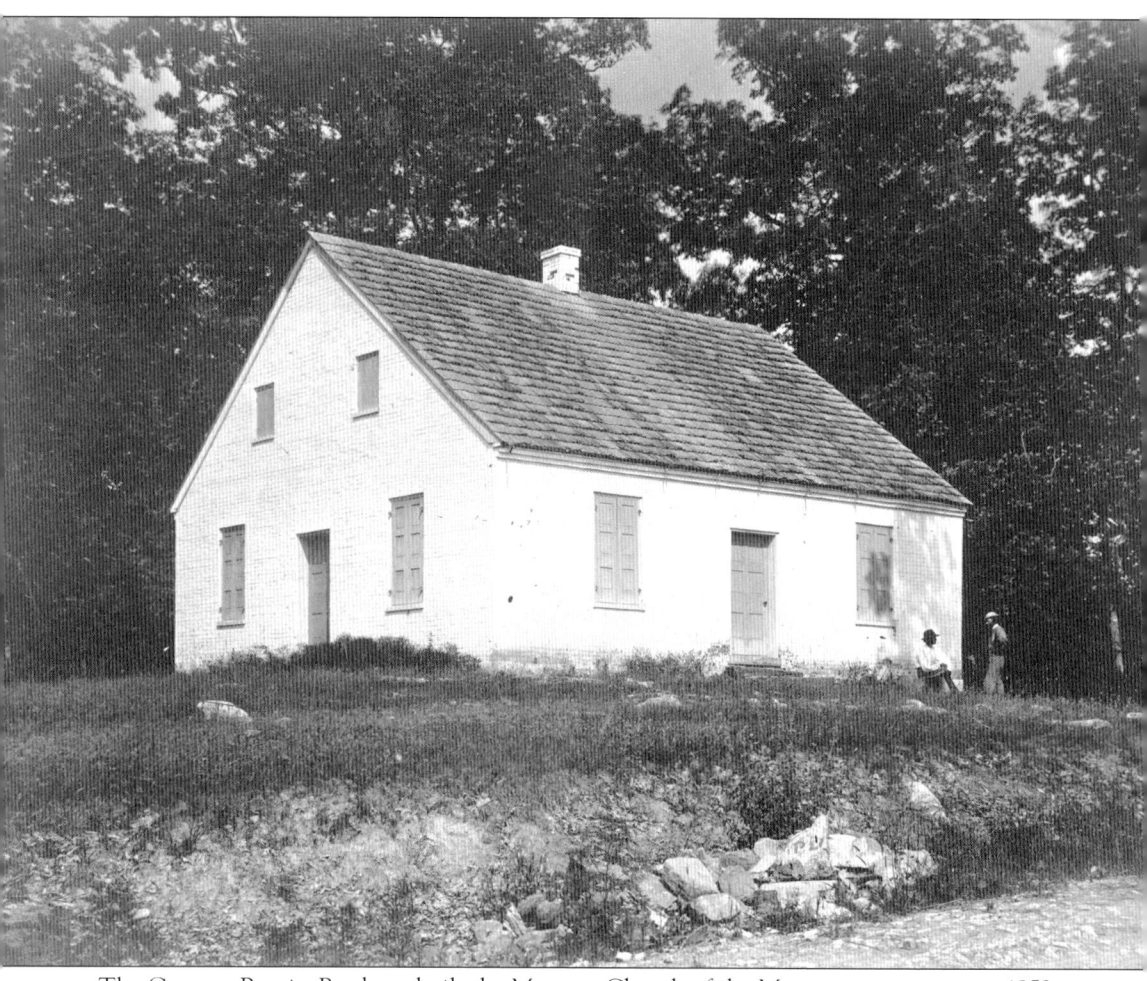

The German Baptist Brethren built the Mumma Church of the Manor congregation in 1853 on land donated by local farmer Samuel Mumma. The Brethren, a pacifist group, were informally known as Dunkers for their belief in full immersion baptism. Therefore, history has remembered this building as the Dunker Church. On Sunday, September 14, while the armies battled atop South Mountain about eight miles east of Sharpsburg, the congregation worshipped within the humble dwelling. They could easily hear the rumble of cannon in the distance. Lee's Confederate army began arriving around Sharpsburg the next day. With an impending battle, many of the local families fled, and the Dunker Church was never the same. It sustained heavy damage inside and outside, including the loss of the church's Bible, which New York soldier Nathan Dykeman took. It was returned in 1903. (Courtesy of the Library of Congress.)

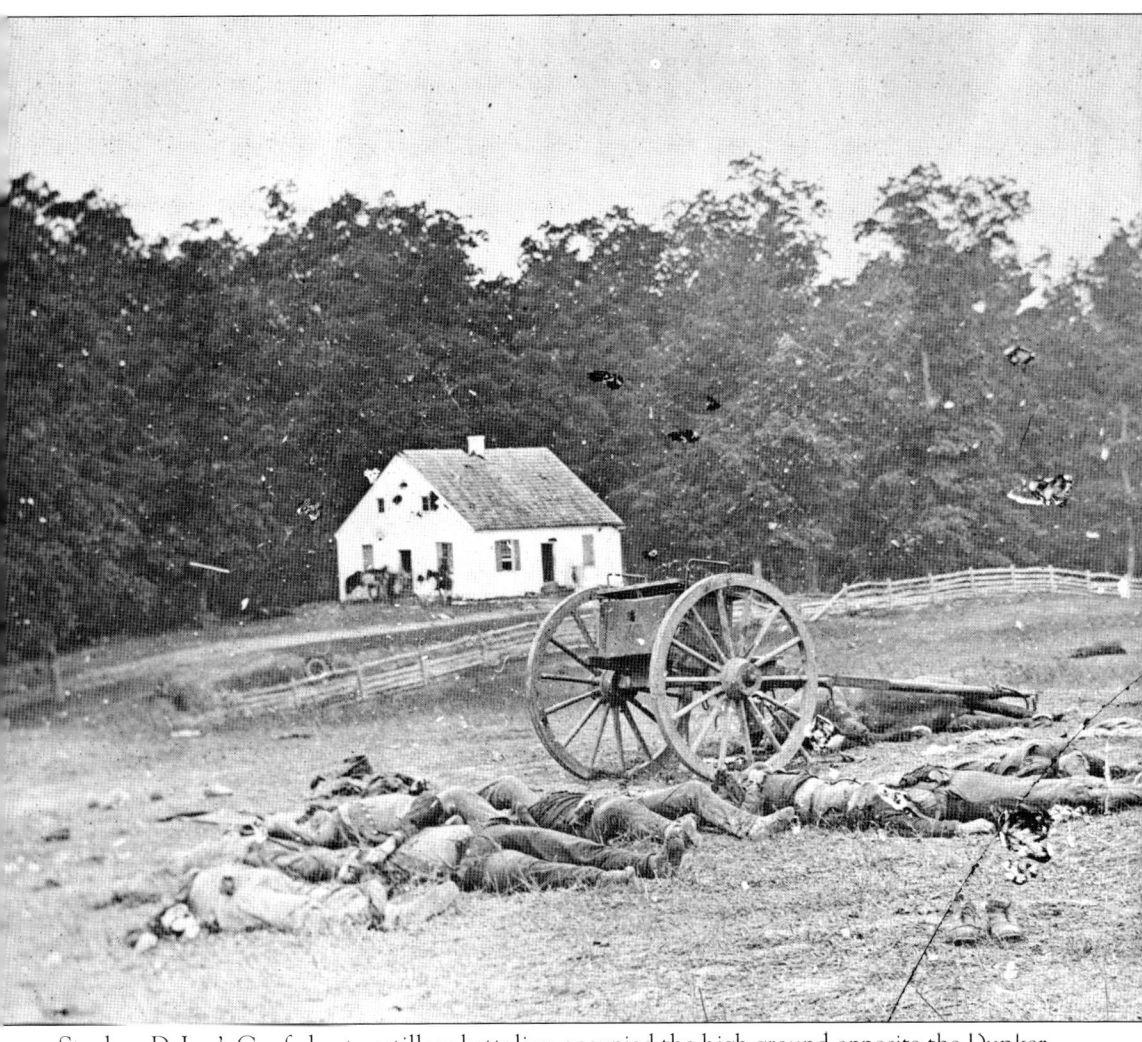

Stephen D. Lee's Confederate artillery battalion occupied the high ground opposite the Dunker Church on the morning of September 17. While dealing death and destruction to the advancing Union foe, Lee's men equally suffered, losing 25 percent of 300 men as well as 60 horses. In the background, the damage inflicted on the church is easily visible. Bullet holes pocked the church's brick walls while at least 30 artillery rounds passed entirely through the structure. The church served as a temporary hospital after the battle while burial parties collected the dead that lay around the building. Many Dunkers opposed repairing the church. Samuel Mumma declared it should be fixed "as a symbol of peace and goodwill among men of all creeds and differences." The building was renovated by early 1864 and regularly used for worship until 1899. (Courtesy of the Library of Congress.)

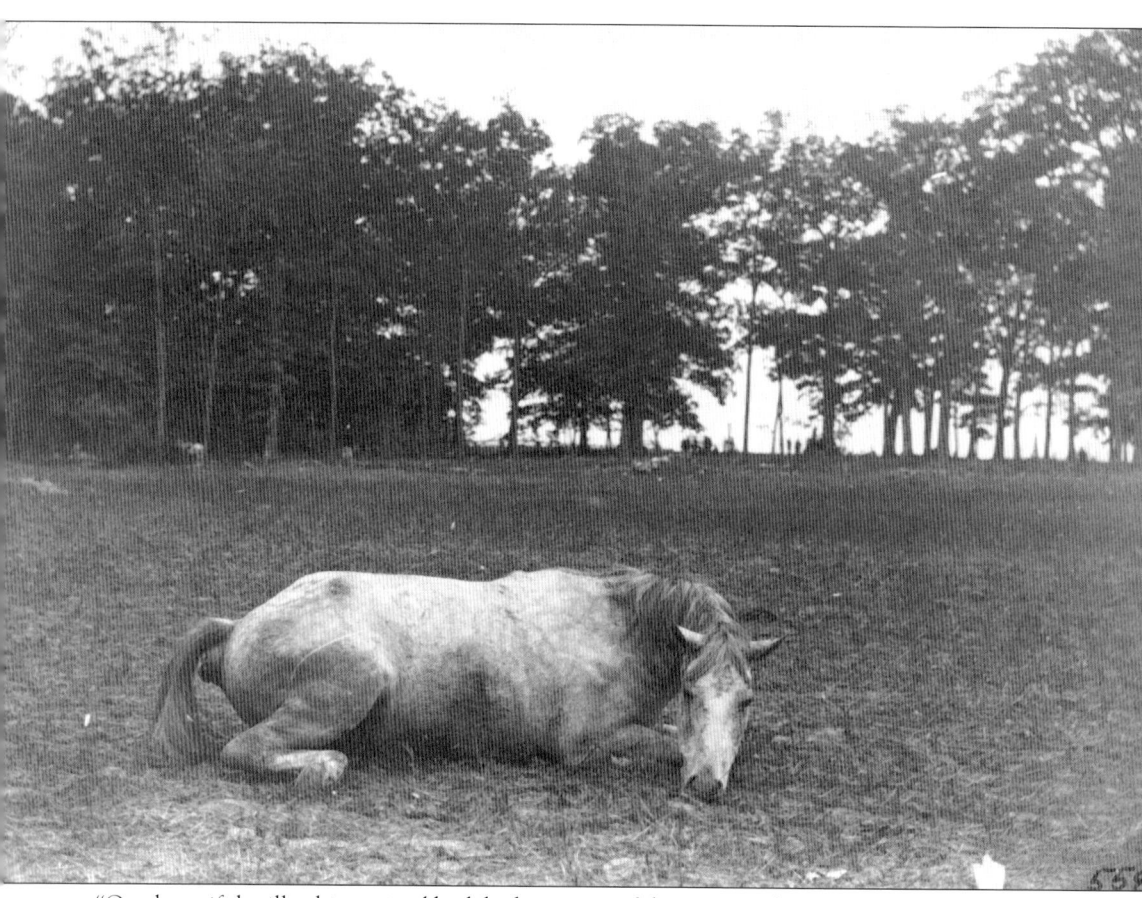

"One beautiful milk-white animal had died in so graceful a position that I wished for its photograph. Its legs were doubled under and its arched neck gracefully turned to one side, as if looking back to the ball-hole in its side. Until you got to it, it was hard to believe the horse was dead," wrote Union general Alpheus Williams of this same horse. Gardner captured this haunting image, showing a dead horse as if it is resting, south of the Cornfield along the edge of the East Woods. Incredibly, research has shown that this horse belonged to Col. Henry B. Strong of the 6th Louisiana. Strong was a Scottish native who led his men into action early in the battle. Known for riding this conspicuous steed, Strong and his mount both died during the fighting. One of Strong's comrades tried to carry some of the colonel's possessions off the field but was struck four times in the attempt. (Courtesy of the Library of Congress.)

The lone grave in this image is that of 50-year-old Pvt. John Marshall of the 28th Pennsylvania Infantry. Marshall enlisted in July 1861, leaving behind a wife and three children. Like many other casualties of the battle, Marshall's remains were hastily buried on the battlefield near where he fell. His remains were reinterred and rest in Grave 3600 at Antietam National Cemetery. (Courtesy of the Library of Congress.)

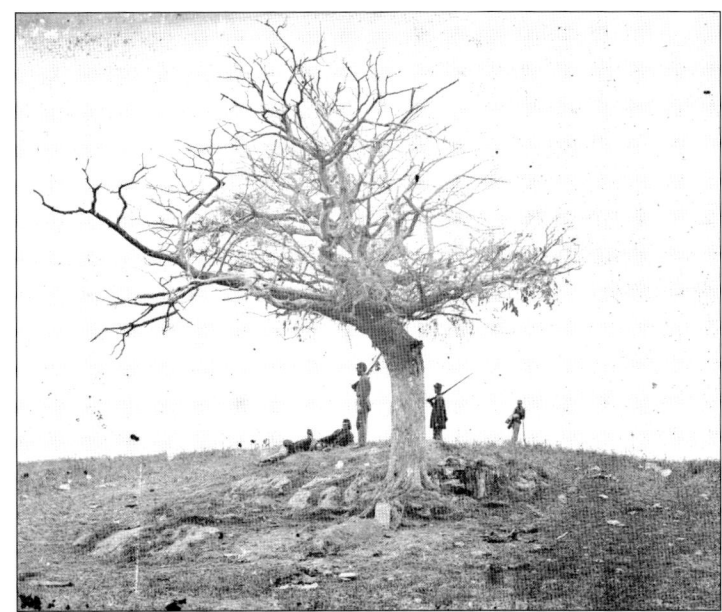

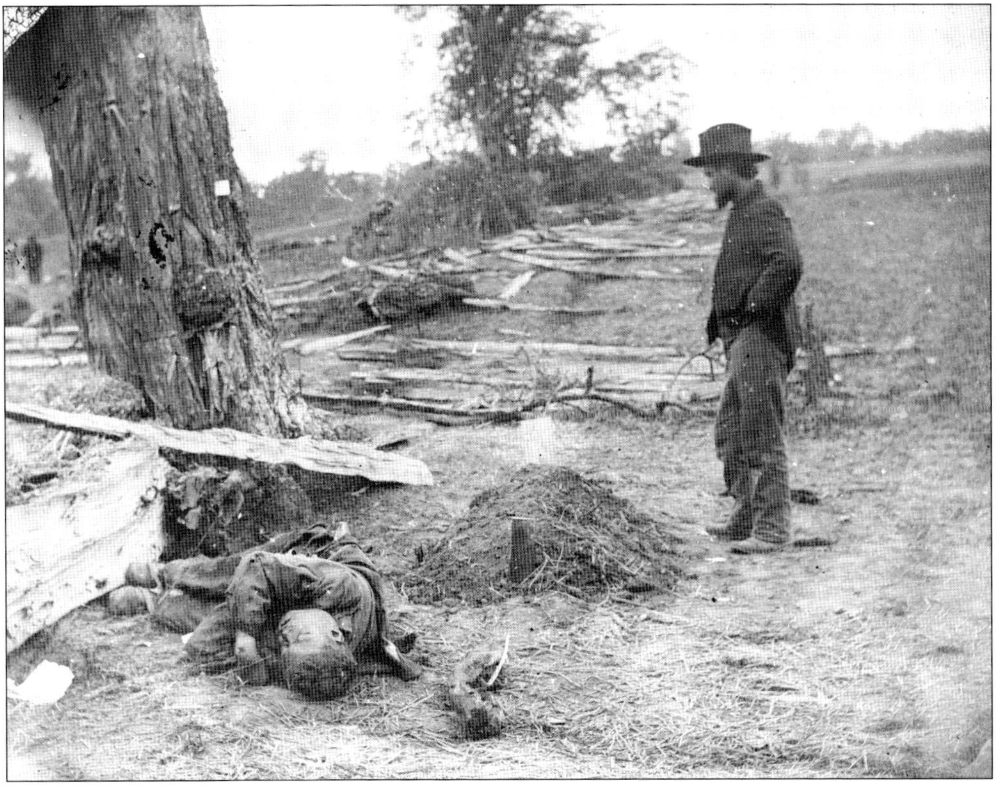

Alexander Gardner captured this haunting photograph just two days after the Battle of Antietam. The dead Confederate soldier and the onlooking Federal remain unknown, but historian William Frassanito discovered the shallow battlefield grave to be that of Lt. John A. Clark of the 7th Michigan Infantry. Clark's family traveled to the battlefield and removed his remains to Michigan that fall. (Courtesy of the Library of Congress.)

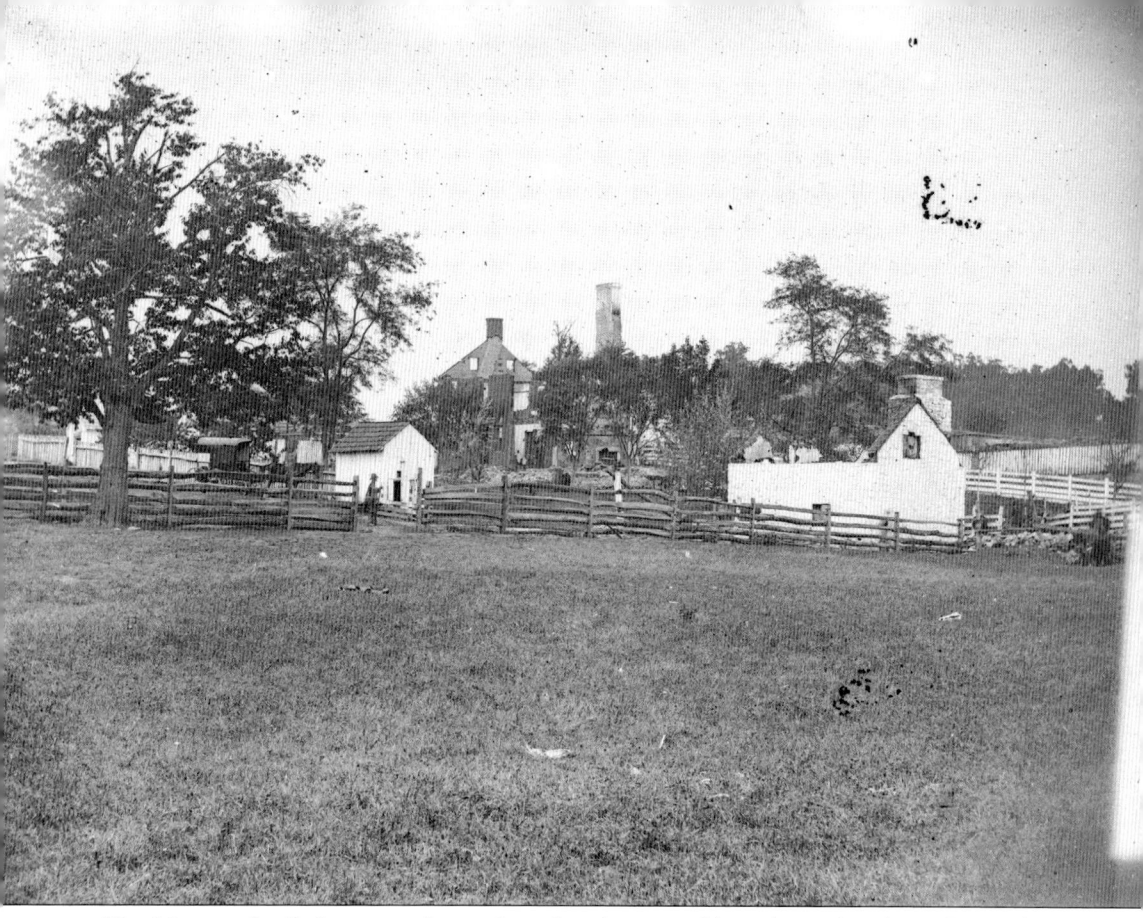

The Mumma family lost everything when their home and barn burned early on September 17. The flames consumed almost all of their earthly possessions. Samuel Mumma Jr., the eldest son, wrote after the war that the damages to their property totaled "from $8,000 to $10,000." Though civilians were often compensated for damages done to their property, the Mummas did not receive

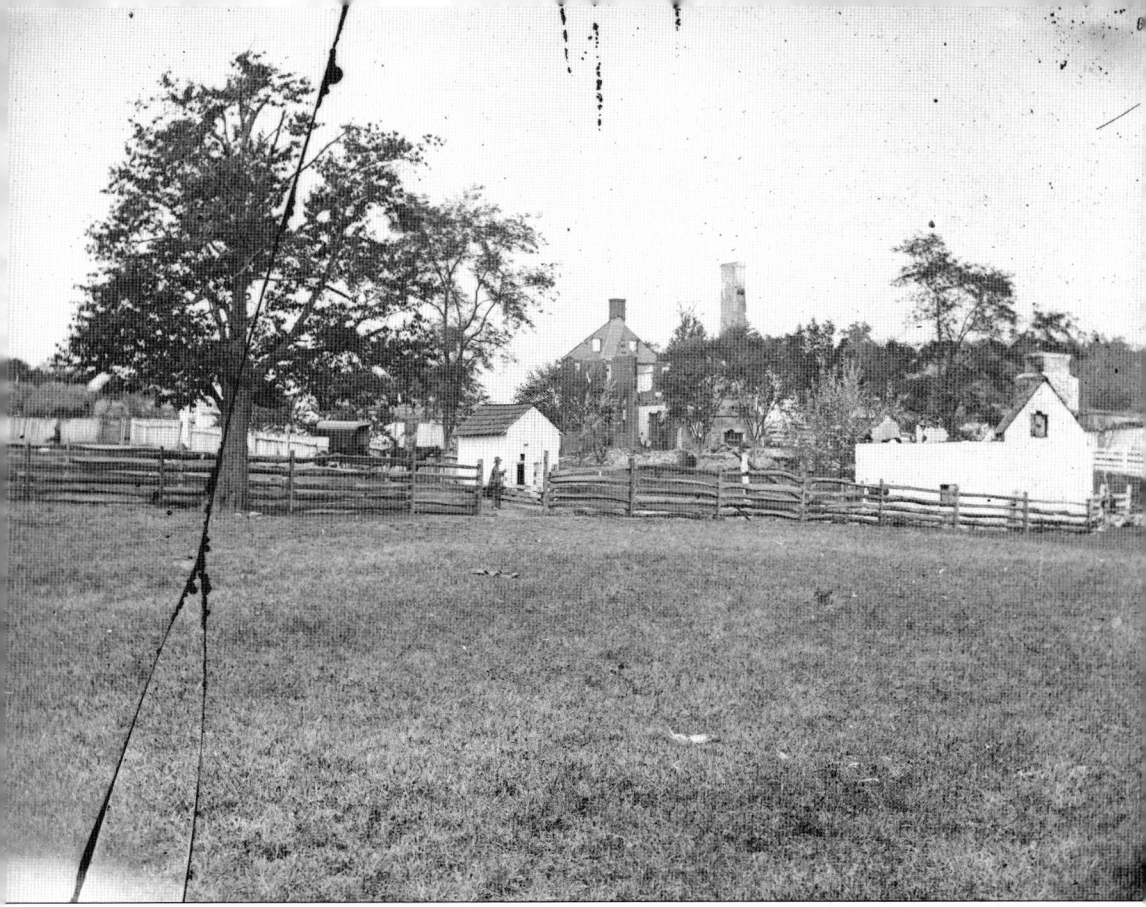

a cent. However, they managed to rebuild their home by the next summer. The family owned the farm until 1886. It came into the possession of the National Park Service in 1961 and today serves as an education center. (Courtesy of the Library of Congress.)

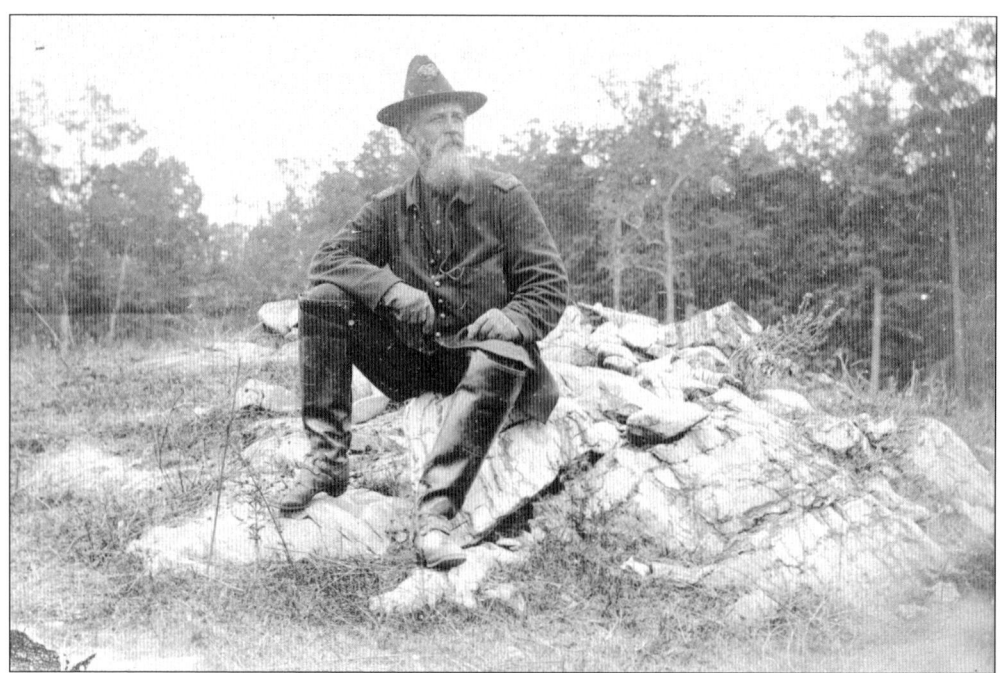

Col. Turner Gustavus Morehead led the 106th Pennsylvania Infantry into the West Woods on September 17. The regiment lost 77 men. Morehead himself fell when his horse was shot and tumbled to the ground. The colonel retreated with his men until he realized he lost his sword. He returned to the fighting, recovered it, and lived to pose for Gardner's camera on September 19. (Courtesy of the Library of Congress.)

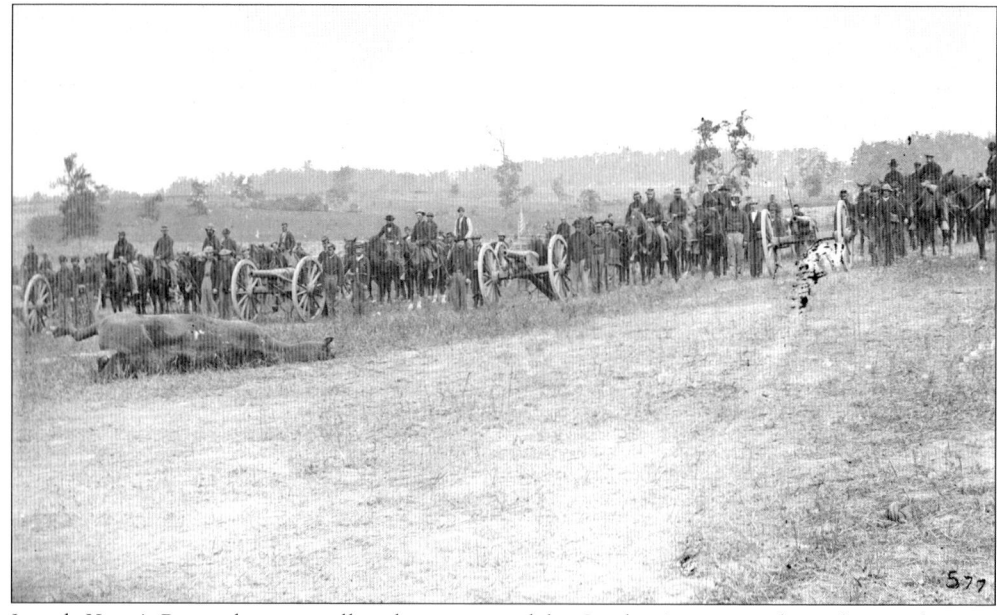

Joseph Knap's Pennsylvania artillery battery posed for Gardner's camera along the Smoketown Road two days after the battle. Knap's battery fought in various positions on September 17. The battery lost one man killed, six wounded, and one missing during the battle. Note the dead horse in front of the battery. (Courtesy of the Library of Congress.)

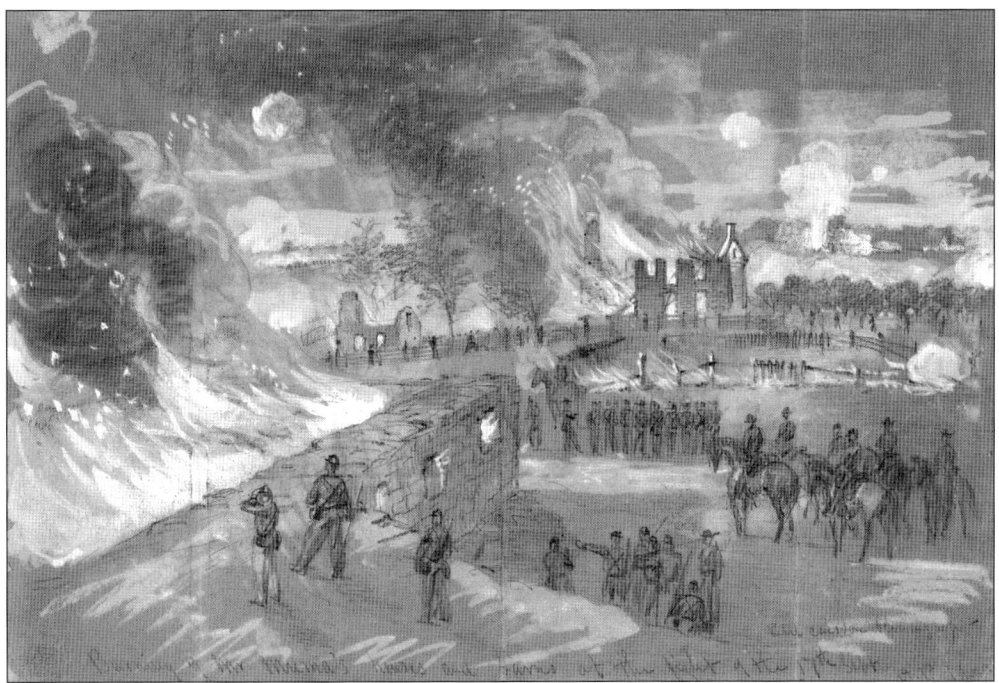

Alfred Waud sketched these contemporary depictions of the destruction of the Mumma farm. Many Americans viewed the Civil War through Waud's dramatic sketches as his preliminary drawings were refined and reproduced in newspapers read by people across the United States. Confederates burned the Mumma house and barn on the morning of the battle to prevent its use by the enemy. James Clark of the 3rd North Carolina Infantry led the soldiers who destroyed the farm. Clark contacted the Sharpsburg postmaster in 1906 asking for particulars of the family whose home he had burned. Ironically, the postmaster was Samuel Mumma Jr., one of the sons occupying the house at the time of the war. Mumma consoled Clark: "As to your burning our house, we know that in doing so, you were carrying out orders." (Both, courtesy of the Library of Congress.)

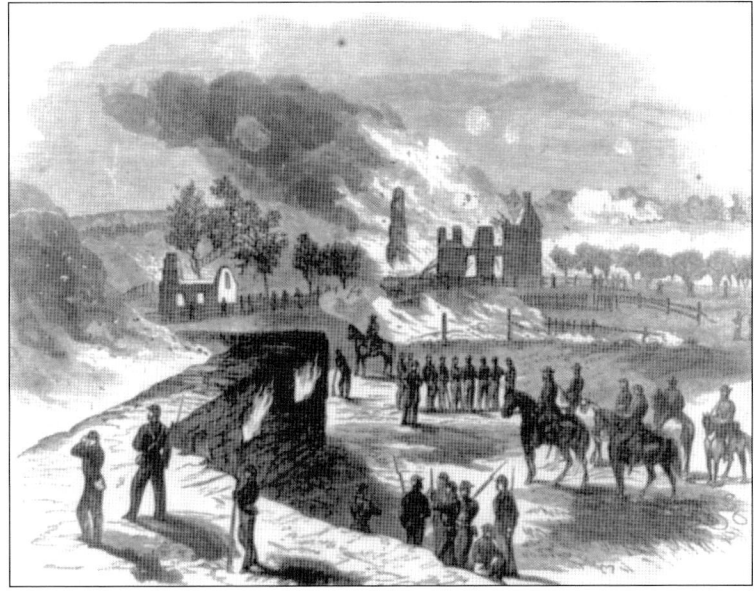

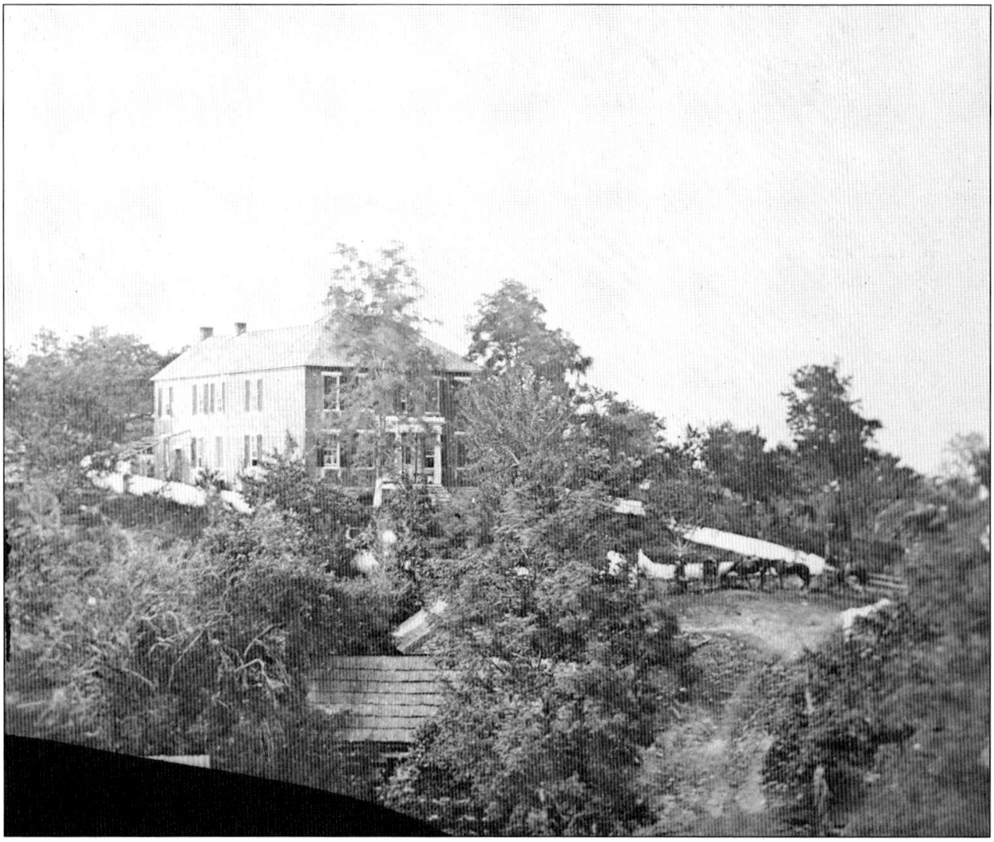

Philip and Elizabeth Pry lived in this farmhouse above Antietam Creek. The battle ruined their prosperity and their lives. George B. McClellan slept there the night before the battle, and at least two wounded Federal generals received medical treatment in the home. The Prys filed for damage claims amounting to $2,459 but never received recompense. They sold the farm in 1874 and moved to Tennessee. (Courtesy of the Library of Congress.)

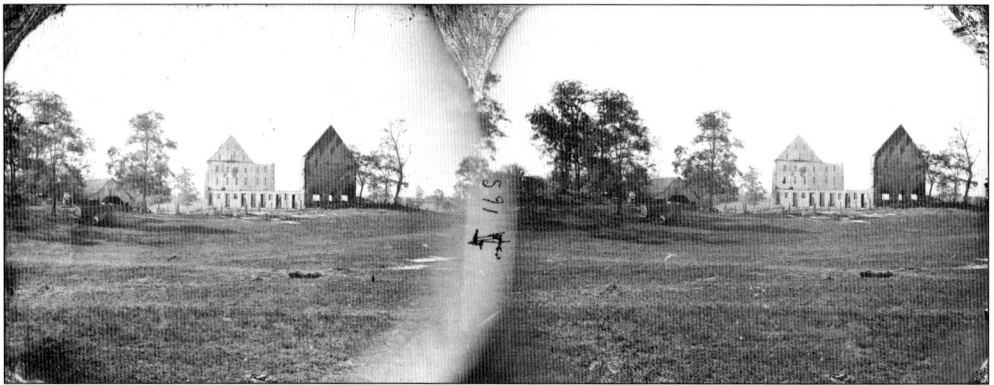

David Reel's barn became a Confederate hospital in the midst of the Battle of Antietam. Unfortunately, an errant Federal artillery shell struck the barn and set it on fire. Many of the Confederate wounded there could not be removed and were consumed by the flames. Civilians digging through the charred remnants found lumps of melted lead and charred bones after the fire subsided. (Courtesy of the Library of Congress.)

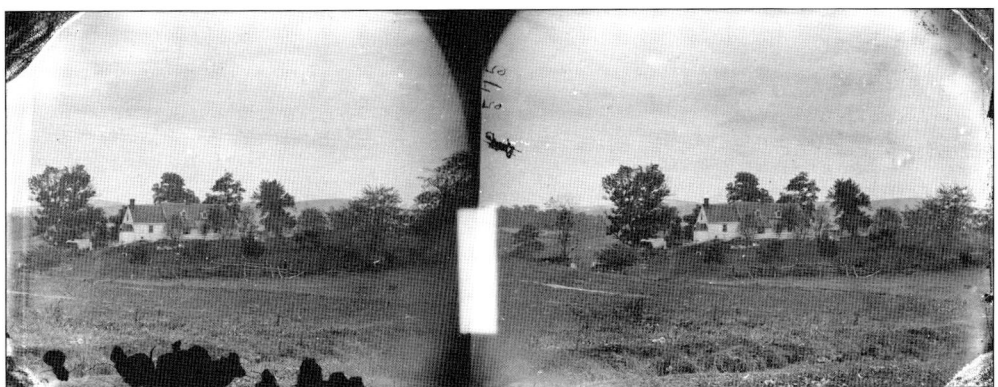

William and Margaret Roulette's home sits near the Sunken Road. Federal soldiers advanced across the Roulette property. The farm became a hospital and burial ground in the wake of the fighting. William Roulette requested $2,496.27 from the government for damage to his property. (Courtesy of the Library of Congress.)

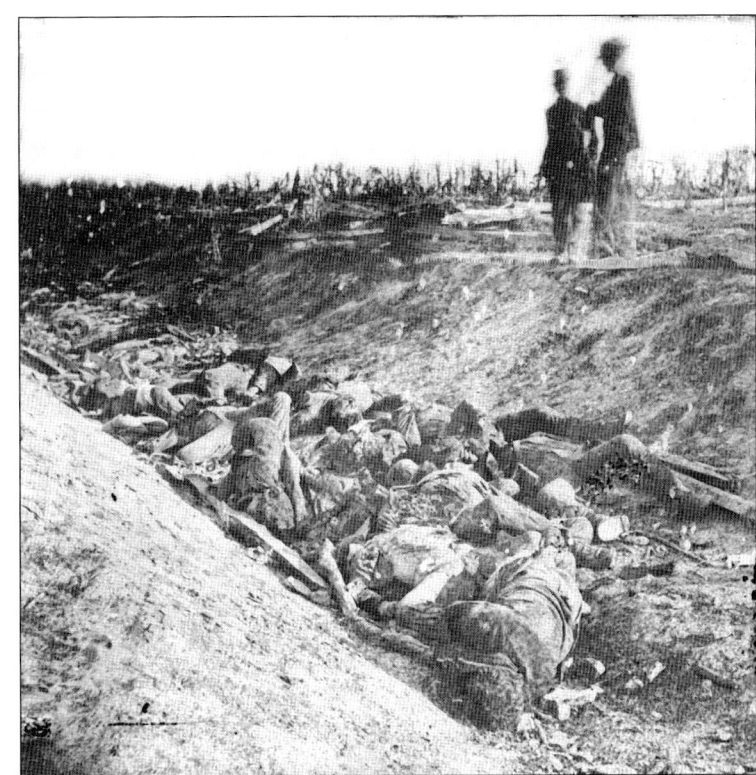

Confederate soldiers tenaciously defended their positions in the Sunken Road, but 2,600 of them became casualties during the fight. Newspaper correspondent Charles Coffin wrote of the scene in the road, recalling that bodies "were lying in rows like the ties of a railroad, in heaps, like cordwood mingled with the splintered and shattered fence rails. Words are inadequate to portray the scene." (Courtesy of the Library of Congress.)

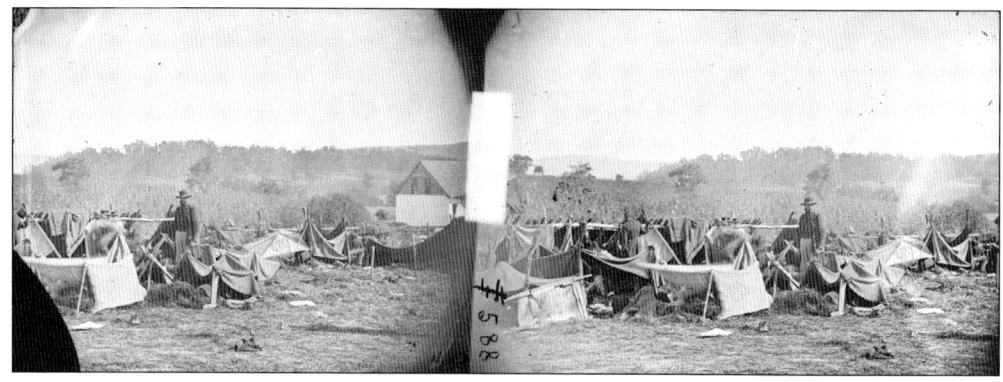

These two images show the hospital of William French's Federal division, which fought for possession of the Sunken Road on September 17. The man standing at the center of the image above is identified by Alexander Gardner as Dr. Anson Hurd of the 14th Indiana Infantry. During the battle, Hurd came under fire while working at a field hospital on the Roulette farm. Subsequently, he moved his operations farther behind the lines to the Otho J. Smith farm on the west bank of Antietam Creek. Both Union and Confederate soldiers received treatment at this hospital, which served as many as 1,400 soldiers at one time during its peak. (Both, courtesy of the Library of Congress.)

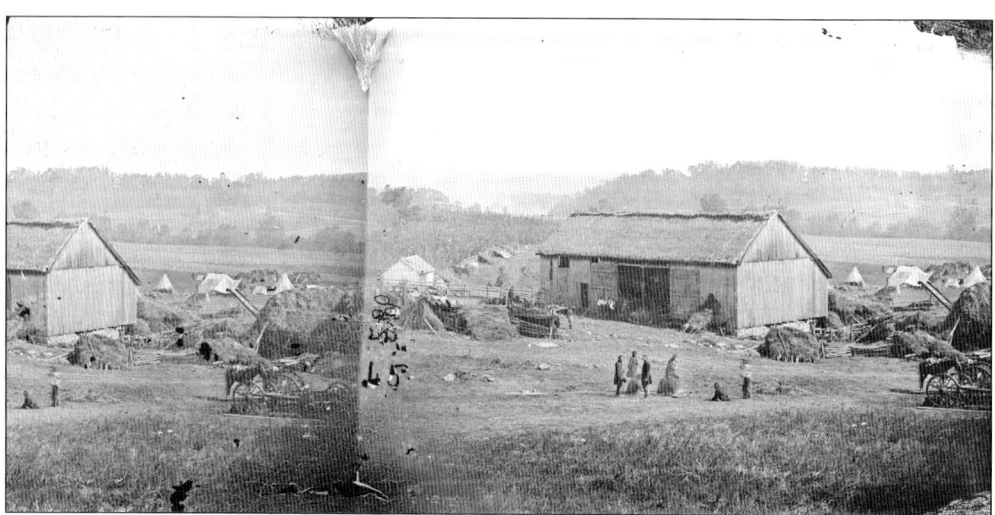

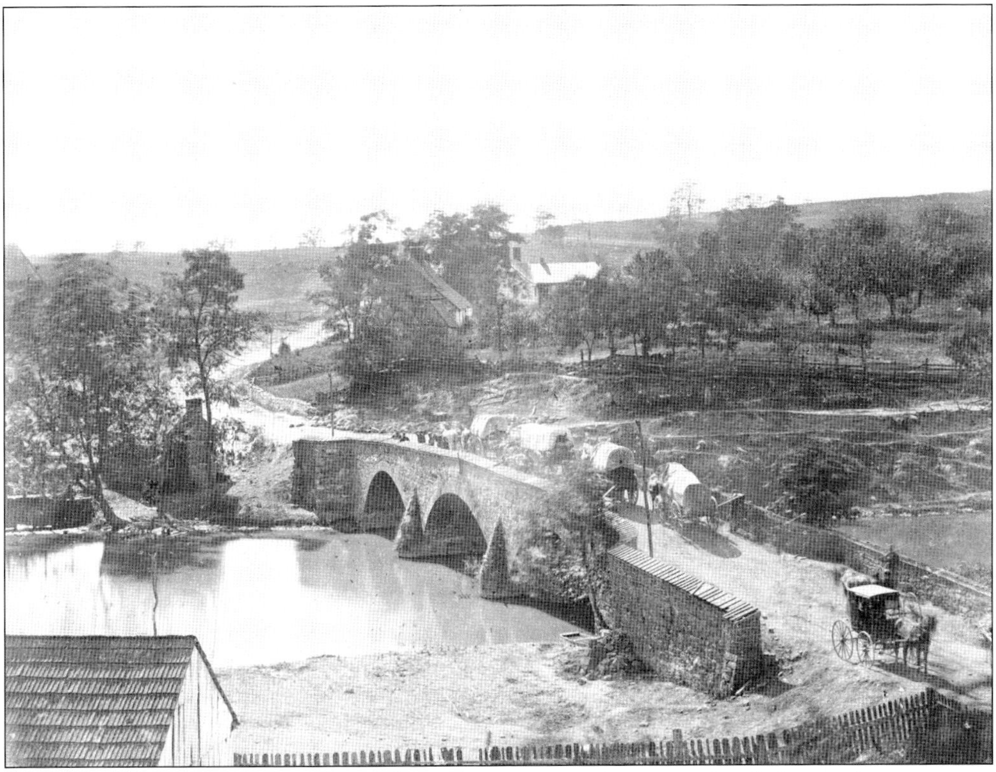

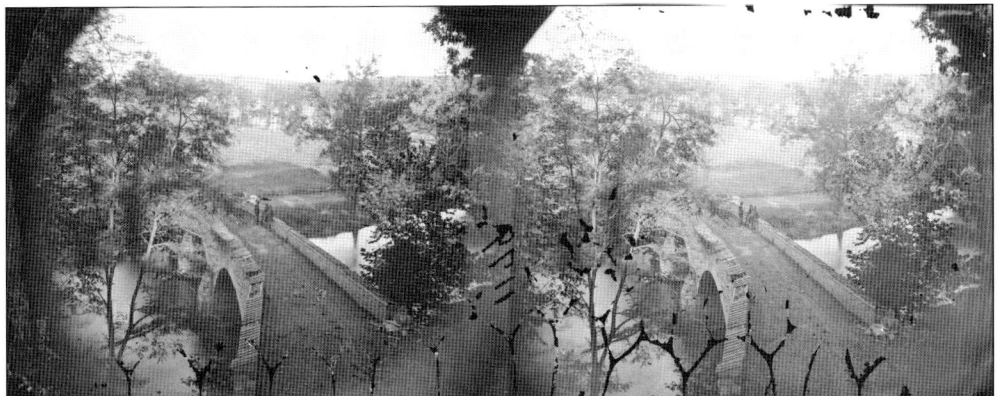

Portions of both armies used the Middle Bridge spanning Antietam Creek during the operations along the creek. Joshua and Mary Newcomer and their seven children occupied the L-shaped farmhouse in the middle ground. The government remunerated their damage claims, but only in the amount of $145. This ruined the Newcomers and forced them to leave the farm. (Courtesy of the Library of Congress.)

Barely 400 Georgians led by Col. Henry Benning defended the Burnside Bridge crossing for three hours on September 17. Gardner captured their strategic vantage point overlooking the bridge with this image looking east across the creek. Three separate Federal attacks attempted to carry the crossing, and only the third succeeded. (Courtesy of the Library of Congress.)

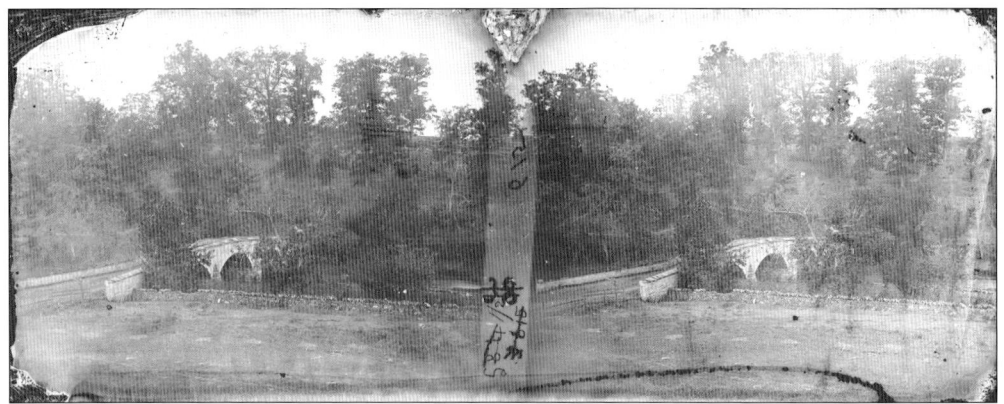

This photograph presents a view of the famous Burnside Bridge from the perspective of the Federal attackers. Northern soldiers occupied the high ground from where Alexander Gardner captured the image. In the final assault to carry the bridge, Pennsylvania soldiers used the stone wall featured prominently in the photograph for cover. (Courtesy of the Library of Congress.)

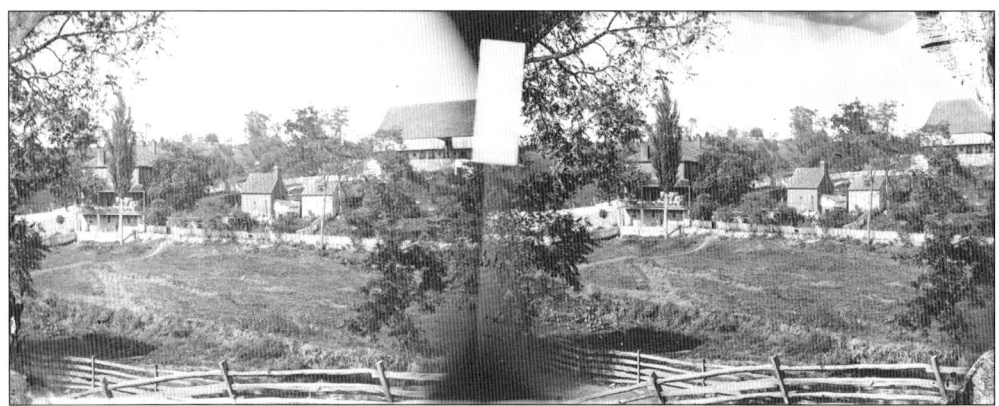

Alexander Gardner snapped this post-battle image of the Sherrick farm from the front yard of John Otto's nearby house. The farm sat in the middle of the afternoon's battle southeast of Sharpsburg. Massachusetts soldier Robert Goldthwaite Carter visited the home shortly after the battle and wrote that the soldiers of both armies acted "absurdly . . . on that deathstrewn ground about Sherrick's yard and orchard." (Courtesy of the Library of Congress.)

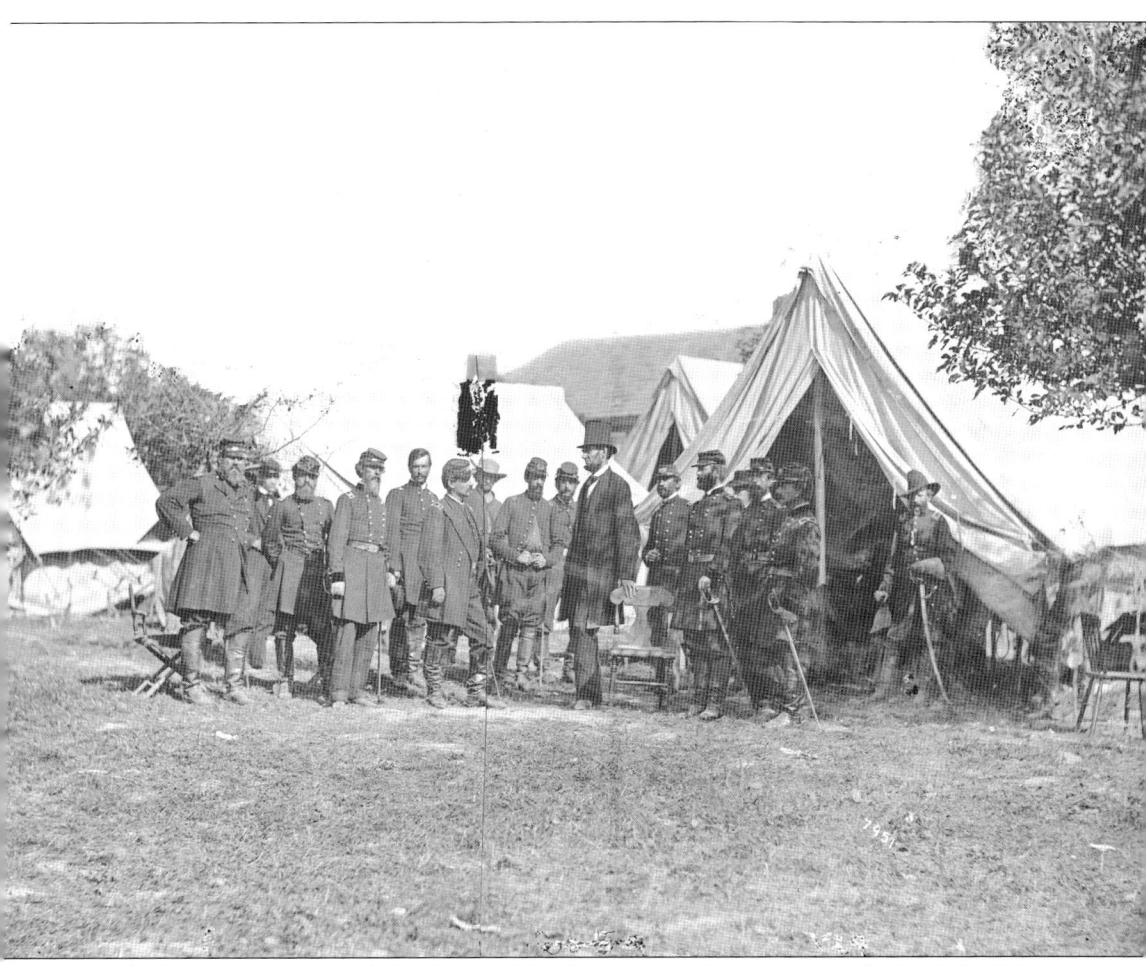

Pres. Abraham Lincoln visited the Army of the Potomac in the vicinity of the battlefield for four days in October 1862. He met with commanding general George McClellan, reviewed the army, and toured the battlefield. Alexander Gardner captured this scene on October 3 in front of the Grove house, whose roof can be seen in the background, on the west end of Sharpsburg. Lincoln reviewed the Union 5th Corps here and visited with the wounded of both sides. Inside the house, Lincoln, according to the *Cincinnati Commercial*, "remarked to the wounded Confederates that if they had no objection he would be pleased to take them by the hand. He said the solemn obligations which we owe to our country and posterity compel the prosecution of this war, and it followed that many were our enemies through uncontrollable circumstances, and he bore them no malice, and could take them by the hand with sympathy and good feeling. After a short silence the Confederates came forward, and each silently but fervently shook the hand of the President." (Courtesy of the Library of Congress.)

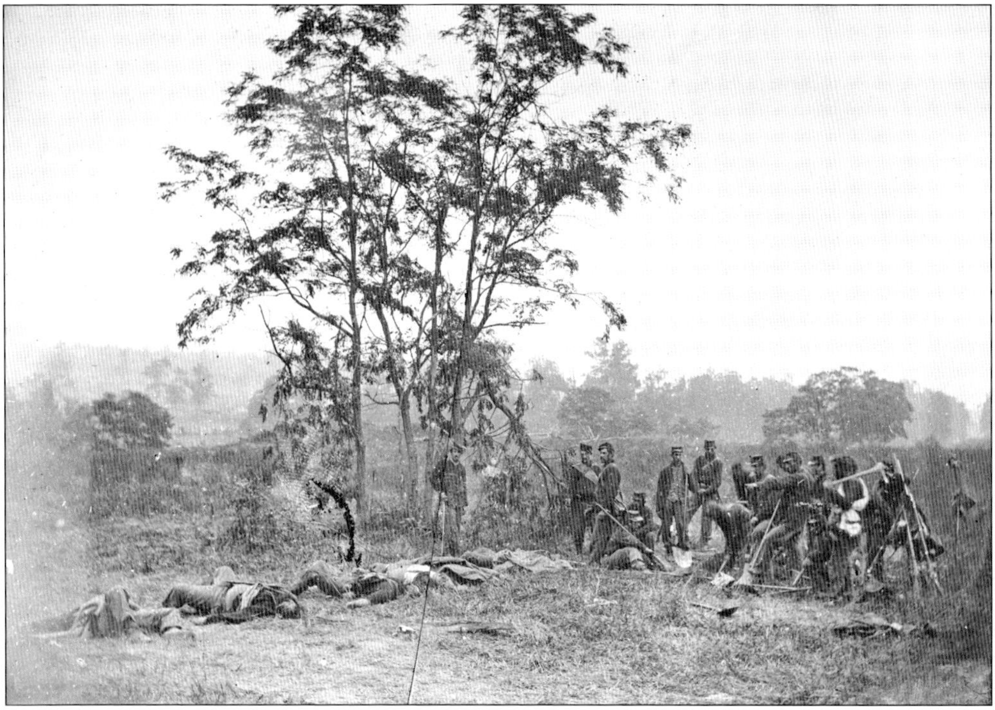

Because the Confederate army left the battlefield on the night of September 18, the grisly task of burying the approximately 4,000 dead fell to the Union victors. Typically, burial parties performed this duty in great haste, often digging shallow trenches and throwing a thin layer of dirt across the top. Skeletal remains frequently reappeared from under this natural canopy. (Courtesy of the Library of Congress.)

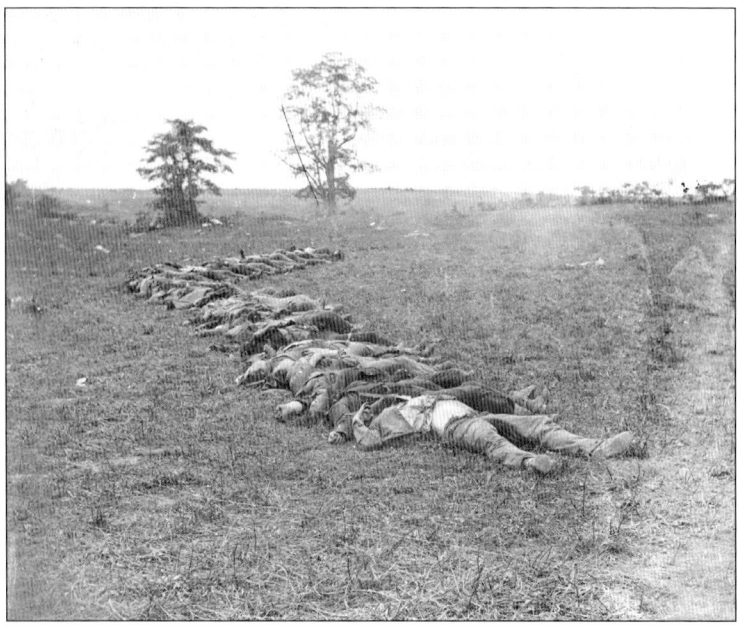

Federal burying parties laid out the Confederate dead for burial in mass graves, as seen here. In 1872, in an effort to disinter the dead from the battlefield, 758 of the buried Confederates were identified while another 2,481 rest unknown in their graves. The remains were removed to a distinct plot in Rose Hill Cemetery in nearby Hagerstown. (Courtesy of the Library of Congress.)

Two

The Cemetery

Even though the armies eventually left the Antietam battlefield behind, the citizens of Sharpsburg sought to pick up the shattered pieces of their lives and homes and likewise move on from the terrible September struggle that engulfed their land. They rebuilt and repaired their homes, erected new fences, and plowed their fields for the next harvest. Unfortunately, none of this could permanently erase memories of the battle. "The eye rests upon something to remind the traveler of that awful day of carnage," wrote a Union soldier passing through the area two years later.

As the civilians attempted to return to some level of normalcy in the weeks and months after the battle, actually achieving that became difficult or even impossible. Rains washed away the covering dirt of shallow graves, exposing the casualties of battle. Broken guns, accoutrements, and artillery shells littered the fields and woodlots.

Amongst all of this, the State of Maryland passed legislation in March 1865 authorizing a central burying place in Sharpsburg for the dead, designated Antietam National Cemetery. Maryland, its wartime status as a border state never far from anyone's minds, initially mandated that both Union and Confederate remains would be reinterred in the cemetery. This touched off a heated debate, as did the discussion about what to do with Lee's Rock, a stone within the cemetery's boundary that was said to be where General Lee watched the battle. The rock was removed, and the cemetery's board of trustees later voted to allow only Union remains in the cemetery. Amidst the disagreements, Pres. Andrew Johnson dedicated the cemetery on September 17, 1867.

The cemetery closed to further burials in 1953, though an exception was made in 2000 for nearby Keedysville native Patrick Howard Roy of the US Navy, who died in the attack on the USS *Cole*. A total of 5,044 American veterans from the Civil War, Spanish-American War, the Boxer Rebellion, World War I, World War II, and the Korean War now rest within the cemetery's stone walls.

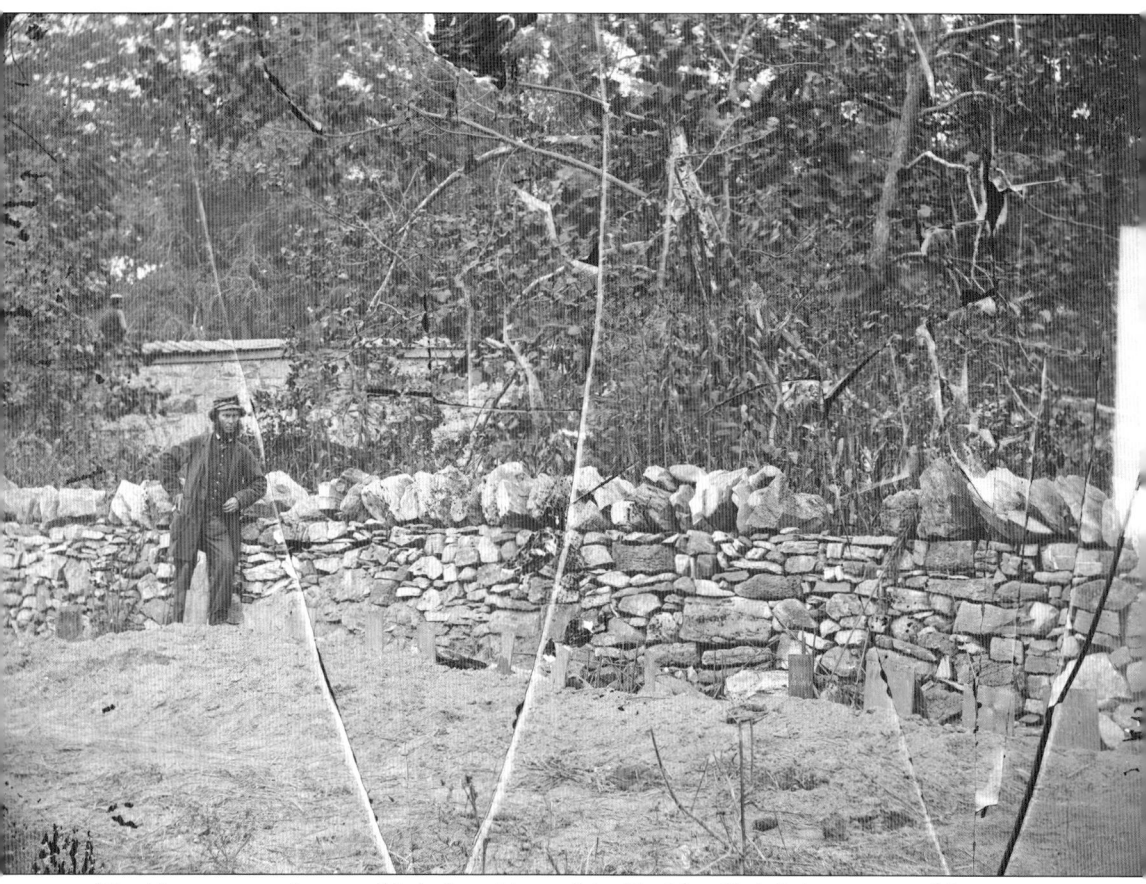

The 12 graves seen here are likely for soldiers of the 51st New York Infantry, one of the regiments responsible for carrying the Burnside Bridge. Four of the graves next to the bridge shown in this Gardner photograph are decipherable: Sgt. George W. Loud, Pvt. Edward Miller, Pvt. John Thompson, and Cpl. Michael Keefe, all members of the 51st New York. The remains of these four

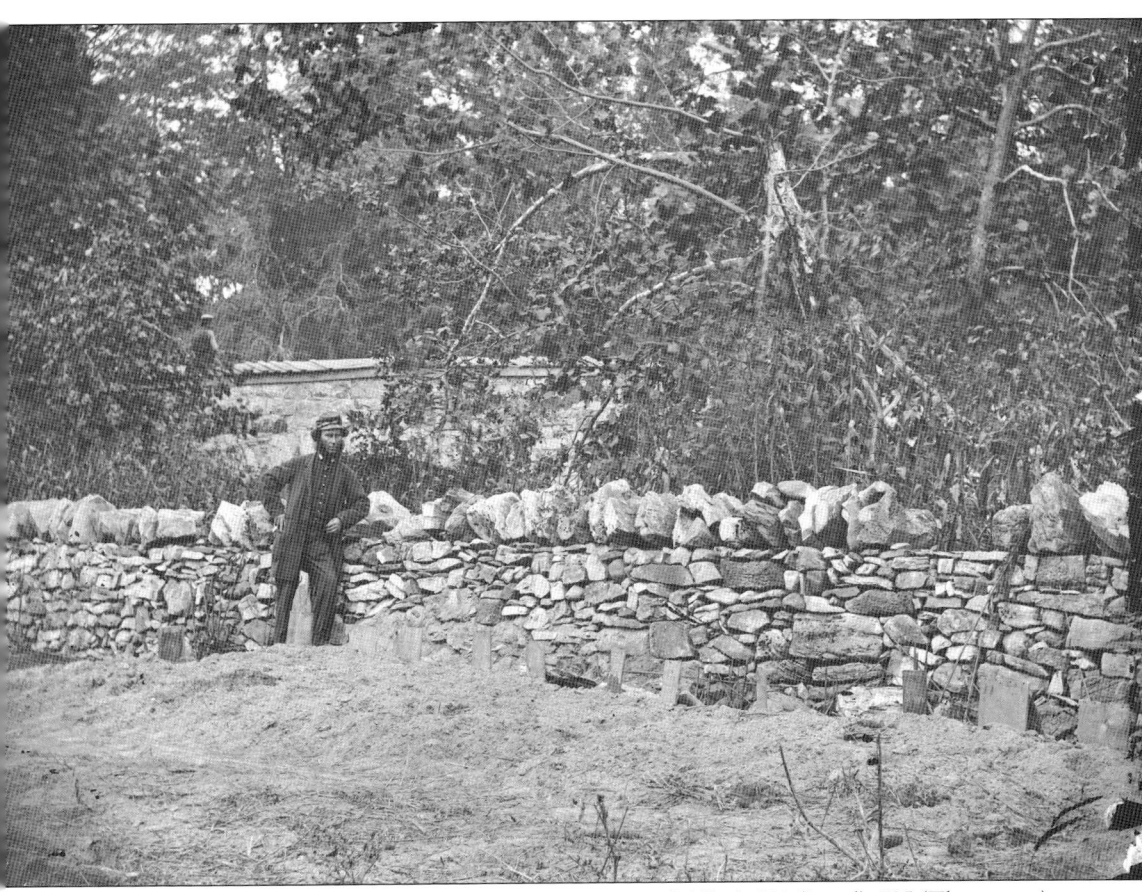

soldiers rest in Antietam National Cemetery in graves 782 (Miller), 783 (Loud), 785 (Thompson), and 786 (Keefe). At the far left of this stereographic image can be seen the branches of a young sycamore tree. This witness tree still stands today near the Burnside Bridge. (Courtesy of the Library of Congress.)

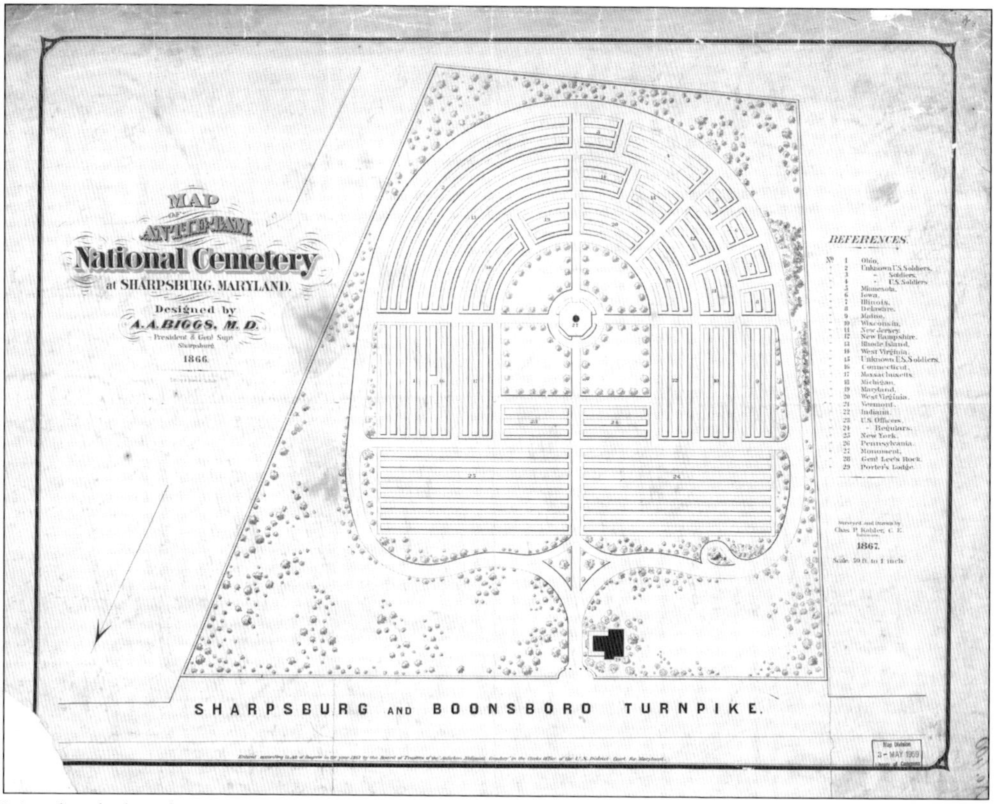

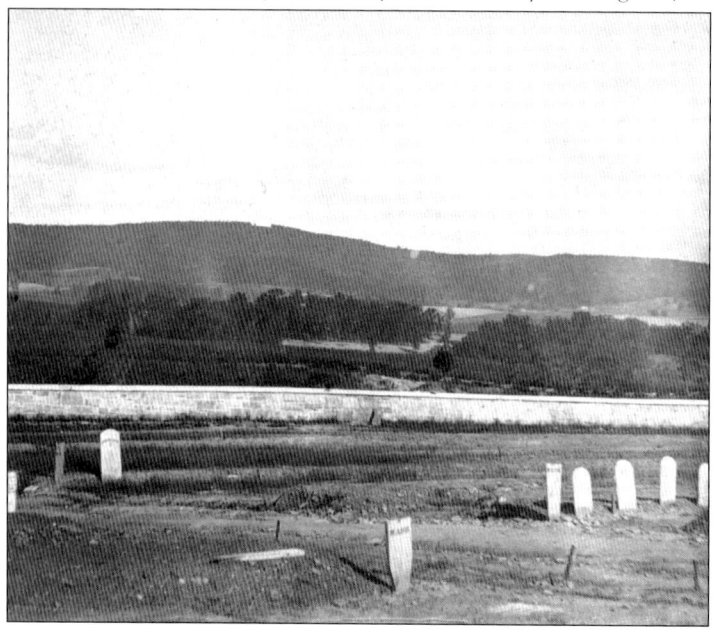

Maryland's legislature passed an act establishing Antietam National Cemetery in March 1865. The legislature selected four trustees to make the act come to fruition. Fifteen-year-old Charles Biggs, the son of trustee Augustin Biggs, won a competition to design the cemetery's layout, which is shown in this 1867 map. (Courtesy of the Library of Congress.)

This early image of the Antietam National Cemetery shows the work in progress. Before the uniform stone markers currently seen in the cemetery stood over the graves of the fallen, wooden markers held their place. Altogether, the remains of 4,776 US soldiers from the Civil War rest within the walls of the cemetery. (Courtesy of the Library of Congress.)

Pres. Andrew Johnson dedicated Antietam National Cemetery on September 17, 1867. In his address, Johnson said, "When we look on yon battlefield, I think of the brave men who fell in the fierce struggle of battle, and who sleep silent in their graves." Approximately 15,000 people attended the ceremony. (Courtesy of the Library of Congress.)

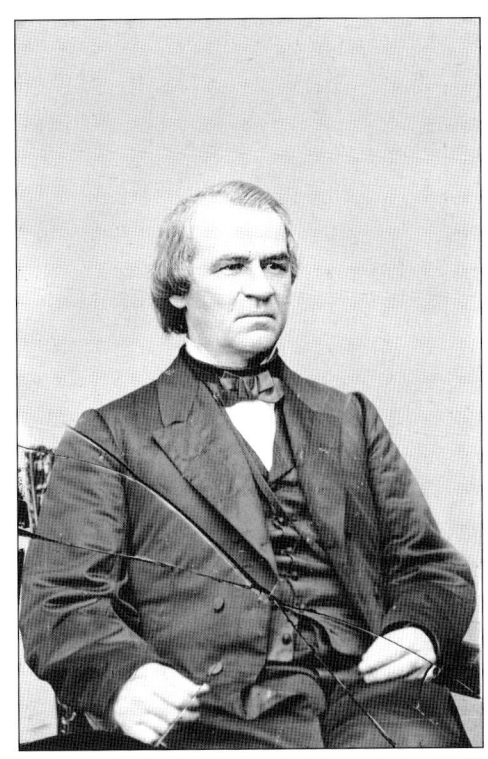

Concurrent with the dedication of the cemetery was the completion of the cemetery lodge building, seen at right in this post-1880 photograph. The architect of the Library of Congress, Paul Pelz, designed the lodge building. It served as the cemetery superintendent's quarters originally and later as a visitor center until 1962. (Courtesy of MOLLUS, US Army Heritage and Education Center, Carlisle, Pennsylvania.)

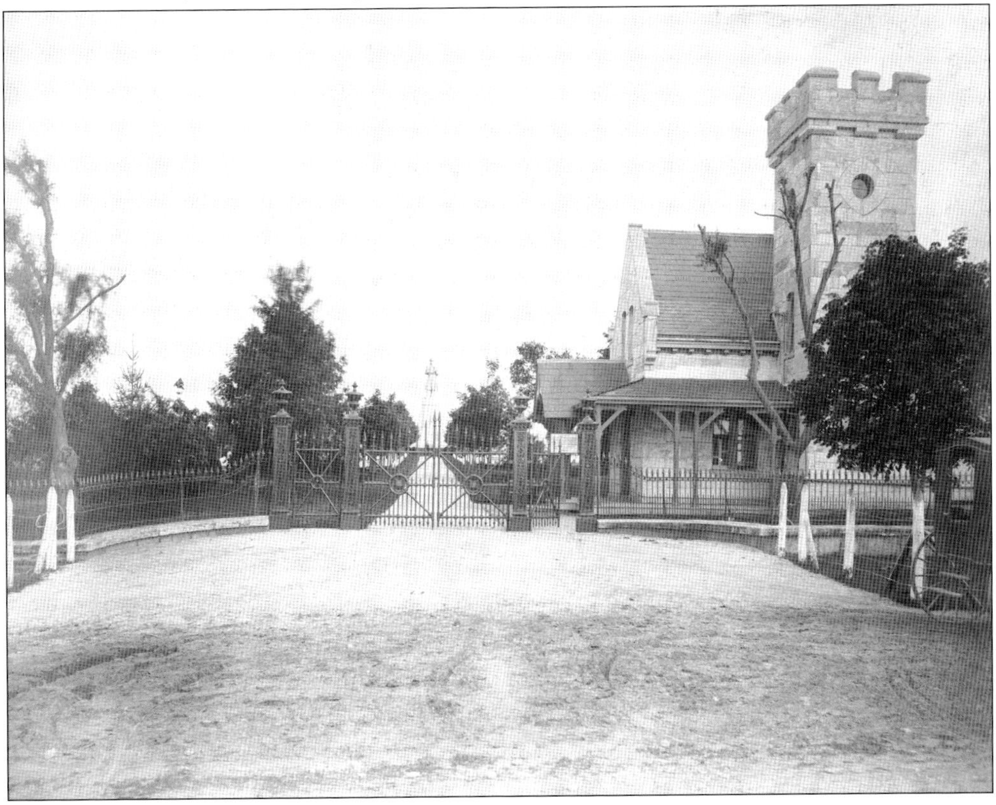

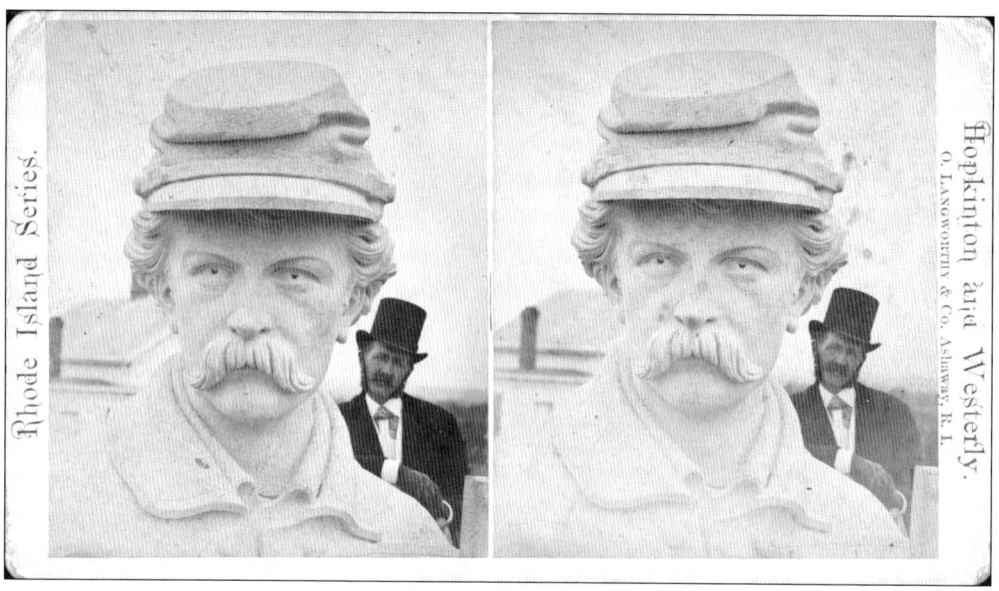

The original plans for the cemetery purposely left an empty plot in the middle "devoted to the erection of a monument commemorative of the great event of the battle, and the heroism of those who sleep at its foot and around it," wrote the cemetery's trustees. A large stone soldier was meant to fill the space. The board of trustees contracted with Connecticut stone designer James Batterson to create the colossal soldier. Payments came slowly to Batterson, and the monument remained in Batterson's hands for several years. While Batterson planned the monument, James W. Poletto sculpted it in Westerly, Rhode Island. Poletto appears in each of these images next to his masterpiece. (Both, courtesy of the New York Public Library.)

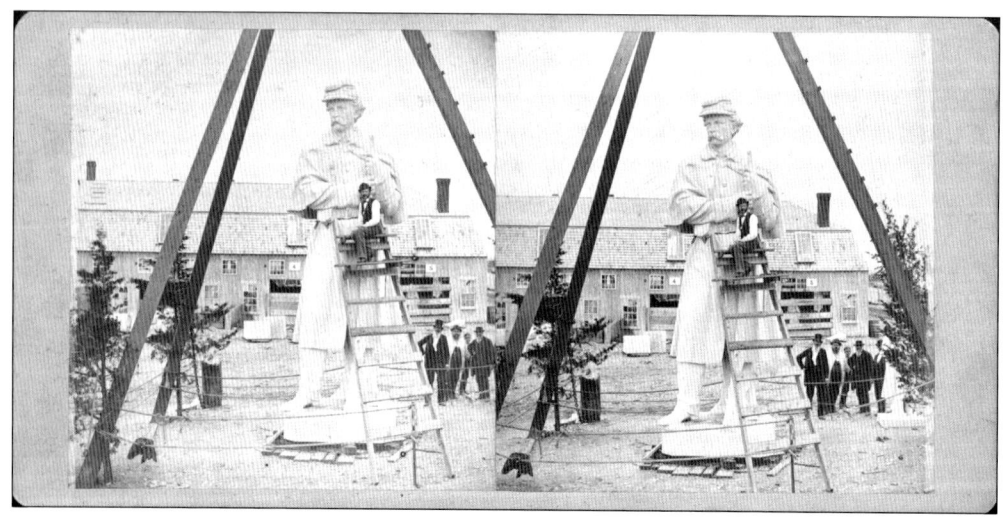

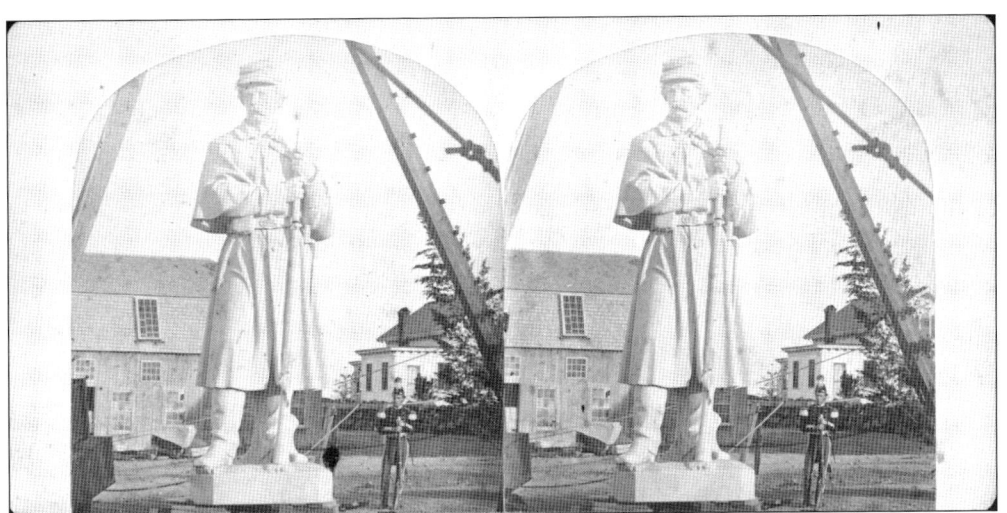

Known officially as *The Private Soldier,*"this impressive monument consists of 27 pieces that collectively weigh 250 tons. The entire monument stands at 44 feet, 7 inches tall while the soldier itself weighs in at 30 tons and rises 21 feet, 6 inches into the air. It cost over $32,000. (Courtesy of the New York Public Library.)

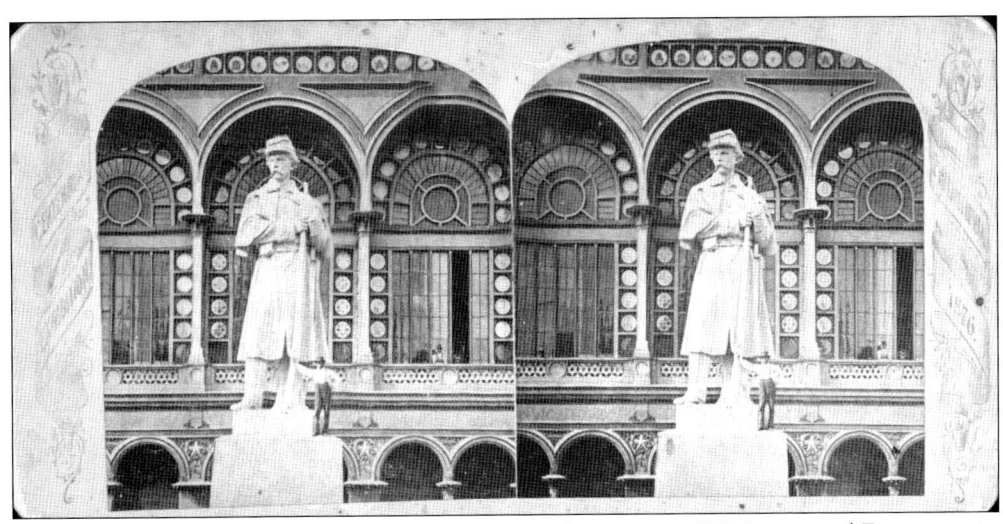

Batterson displayed the monument at the entrance of America's 1876 Centennial Exposition in Philadelphia. Critic Phillip T. Sandhurst wrote of the imposing soldier there, "Like the nation he defends, this colossus is in the bloom of youth. . . . Something rocky, rude and large-grained is obvious in this stalwart American; his head, with masculine chin and moustache [sic] of barbaric proportions." (Courtesy of the New York Public Library.)

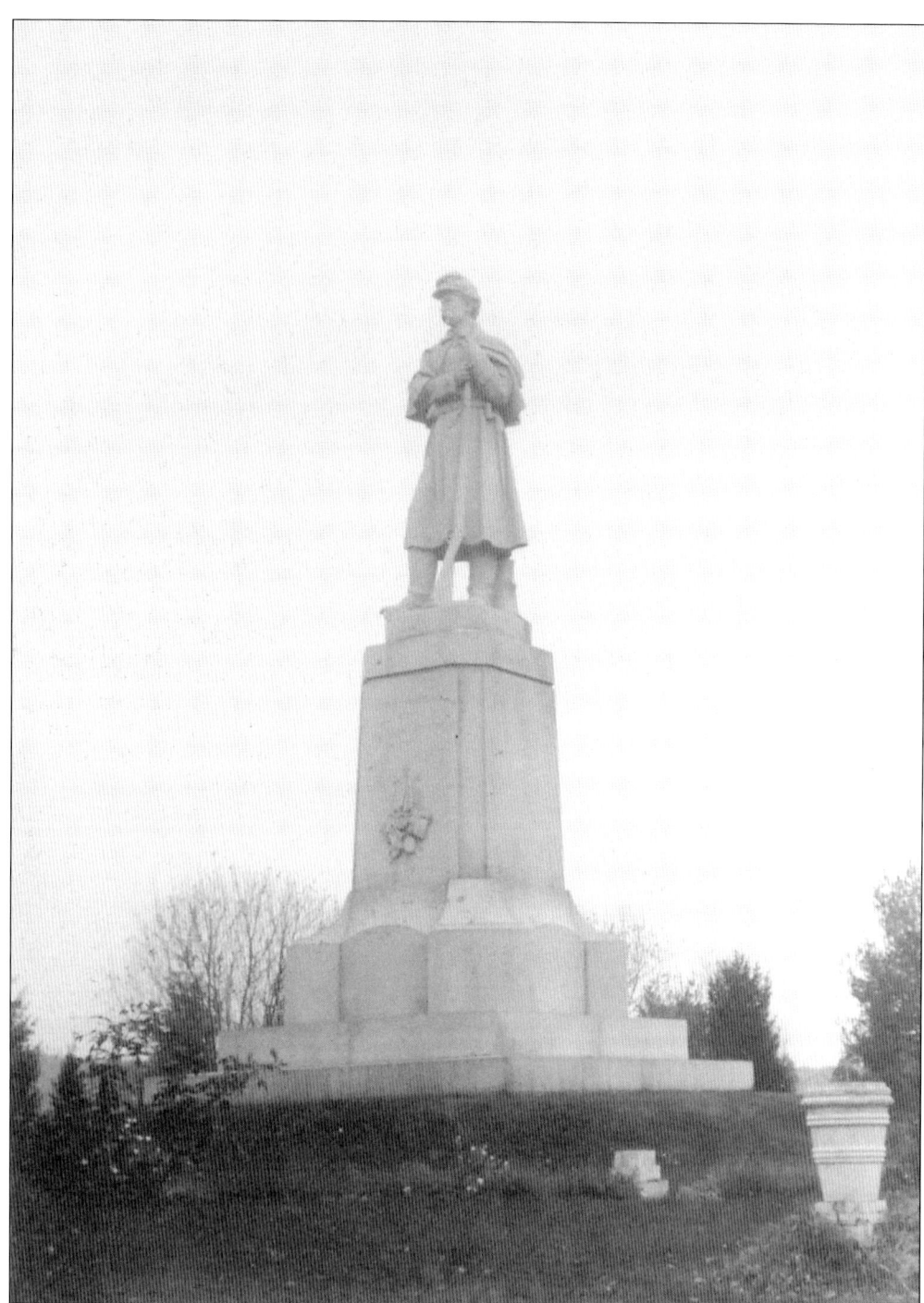

The monument was erected in the cemetery in January 1880, though even that was delayed. While transferring the monument—in pieces—from a barge in the Potomac River to a canal boat for conveyance to Sharpsburg, the top piece fell into the river. It finally arrived in Sharpsburg and had to be rolled to the cemetery on large wooden rollers. It was dedicated on September 17, 1880. (Courtesy of the Western Maryland Room, Washington County Free Library.)

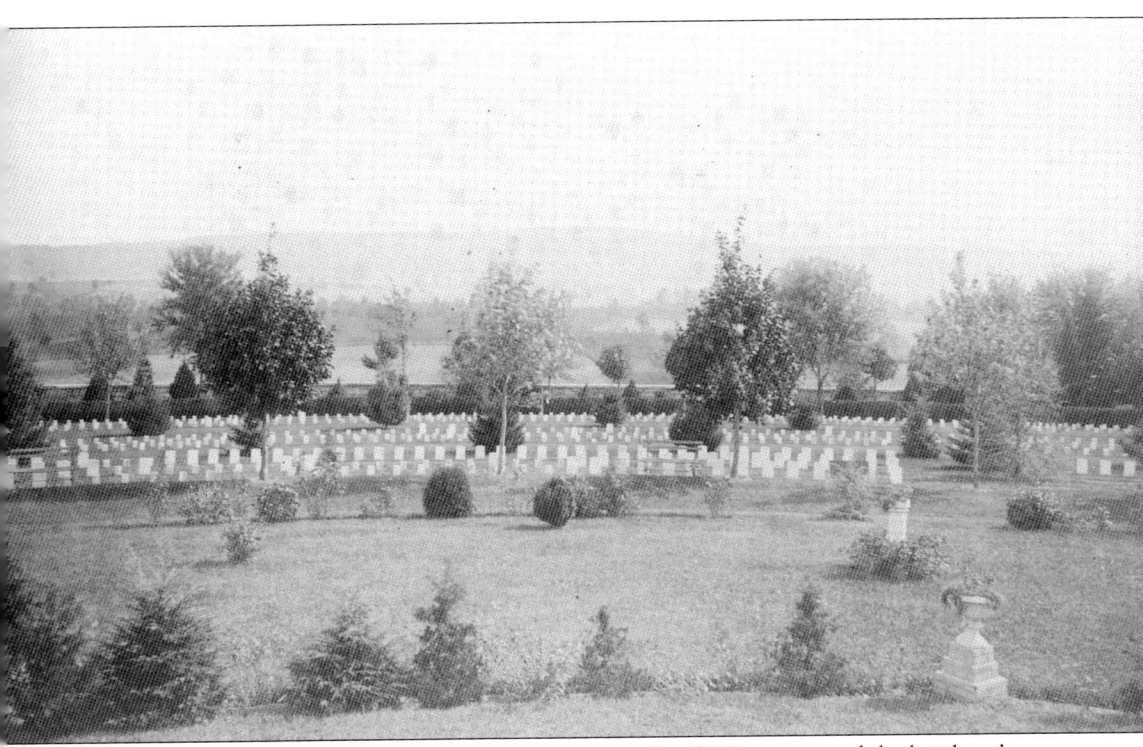

This early view of the cemetery looks east from its center. South Mountain and the heights above Antietam Creek can be discerned in the background. The urns and benches in the cemetery highlight the 19th-century idea of cemeteries also being used as public parks. (Courtesy of MOLLUS, US Army Heritage and Education Center, Carlisle, Pennsylvania.)

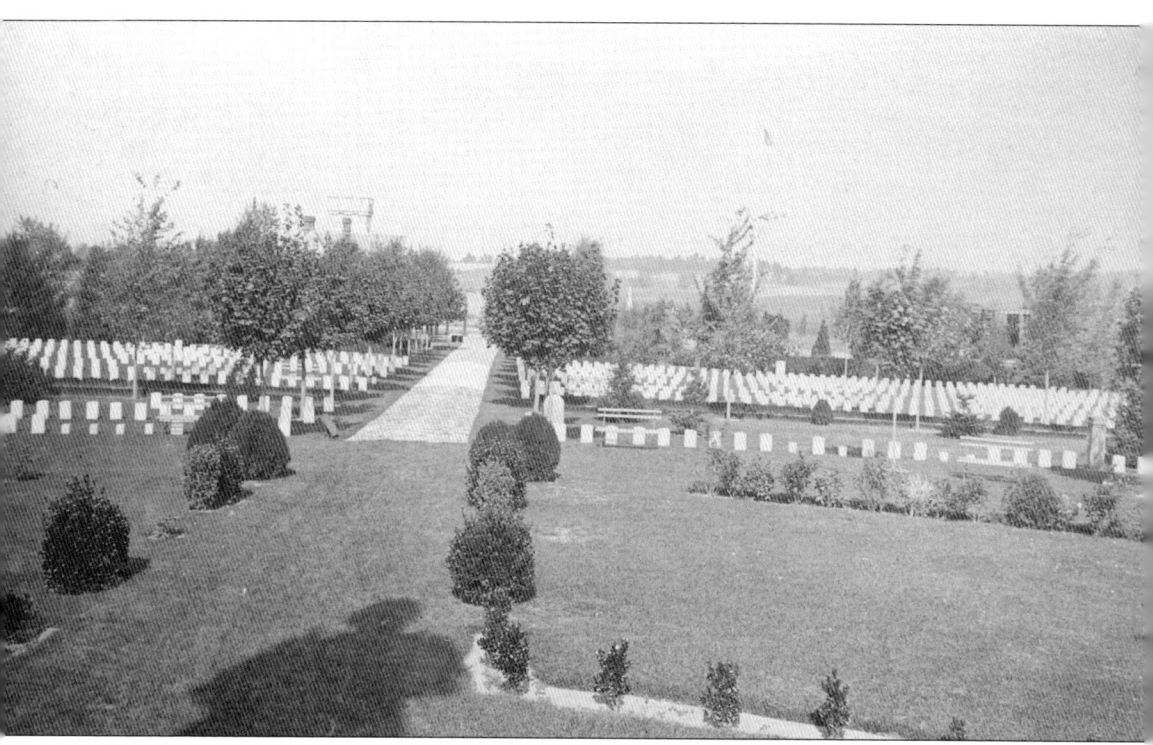

Wooden markers originally adorned each gravesite when remains from across Maryland were first buried within the grounds of the cemetery. This process took place between October 1866 and August 1867. By the late 1870s, those markers were gone, victims of the elements. The rest of the cemetery fell into disrepair until the War Department became the owner of the grounds in September 1877. The new caretakers immediately began to repair the grounds, and by 1878, the process of planting stone military headstones at each grave commenced. "The improvement in the appearance and condition of the Antietam Cemetery since the Govt. assumed charge of it is great," wrote Capt. A.F. Rockwell, the officer in charge of all national cemeteries, in 1879. The upgrades were "generally remarked by the visitors and neighborhood residents, and each year will add to the beauty and attractiveness of the place." (Courtesy of MOLLUS, US Army Heritage and Education Center, Carlisle, Pennsylvania.)

Looking north from the cemetery lodge reveals the entire northern half of the Antietam battlefield. In this picture, dated 1885, the Piper Barn (center) and the reconstructed Mumma Barn (right) can clearly be seen. Mountain View Cemetery, Sharpsburg's town cemetery, was established in 1883 and can be seen in the foreground. (Courtesy of MOLLUS, US Army Heritage and Education Center, Carlisle, Pennsylvania.)

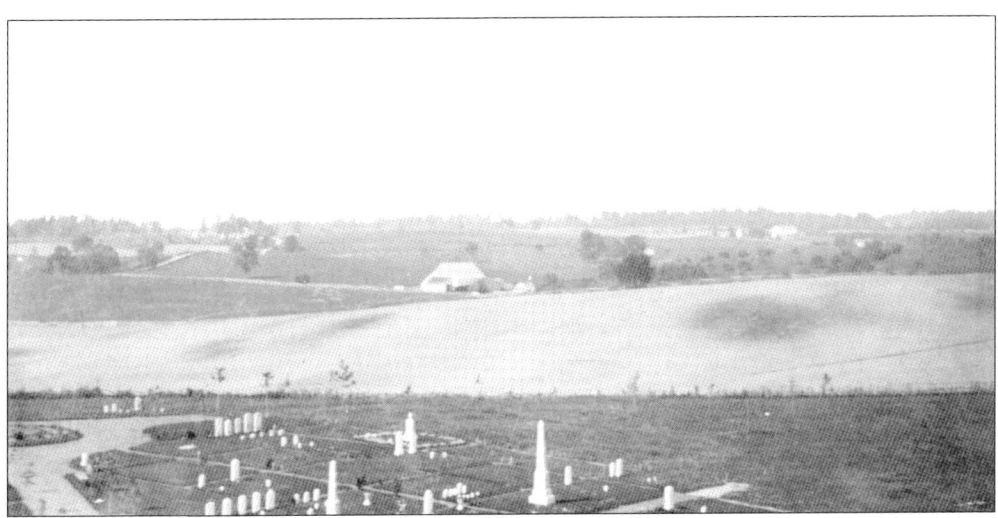

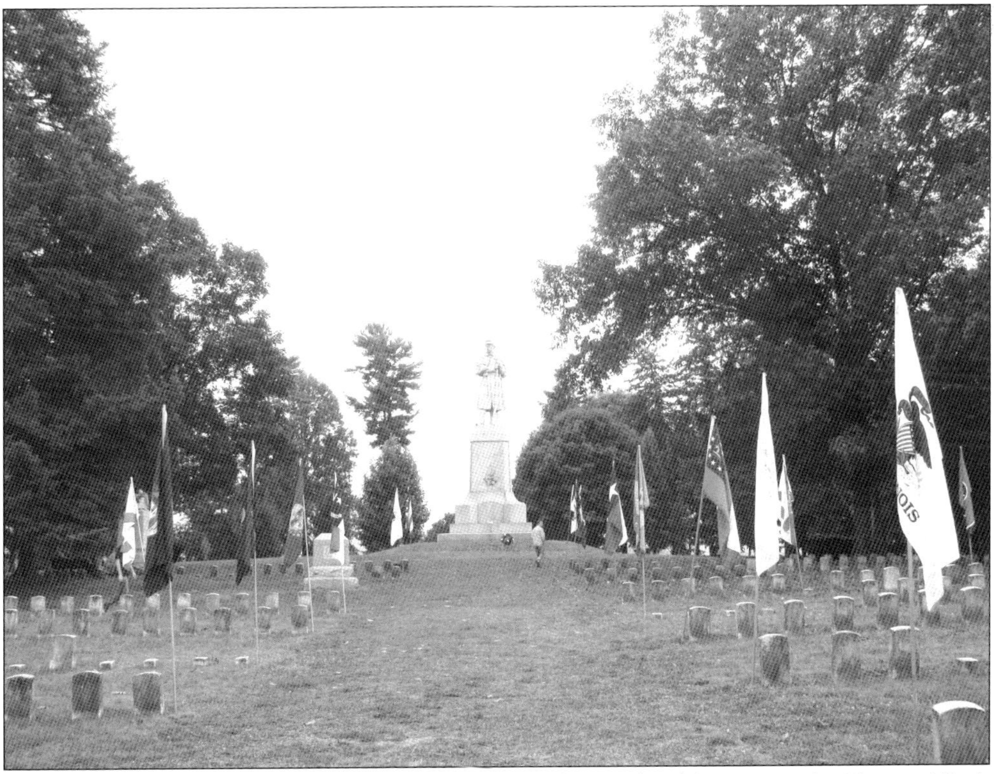

During the sesquicentennial (150th) anniversary of the Battle of Antietam, the National Park Service held a ceremony throughout the day that involved a public reading of the names of every soldier, Union and Confederate, killed in action on September 17, 1862. It lasted many hours and consisted of approximately 4,000 names. (Author's collection.)

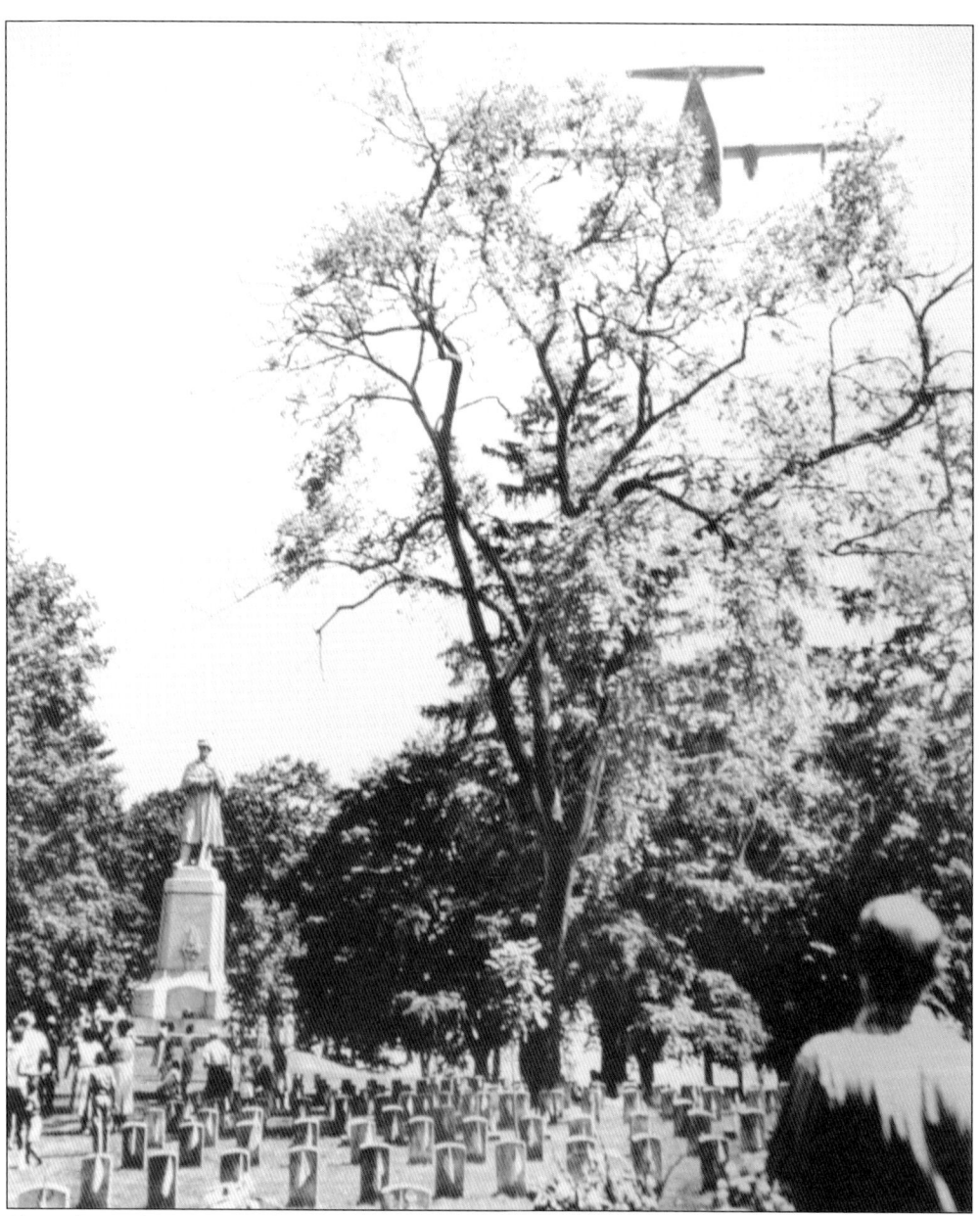

Sharpsburg's first Memorial Day celebration occurred on May 30, 1869. Citizens of the surrounding countryside gathered at the town's train station and walked to Antietam National Cemetery where they placed flowers at each grave. One of the attendees spoke briefly. Before the ceremony adjourned, the participants "resolved that, on next 'Memorial Day,' should their lives be spared, they would return again to strew flowers over the graves, and renew their vows of devotion to the memory of the sacred dead." Those that survived the year returned in 1870, and the ceremonial gathering at Antietam National Cemetery on Memorial Day has continued ever since, featuring different guest speakers each year, including former Civil War generals Ambrose Burnside, John Logan, and George B. McClellan. Pictured here is the 1958 Memorial Day ceremony, where organizers recruited a Fairchild C-123 to sprinkle flowers over the graves of the fallen. (Courtesy of the Western Maryland Room, Washington County Free Library.)

Three

THE BATTLEFIELD

Thousands of visitors travel to Sharpsburg every year to visit Antietam National Battlefield. The ground they tread on a daily basis looks much the same in the 21st century as it did in 1862. Historic homes, roads, fence lines, and farm fields still exist. One can walk in the footsteps of Union and Confederate soldiers from one end of the field to the other with few modern intrusions.

This virtually unchanged appearance did not always exist, though. Once the armies moved on from the fields of Antietam, Sharpsburg's citizens had to turn the area into a habitable place again. They built new homes, cut down historic trees, and planted new crops. Throughout the years, these post–Civil War homes became problematic on the battlefield landscape. A convenience store stood along the edge of the Bloody Lane while another used the foundation of the fallen Dunker Church. But the more things changed, the more things stayed the same at Antietam.

A visiting delegation of North Carolina veterans in 1894 wrote back home, "The locality in the nearly thirty-two years since the battle has undergone remarkably small change. The landmarks are all there." By the time of that visit, several monuments had already been erected on the battlefield. The monuments and the railroad increased visitation to the battlefield. This boon received praise from Sharpsburg's citizens. "Our citizens are beginning to take a deep interest in the work of laying out this battlefield, and have it eventually pass into the hands of the government. Our town has always manifested a loyalty to the Union, and now we have an opportunity—a grand opportunity to demonstrate our patriotism and to show our deepest regard for the faith and work of the heroes now sleeping in Antietam National Cemetery," read one local newspaper.

The US War Department assumed control of the battlefield in 1890 as Antietam became one of America's first five national military parks. In 1933, the National Park Service took charge of the park. The numerous images that appear in this chapter trace the history and preservation of Antietam National Battlefield through the years.

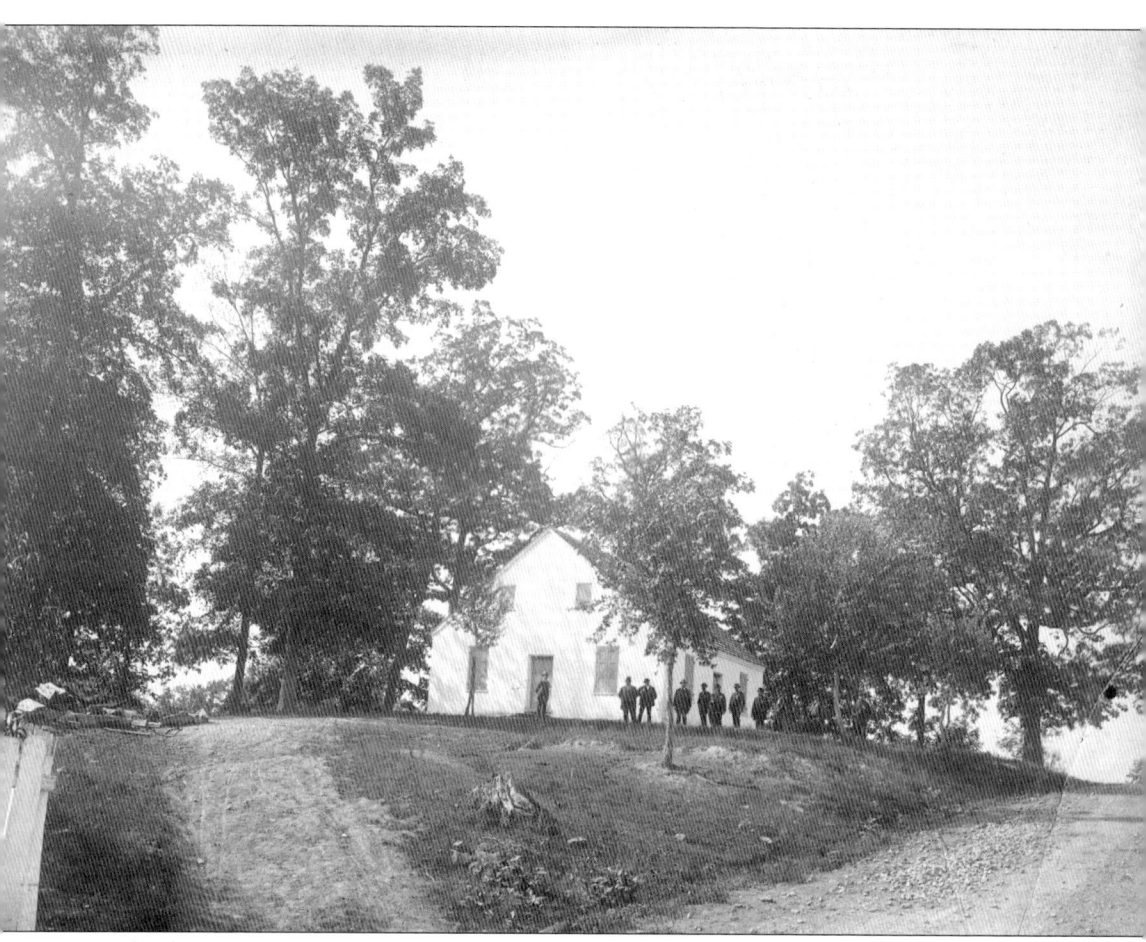

In the decade following the Civil War, only Gettysburg witnessed preservation of its battleground and a subsequent blossoming tourism industry. Sharpsburg's citizens initially showed little interest in preserving the Antietam battlefield in a Gettysburg-like manner. Thus, the field remained in private hands. However, following along with the increased interest in commemorating the Civil War, veterans' organizations began to make excursions to their former fields of battle. Veterans originally did not flock to Antietam like they did Gettysburg. By the late 1870s, though, veteran groups began visiting Antietam. Here, tourists stand by the Dunker Church. Sharpsburg's citizens soon realized that travelers to the battlefield could be a boon to their town. A 1907 visitor noted how many of the town's buildings showed damage from the battle, but the townsfolk showed little inclination to repair it in order for tourists to see it. (Courtesy of MOLLUS, US Army Heritage and Education Center, Carlisle, Pennsylvania.)

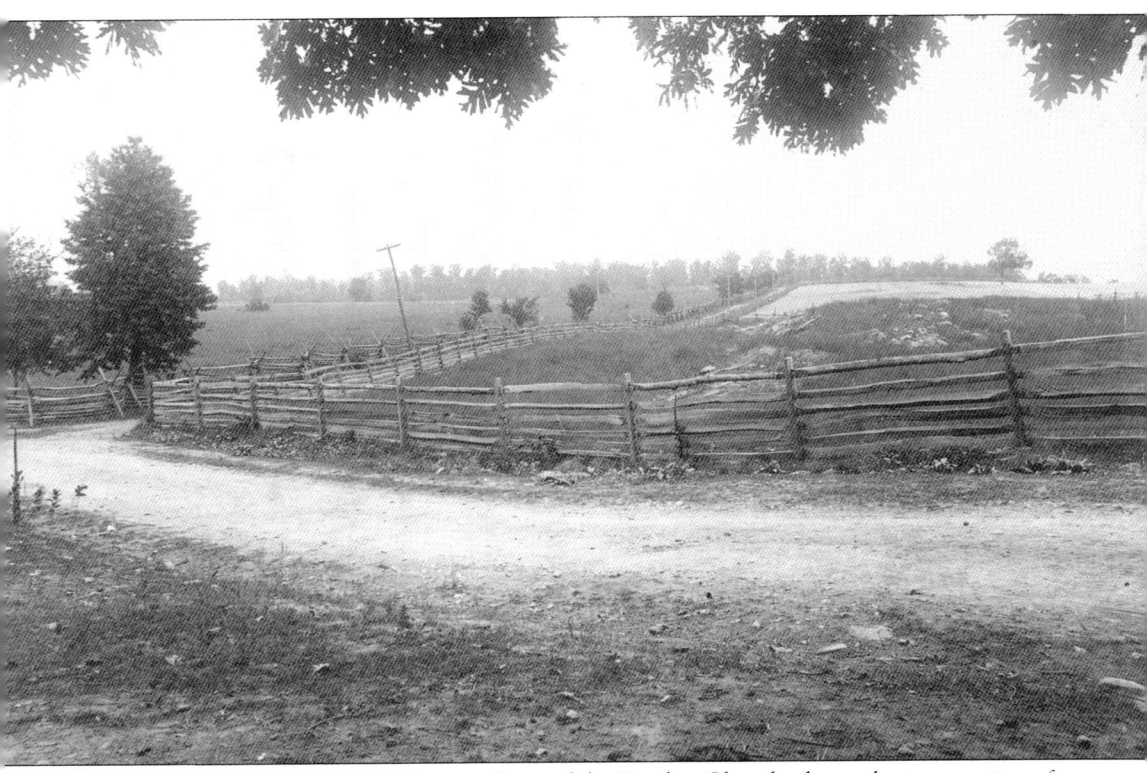

This early battlefield view, taken from in front of the Dunker Church, shows the intersection of the Smoketown Road and the Hagerstown Turnpike. The Hagerstown Turnpike runs from left to right, and the Smoketown Road cuts through the middle of the picture and runs away from the camera. The rocky outcropping toward the right is where the Maryland Monument sits today. The East Woods can be seen in the background. Serious fighting swirled through the field to the left of the Smoketown Road early on the morning of September 17, and some historians believe that more casualties fell in that field than in the Cornfield just to the north. This critical land was recently preserved and will someday be incorporated into Antietam National Battlefield. (Courtesy of MOLLUS, US Army Heritage and Education Center, Carlisle, Pennsylvania.)

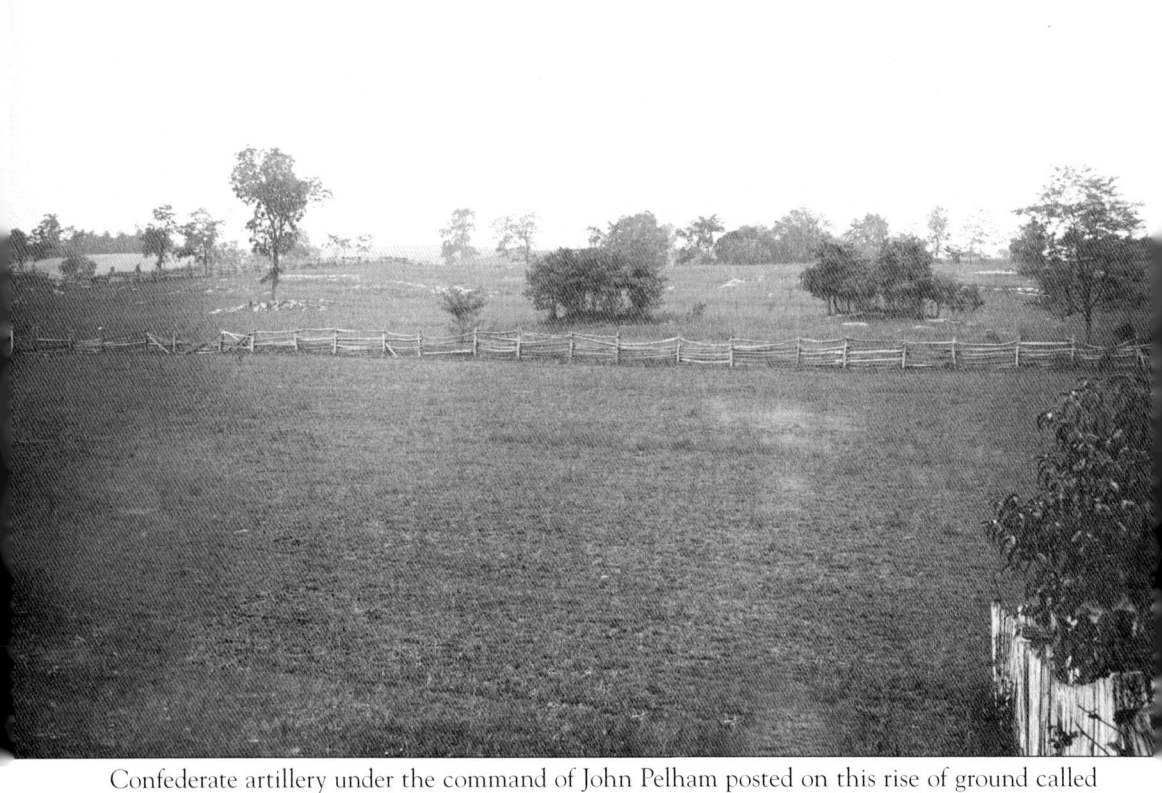

Confederate artillery under the command of John Pelham posted on this rise of ground called Nicodemus Heights opened the Battle of Antietam on the morning of September 17. "We could see the first rays of the sun lighting up the distant hilltops, when there was a sudden flash, and the air around us appeared to be alive with shot and shell," remembered Union artillerist J. Albert Monroe, who was on the receiving end of those first shots. "The opposite hill seemed suddenly to have become an active volcano, belching forth flame and smoke." A mass of Federal artillery behind the Joseph Poffenberger farm eventually forced Pelham's guns off Nicodemus Heights, though it remained a sought-after piece of high ground. This view looks west from near a toll booth on the Hagerstown Turnpike. (Courtesy of MOLLUS, US Army Heritage and Education Center, Carlisle, Pennsylvania.)

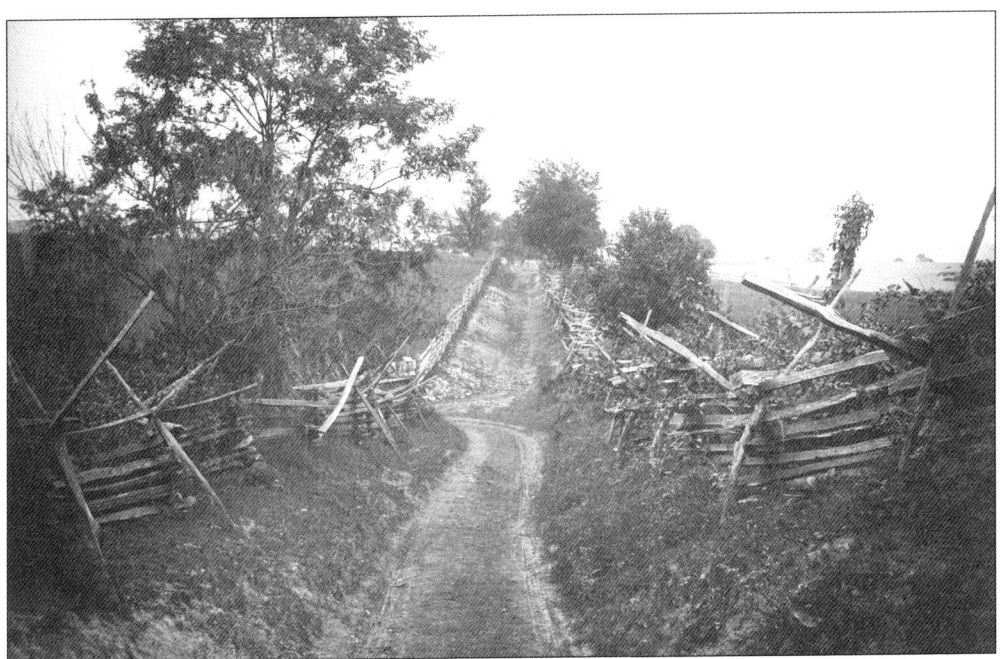

The Sunken Road became a deadly Confederate position in September 1862. According to legend, a local woman saw the piles of dead soldiers in the lane, dropped to her knees, and asked God to bless the dead in that "bloody lane." It was another innocent local landmark that forever became associated with America's bloodiest day. (Courtesy of MOLLUS, US Army Heritage and Education Center, Carlisle, Pennsylvania.)

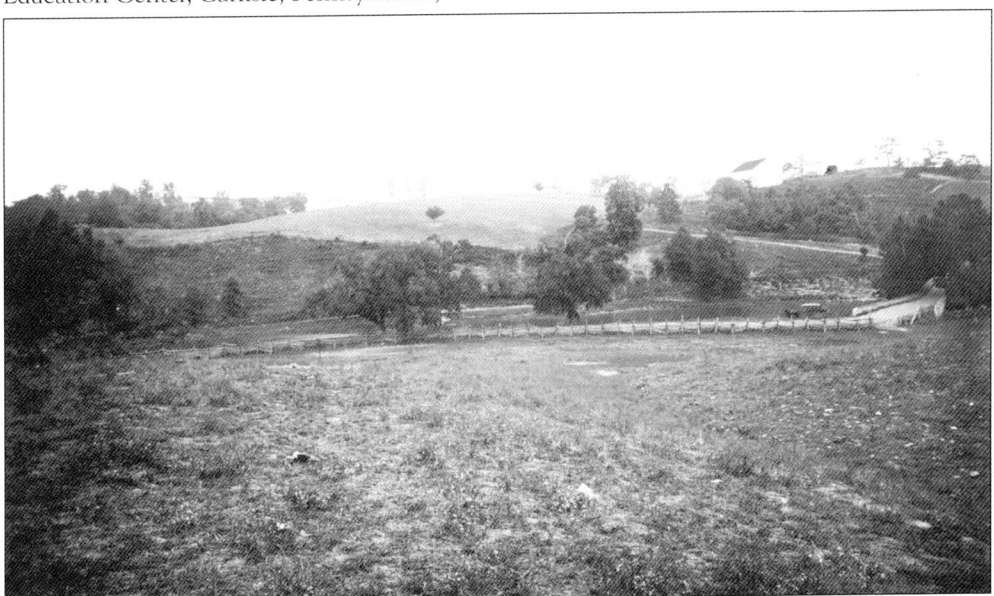

Because the battlefield remained in private hands, postwar development sprouted occasionally on the hallowed ground. Here, above the Burnside Bridge, can be seen the outbuildings of the Benner, or Spong, farm, constructed in 1864. Sadly, a dispute between the Spong family and the War Department led to the murder of battlefield superintendent Charles W. Adams on June 6, 1912. (Courtesy of MOLLUS, US Army Heritage and Education Center, Carlisle, Pennsylvania.)

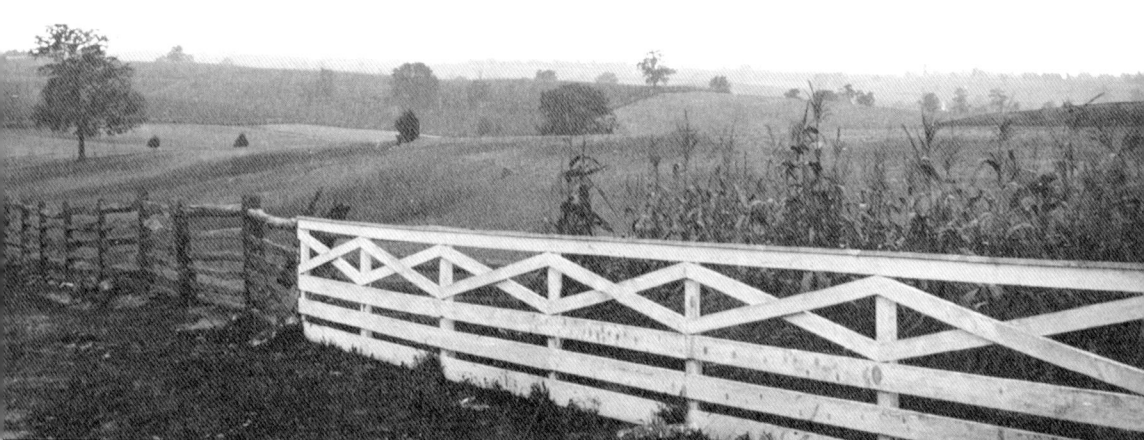

Union commander George McClellan used a vantage point like this from near the Pry House to coordinate his army during the battle. Armed with this view, McClellan wrote that the Confederate position "was one of the strongest to be found in this region of country, which is well adapted to defensive warfare." While the vantage point was impressive and vast, it did not expose the entire Confederate army to the Federals' eyes. The rolling terrain on the battlefield allowed Robert E. Lee to hide his men on the rear slope of the ridge and in numerous ravines. George Smalley of the *New York Tribune* noted this truth for his readers: "Some directions of the rebel lines had been disclosed by the smoke of their guns, but the whole interior formation of the country beyond the hills was completely concealed," he wrote. (Courtesy of MOLLUS, US Army Heritage and Education Center, Carlisle, Pennsylvania.)

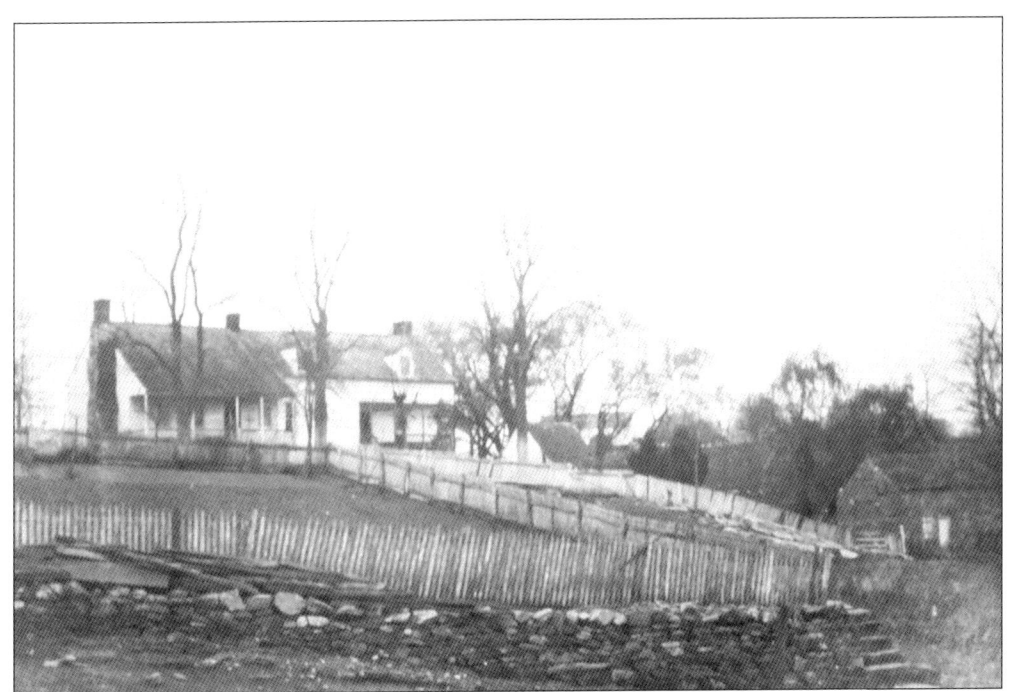

Veterans of the 14th Connecticut Infantry visited the Roulette farm during their trip to Antietam in 1894 when they dedicated their monument near the Bloody Lane. "On its fields perhaps was fought some of the most savage battles of the Civil War," read a 1956 National Park Service report of the Roulette property. The 179-acre farm became a part of Antietam National Battlefield in 1998. (Courtesy of the Western Maryland Room, Washington County Free Library.)

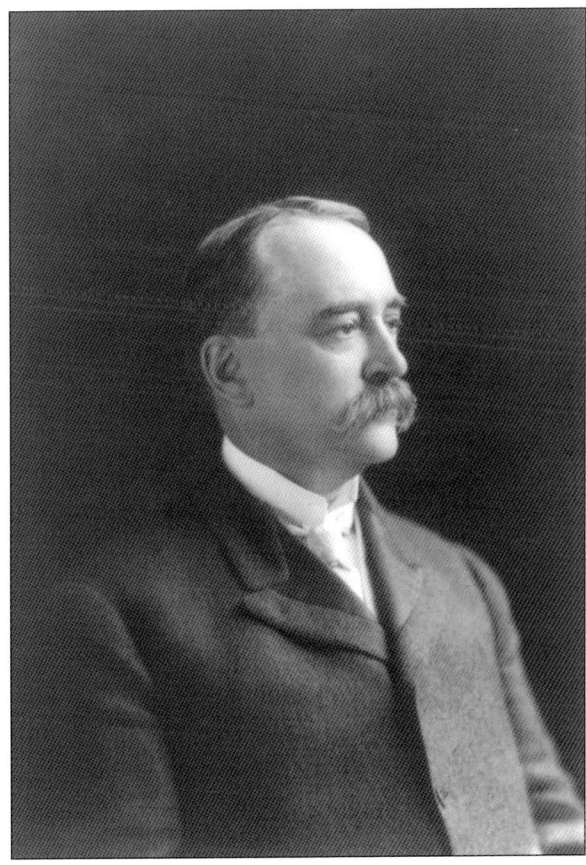

Congressman Louis McComas helped pass legislation on August 30, 1890, appropriating $15,000 "for the purpose of surveying, locating and preserving the lines of battle of the Army of the Potomac and of the Army of Northern Virginia at Antietam, and for marking the same," read the legislation. The road leading from the Antietam Railroad Station to the National Cemetery later bore the name McComas Avenue in his honor. (Courtesy of the Library of Congress.)

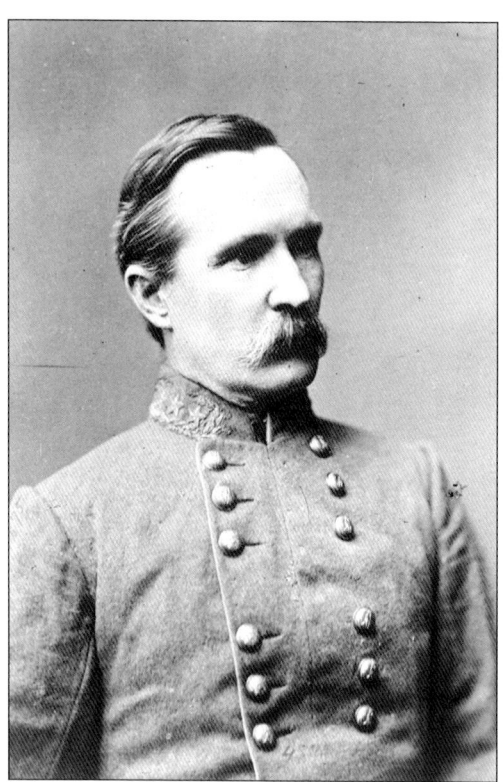

Though not present at the Battle of Antietam, former Confederate general Henry Heth served as the southern representative on the Antietam Battlefield Board alongside his Union counterpart John C. Stearns. The War Department instructed the two men to denote both army's battle lines and map the battlefield. Both men received $250 per month each for the work. (Courtesy of the Library of Congress.)

George Breckenridge Davis was a veteran of the 1st Massachusetts Cavalry during the Civil War. Davis served as the president of the Antietam Battlefield Board from 1894 to 1895. Under his direction, the board laid out the battlefield tour roads, placed and wrote the numerous iron War Department tablets on the battlefield, and supervised the construction of the stone observation tower at the Bloody Lane. (Courtesy of the Library of Congress.)

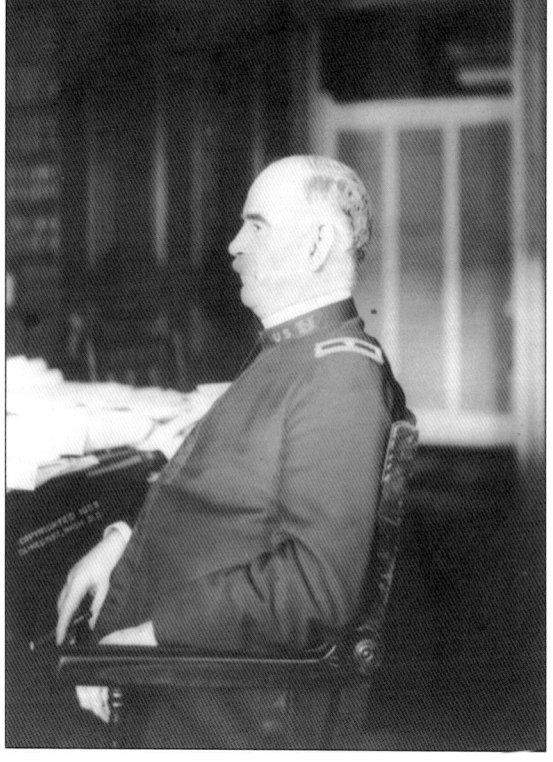

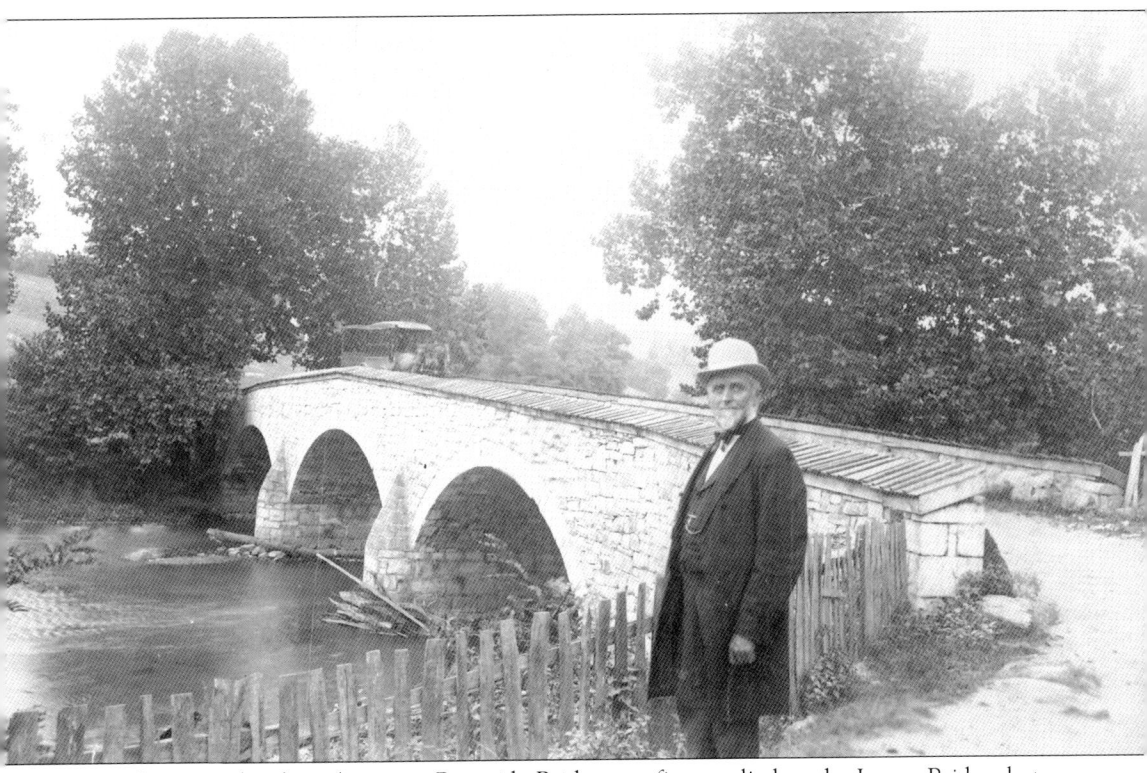

It is unclear exactly when the name Burnside Bridge was first applied to the Lower Bridge, but it was shortly after the battle when the sobriquet stuck. As tourism at Sharpsburg grew, more visitors came to see the battle's famous landmarks. The bridge remains one of the most visited landmarks at Antietam and an iconic American battlefield structure. (Courtesy of MOLLUS, US Army Heritage and Education Center, Carlisle, Pennsylvania.)

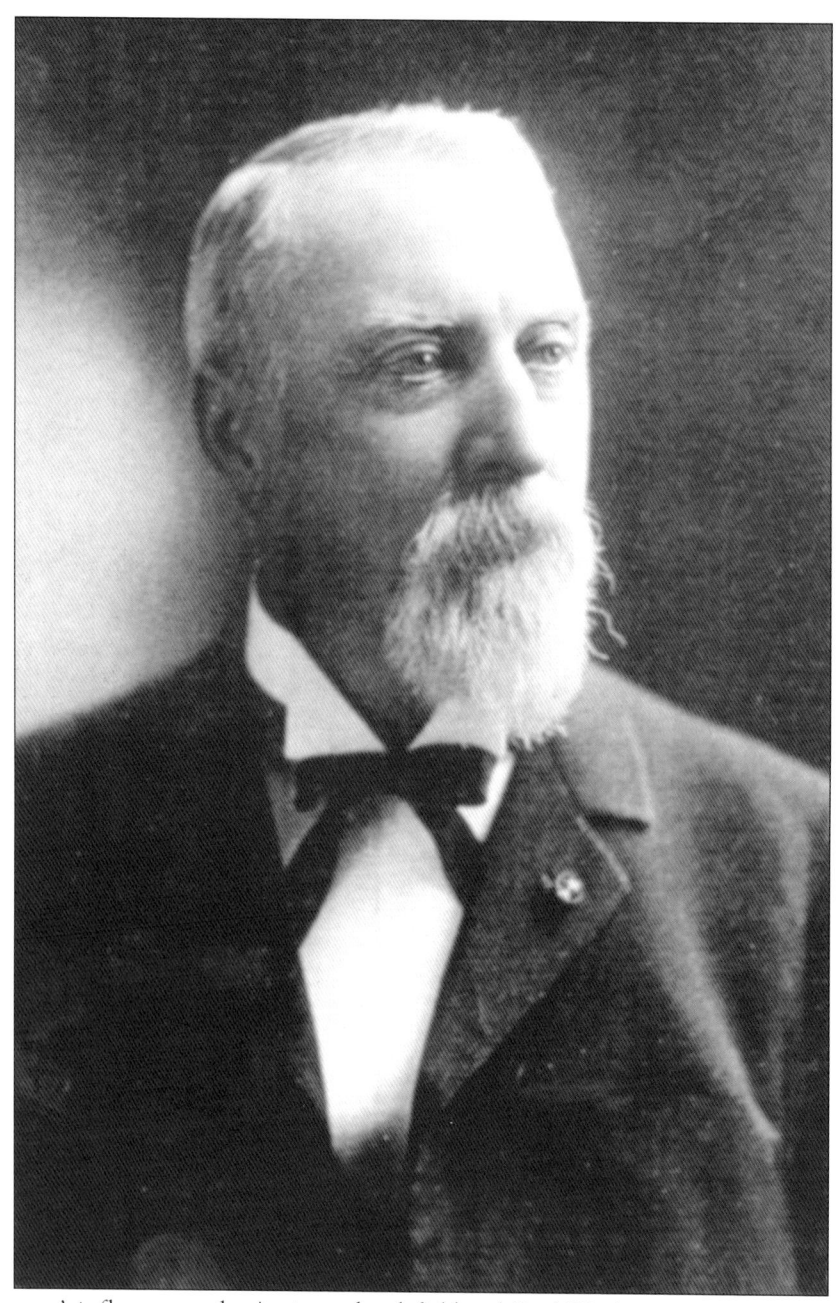

Ezra Carman's influence on the Antietam battlefield and Civil War history remains strong to this day. Carman served as the 13th New Jersey Infantry's colonel during the battle and served on the executive committee of the board of trustees for Antietam National Cemetery. On October 8, 1894, Carman became the historical expert of the Antietam Battlefield Board, earning a salary of $200 per month. His work at the battlefield ultimately produced the iron War Department tablets that dot the landscape today, a series of detailed battle maps tracing troop movements, and an 1,800-page handwritten history of the Maryland Campaign and the Battle of Antietam. Carman's orders to write this history stated that it be pamphlet-sized, though he clearly exceeded that. It is still the go-to work on the battle and campaign. (Courtesy of the National Park Service.)

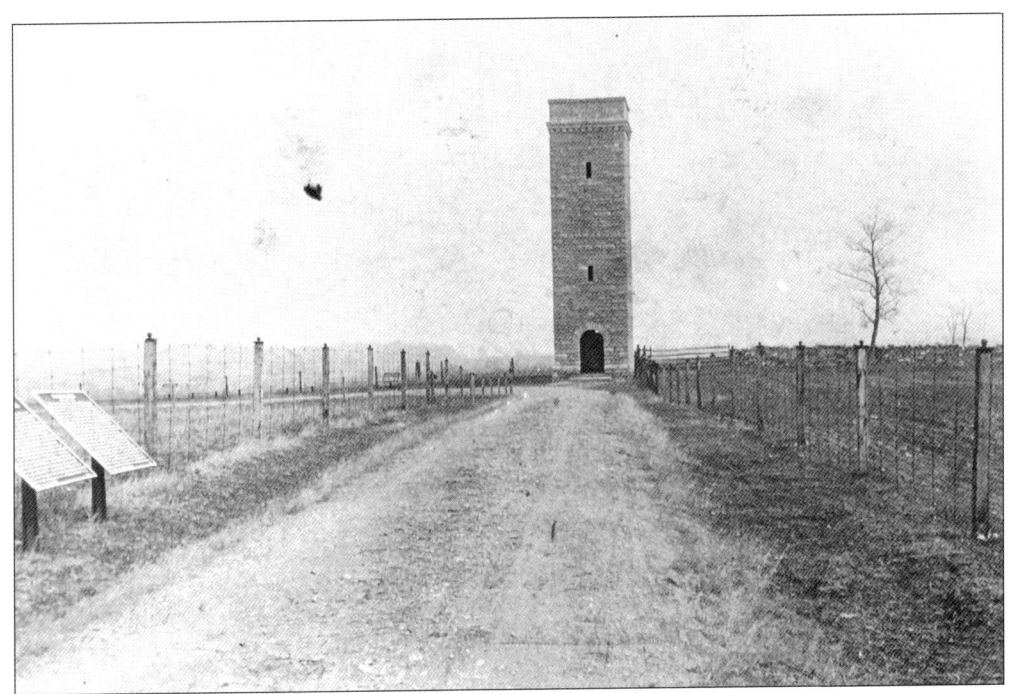

Antietam Battlefield Board president George Davis envisioned two observation towers at Antietam, one near the northern end of the battlefield and another near the southern end. Their purpose was to provide visitors with a unique view of the entire battlefield, much of which remained privately owned. Ultimately, the War Department only built one. Construction of a tower near the Bloody Lane was completed in 1895, though the larger and more substantial stone one, seen here, replaced the original in 1896. The War Department's funding ran out at the time of the stone tower's construction, and the roof was not added until 1909. The tower has remained a popular attraction for visitors throughout subsequent decades. (Above, courtesy of the National Park Service; right, courtesy of the Western Maryland Room, Washington County Free Library.)

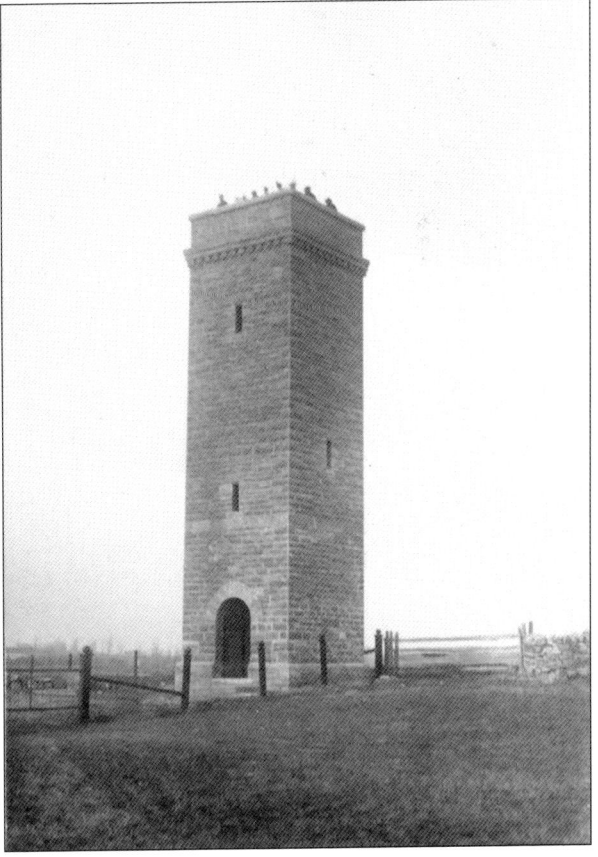

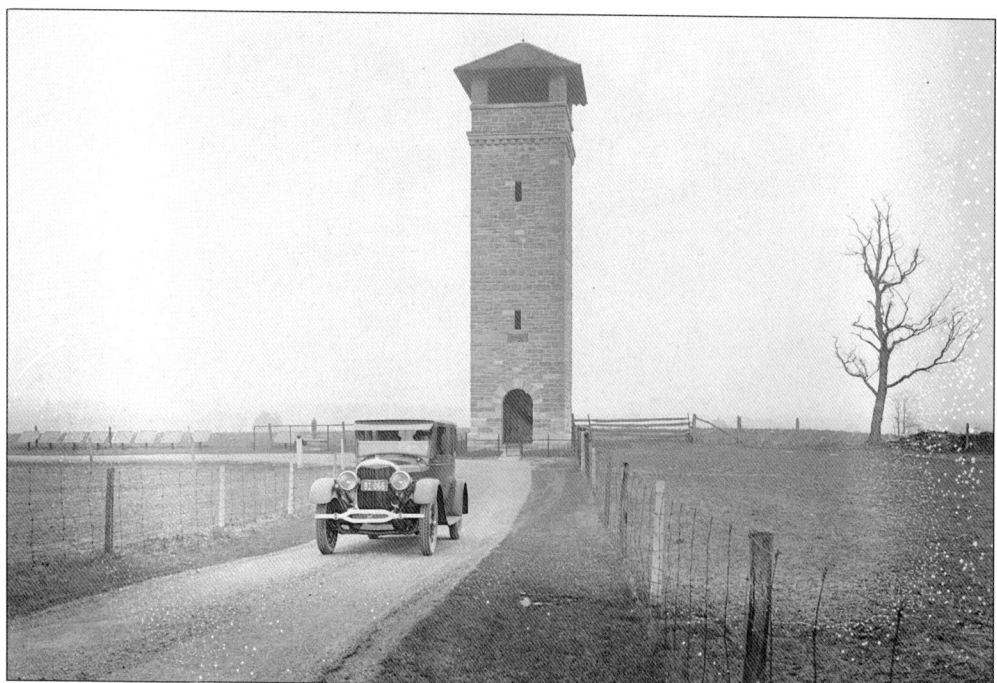

The advent of the automobile brought visitors to Antietam from farther away and shortened the amount of time it took to see the entire battlefield. A 1912 *Leslie's* magazine article described the usefulness of this new technology for such purposes: "The automobile proved a great aid in studying history, for it carried us up hills which would have been exceedingly tiresome in a carriage. It saved time, too, for the three hours spent in the machine on the field were equal to a whole day in a carriage." (Above, courtesy of the Library of Congress; below, courtesy of the National Park Service.)

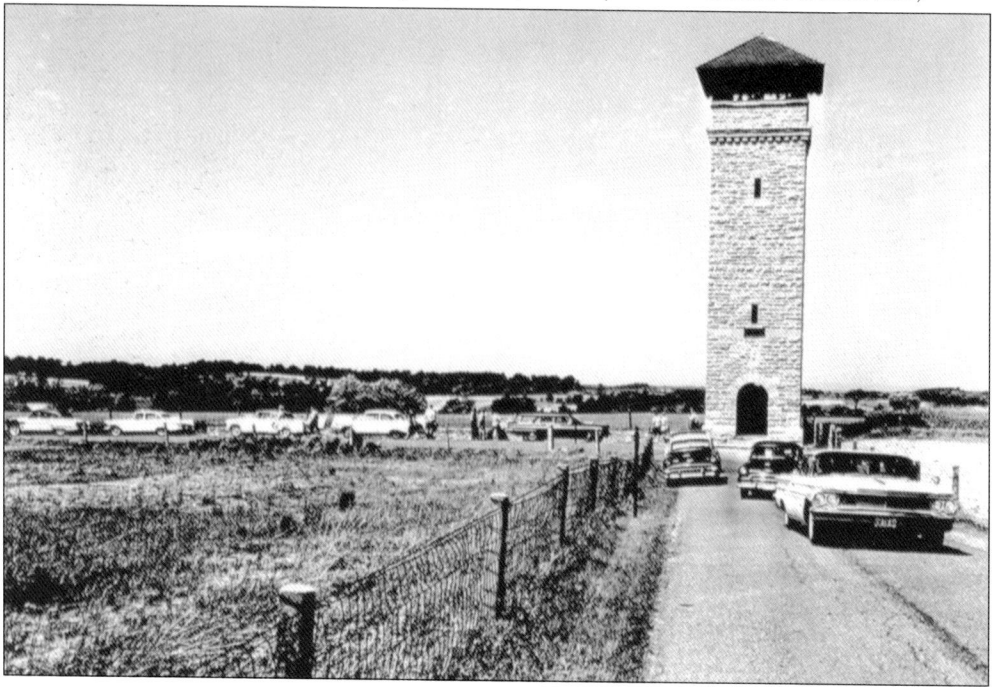

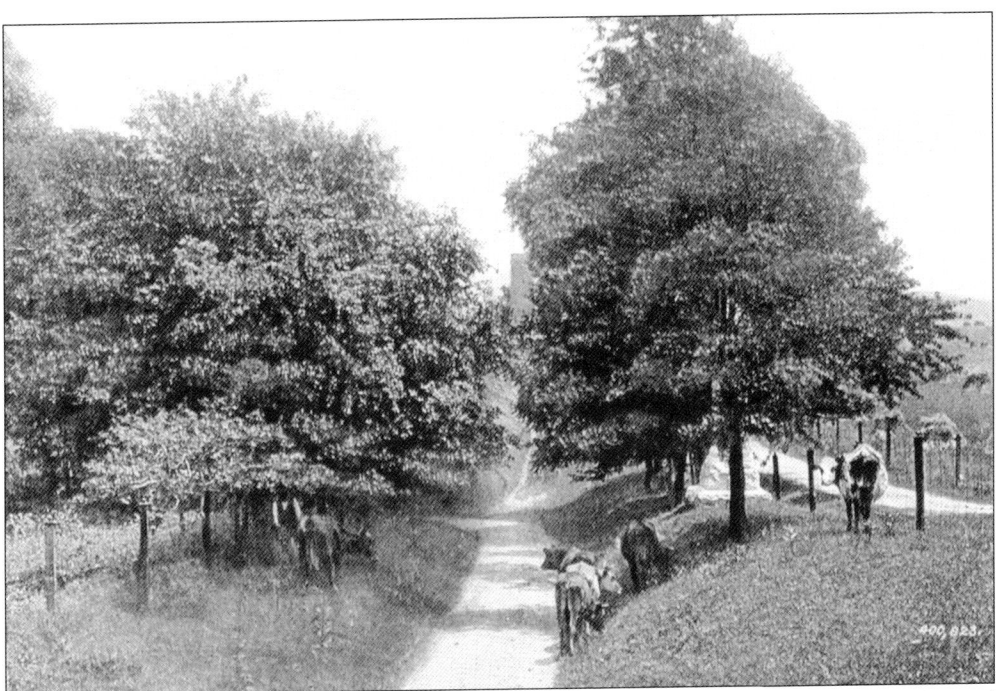

The Sunken Road was one of the first battlefield landmarks that the Antietam Battlefield Board requested specific funds to purchase—$8,000 to be exact. The War Department constructed the bypass around the Sunken Road in 1895, and the 8th Ohio monument, seen to the right of the lane, was dedicated in 1903. The board purchased the road in 1894. (Courtesy of the National Park Service.)

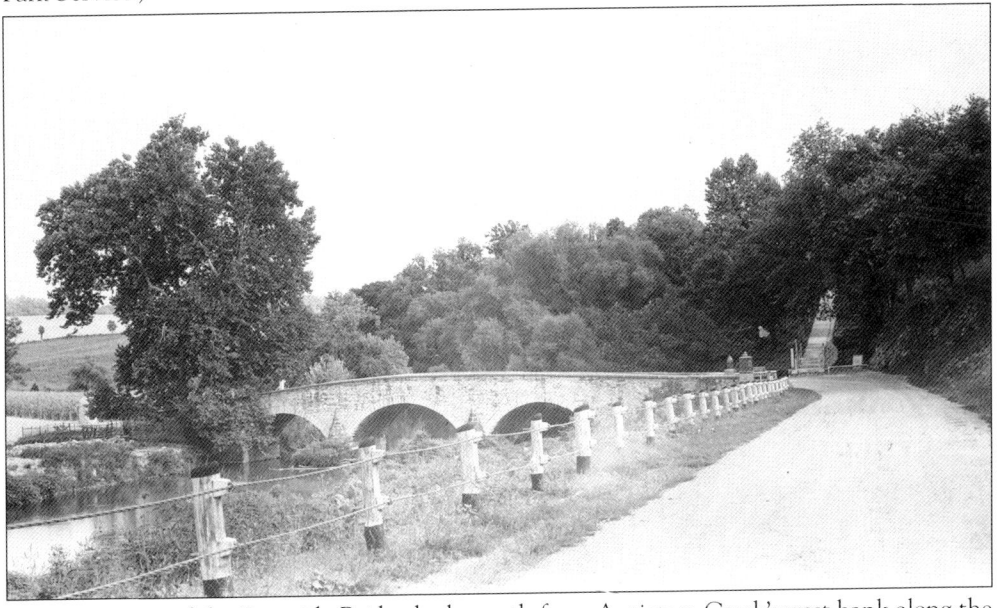

This 1934 view of the Burnside Bridge looks south from Antietam Creek's west bank along the historic trace of the Sharpsburg-Rohrersville Road. At the time this photograph was taken, Supt. John K. Beckenbaugh reported that Antietam National Battlefield consisted of approximately 50 acres of land. (Courtesy of the National Park Service.)

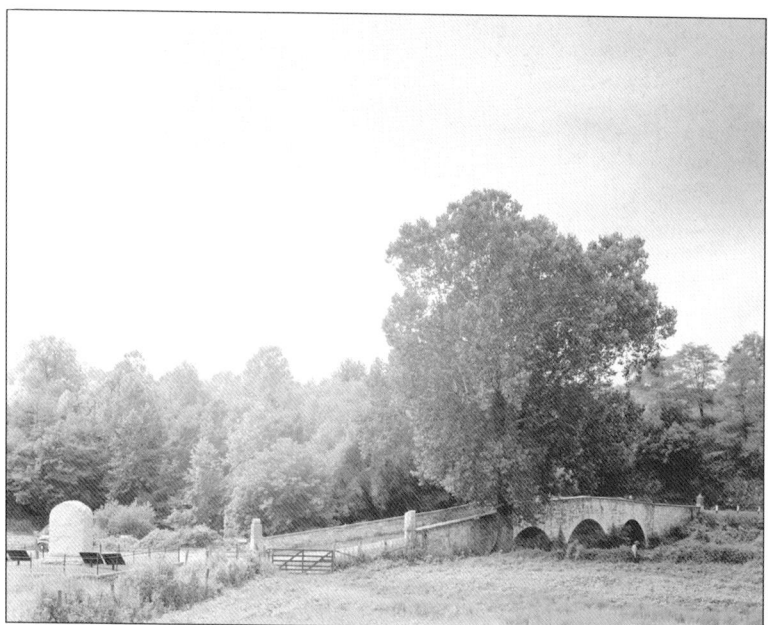

This 1940s view of the Burnside Bridge shows the battlefield in its raw state before more modern preservation and interpretation techniques were applied to the park. Note the four monuments visible on each corner of the bridge as well as the stone wall that the 51st Pennsylvania utilized. (Courtesy of the National Park Service.)

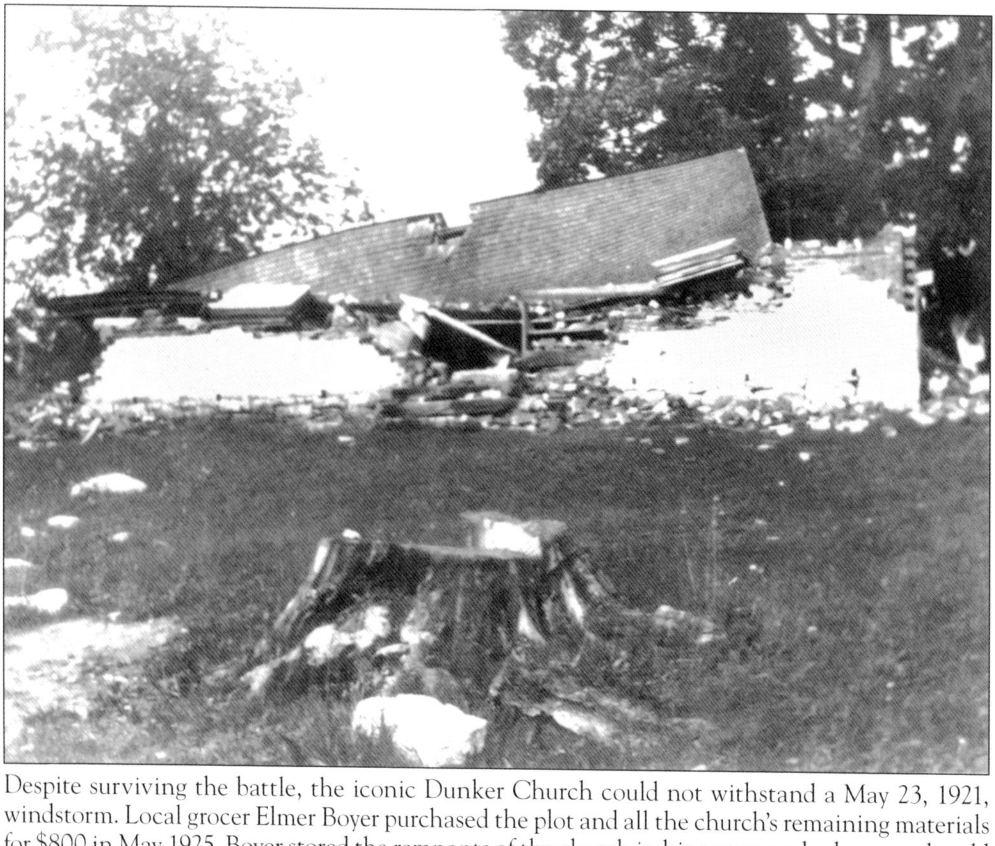

Despite surviving the battle, the iconic Dunker Church could not withstand a May 23, 1921, windstorm. Local grocer Elmer Boyer purchased the plot and all the church's remaining materials for $800 in May 1925. Boyer stored the remnants of the church in his garage and subsequently sold the land. In 1928, Charles Turner built a lunch stand and gas station on the church's foundation. (Courtesy of the National Park Service.)

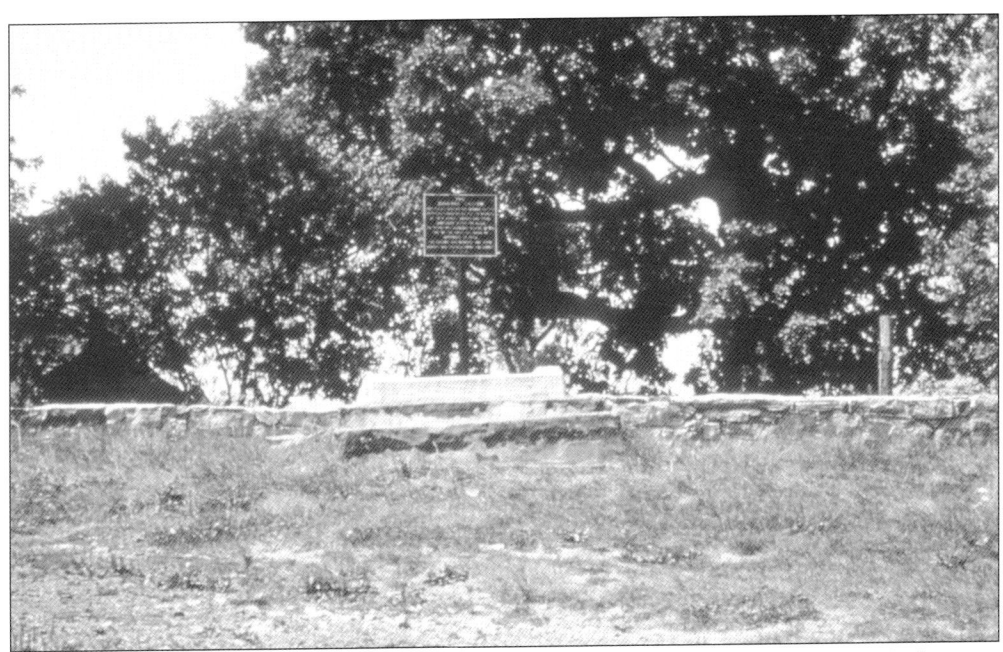

This lone sign (above) and the stone foundation were all that marked the Dunker Church's location through much of the 1950s. At the time of this photograph, "a chrome and orange house trailer, complete with tall TV antenna, rests semi-permanently within fifty feet of the historic Dunker Church site," noted a 1959 House of Representatives Interior Committee task force. Embarrassed by the state of the battlefield from a preservation standpoint, the writer quipped, "Tomorrow the ghostly cannonballs may be sailing through scores of living rooms in the Bloody Cornfield and along Bloody Lane." When the committee filed the report, Antietam National Battlefield consisted of only 183 acres. Today, it encompasses approximately 3,250 acres. (Both, courtesy of the National Park Service.)

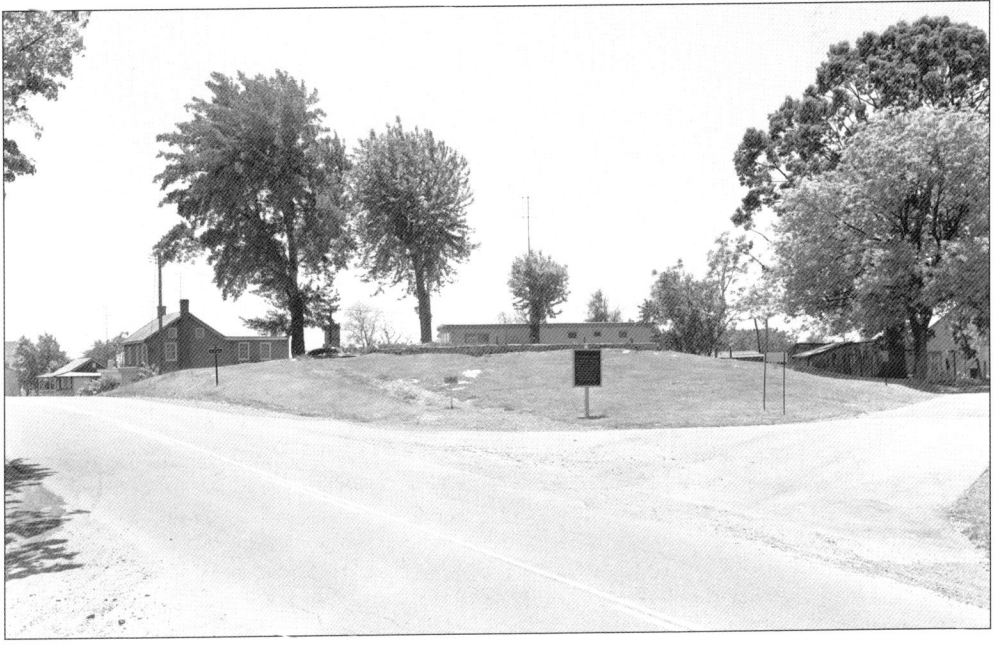

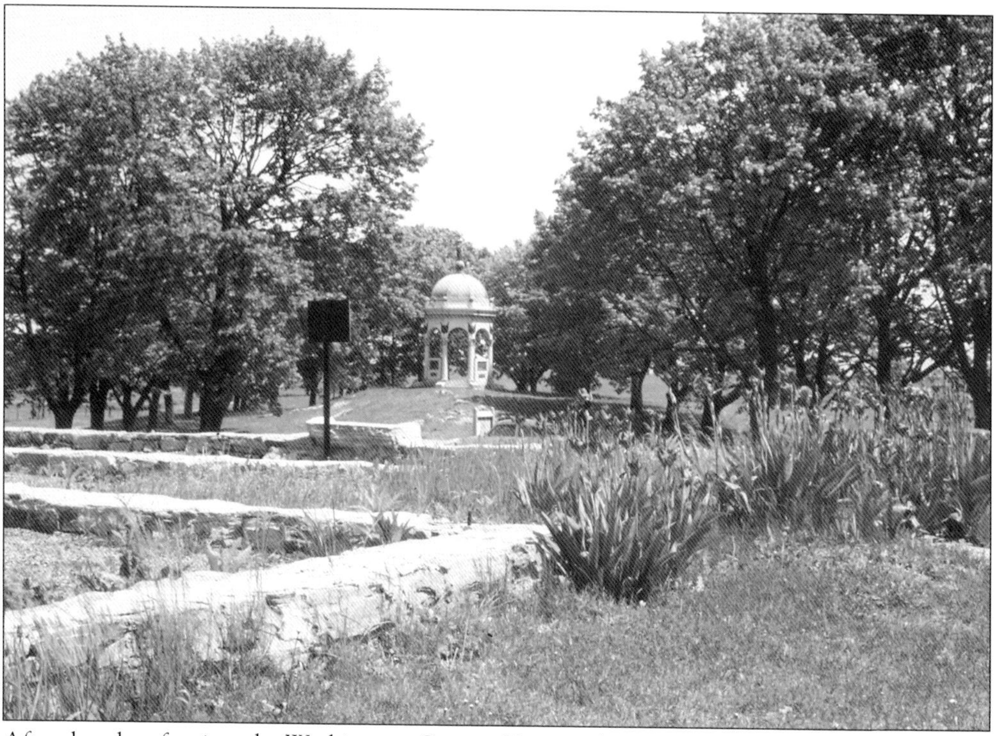

After decades of trying, the Washington County Historical Society purchased the land on which the Dunker Church sat in 1951 for $4,000. Immediately, efforts began to rebuild the historic house of worship, but just as quickly as they began, the exertions hit a snag. Elmer Boyer offered to sell the church's original materials for the exorbitant price of $7,500 and a National Park Service regional director further dowsed any plans to rebuild the church by estimating the cost of such an endeavor to be approximately $50,000. Meanwhile, a simple sign stood within the empty foundation telling the story of the church. (Both, courtesy of the National Park Service.)

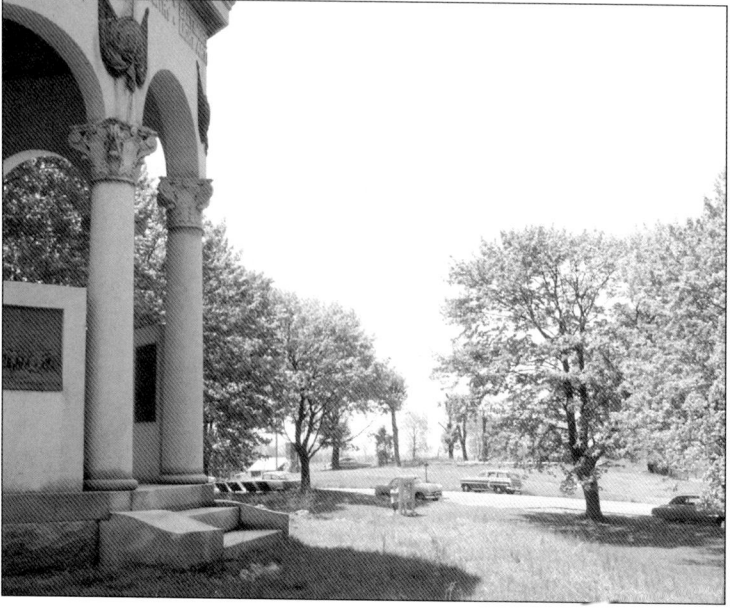

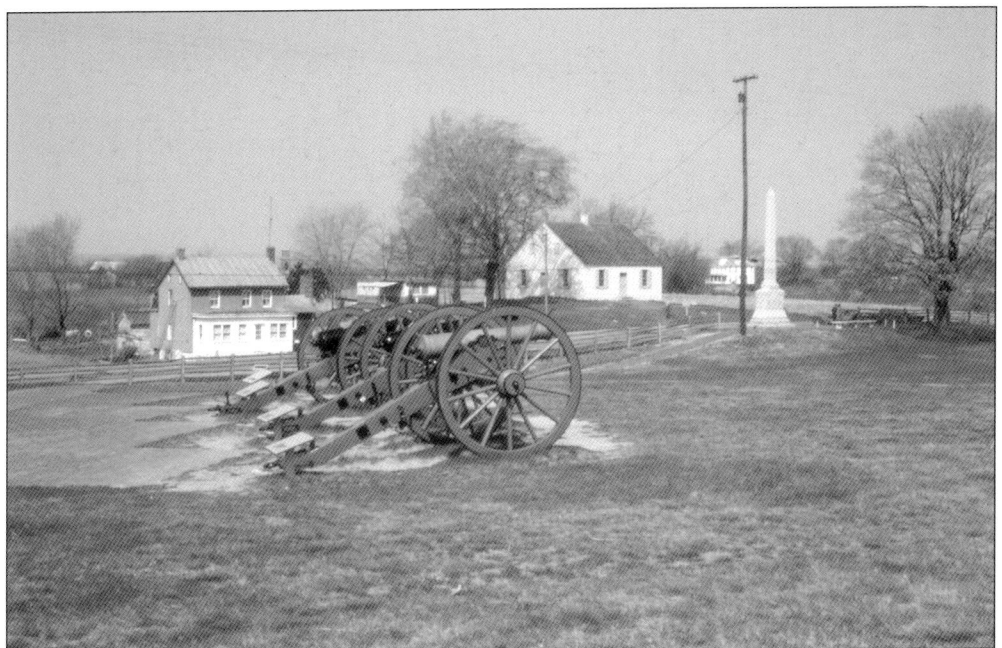

While Maryland governor Millard Tawes proclaimed the Dunker Church "a beacon by which commanders took their direction and men found their way in the smoky chaos of battle" during his 1961 rededication speech, that concept must have been difficult for visitors to grasp with views such as these. Modern buildings surrounded the rebuilt church and the West Woods, which surrounded the church in 1862, was long gone. The National Park Service replanted the historic West Woods to its wartime boundaries. Today, none of the buildings seen here in the immediate vicinity of the church stand, a stark reminder of how far the preservation of Antietam National Battlefield has come. (Both, courtesy of the National Park Service.)

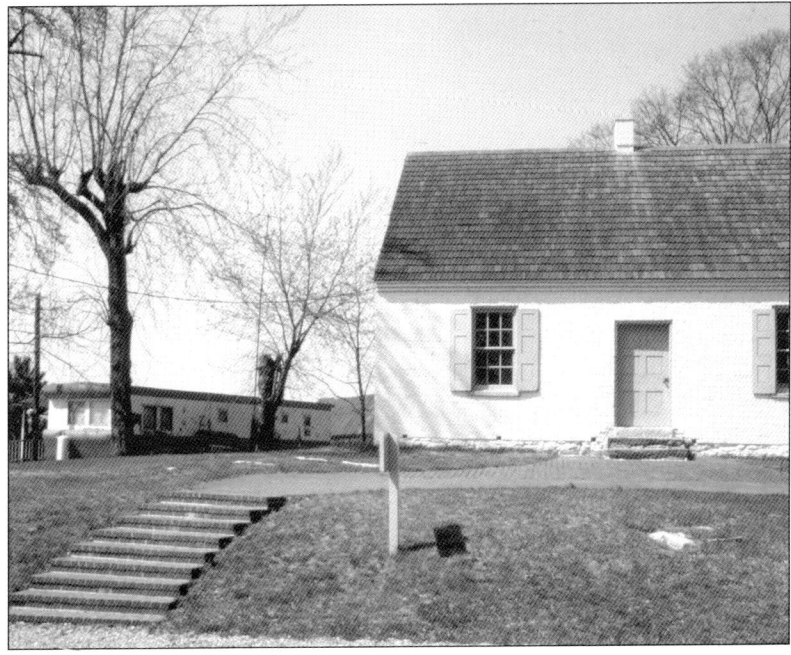

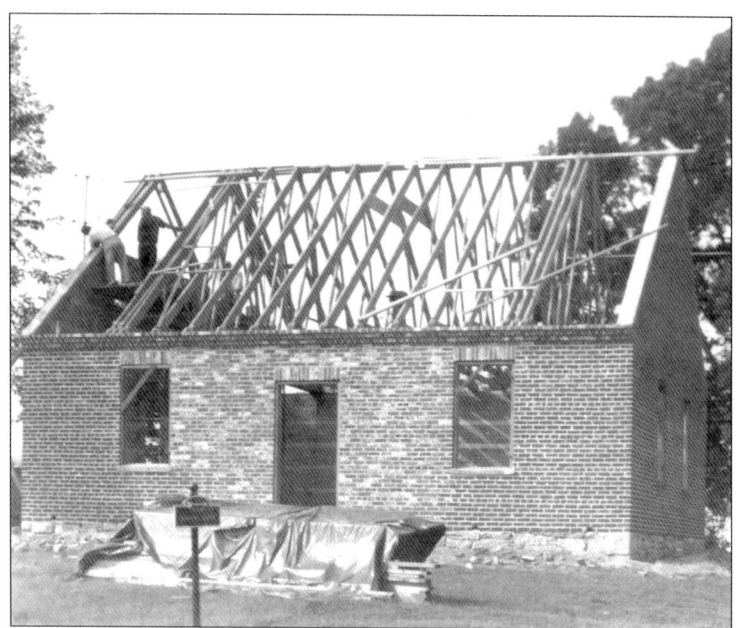

Multiple groups contributed to the rebuilding of the church, which was officially rededicated on September 2, 1962. About 3,000 of the original bricks constitute the rebuilt Dunker Church, while another 22,500 were custom-made for the reconstruction. Cost of the construction project totaled $20,046.90, significantly lower than the earlier $50,000 estimate. (Courtesy of the National Park Service.)

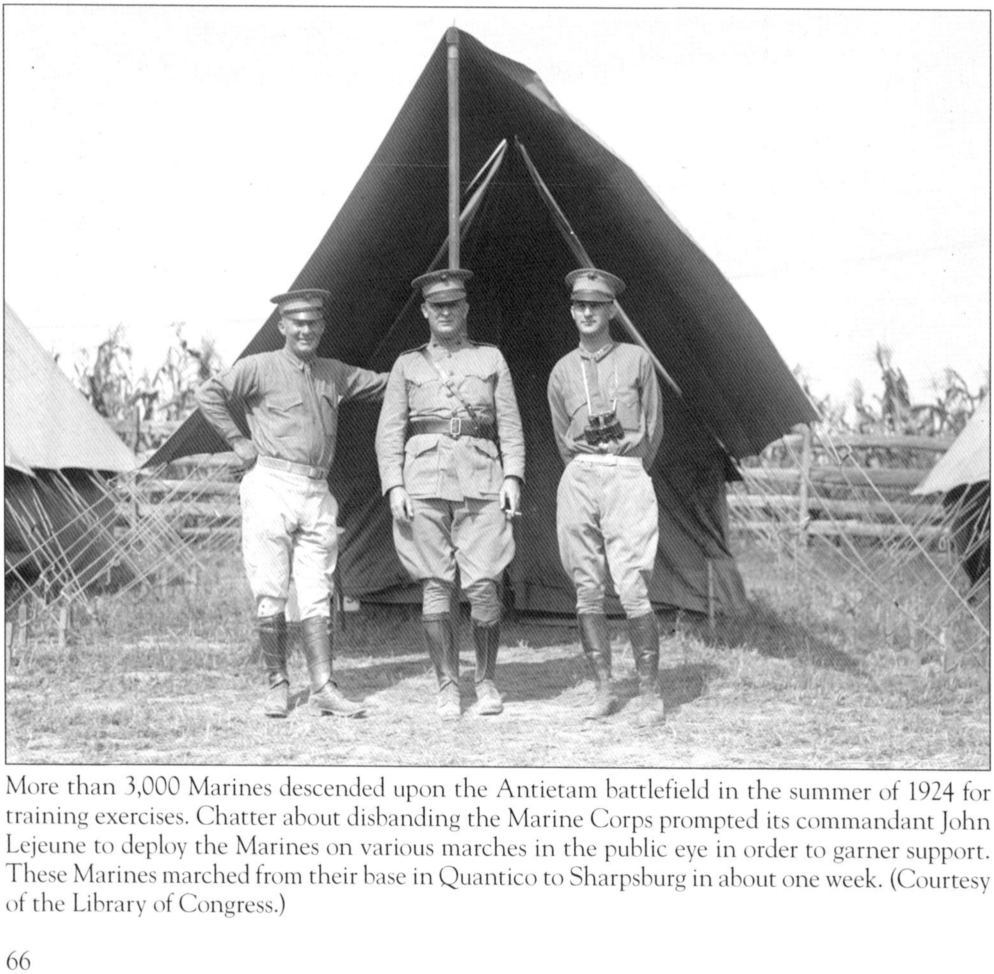

More than 3,000 Marines descended upon the Antietam battlefield in the summer of 1924 for training exercises. Chatter about disbanding the Marine Corps prompted its commandant John Lejeune to deploy the Marines on various marches in the public eye in order to garner support. These Marines marched from their base in Quantico to Sharpsburg in about one week. (Courtesy of the Library of Congress.)

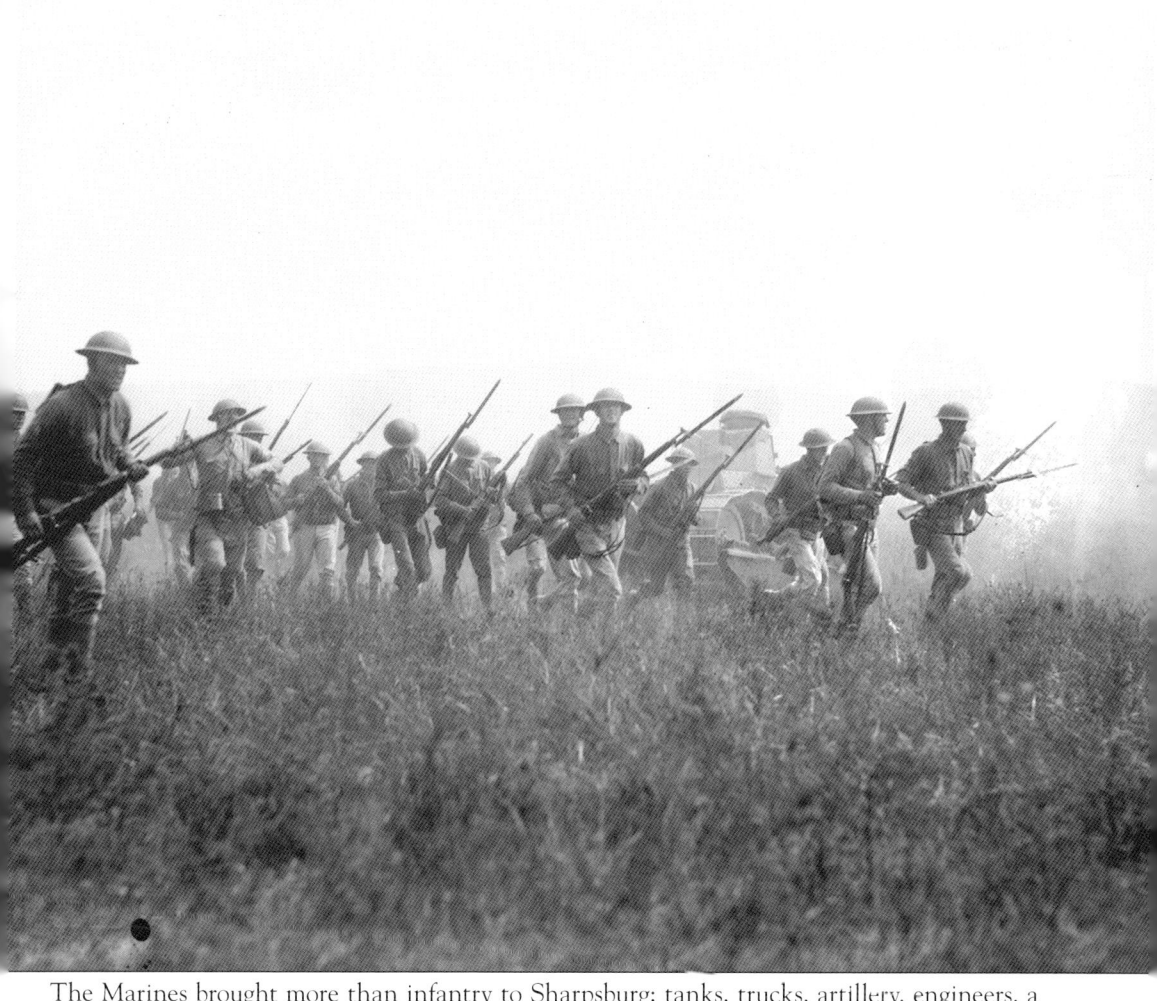

The Marines brought more than infantry to Sharpsburg; tanks, trucks, artillery, engineers, a medical corps, a chemical unit, and even 13 airplanes accompanied the foot soldiers. Approximately 50,000 people visited the Marine camp on September 7, 1924, while planes circled overhead performing "every stunt known to flyers," wrote the *Frederick News-Post*. The public was enamored with the Marines. Between training sessions, the Marines traveled to nearby Hagerstown and Shepherdstown to watch the Marine baseball team play the local clubs. The Hagerstown Hubs defeated the Marines, who subsequently triumphed over both Sharpsburg's and Shepherdstown's teams. But the Marines were also present to stage a planned battle on the old Antietam battlefield. "The ground was the same but that was all," said one witness. "Airplanes circled overhead and swooped down low to bomb the 'enemy' lines. Artillery firing blank shrapnel laid down a barrage for an advancing infantry. The infantry deployed and crept forward, while machine guns rattled on either flank. And finally tanks scurried here and there through the enemy lines, spitting fire and leveling positions." (Courtesy of the Library of Congress.)

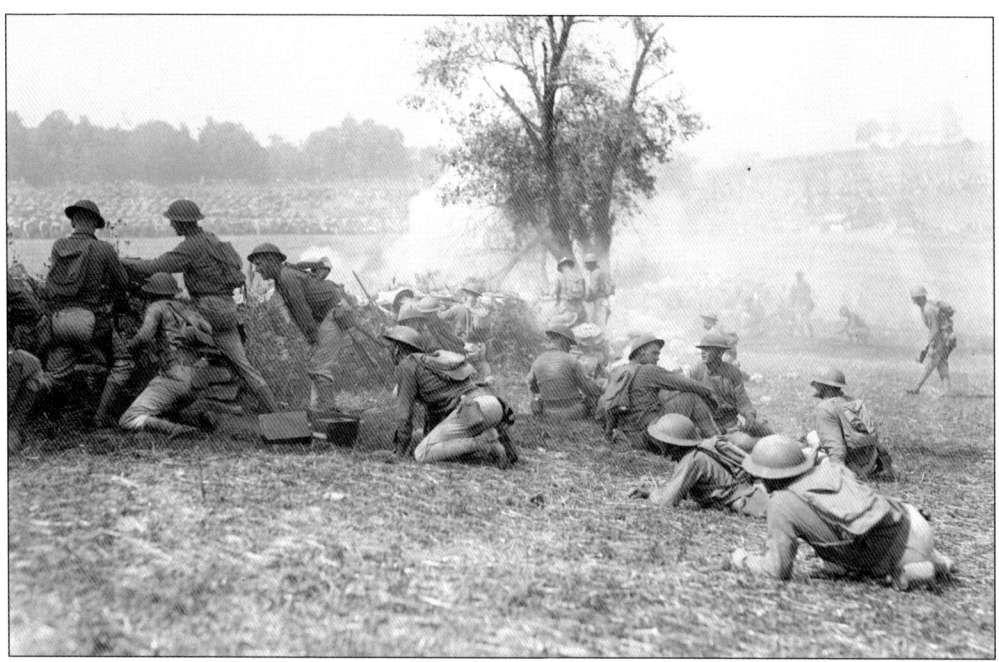

September 12, 1924, was the date of the reenactment. People flocked from the countryside to witness the event (notice the camps and crowds in the background of these images). Baltimore's *Sun* wrote of the occasion, "It was the largest crowd assembled here since that September day in 1862 when General Lee matched his forces against McClellan's fighting Yankees. They began streaming in this morning before the marines were away and they continued to arrive until after the battle was over." The Marines fought from north to south as the battle climaxed on the knoll where the 50th Pennsylvania Infantry monument stands. Infantry, tanks, artillery, and planes participated in the reenactment. (Both, courtesy of the Library of Congress.)

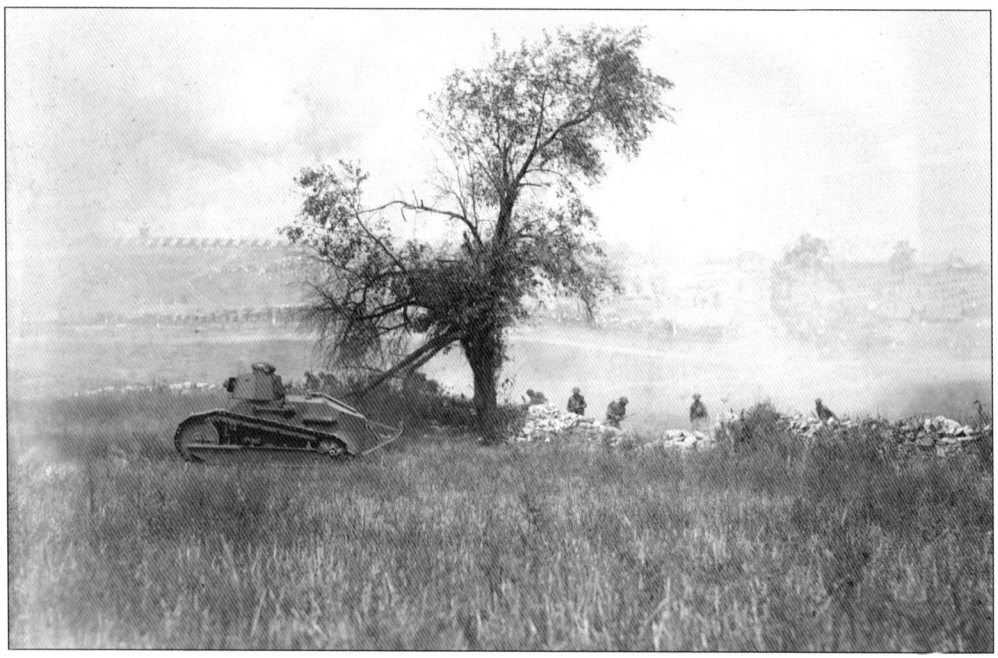

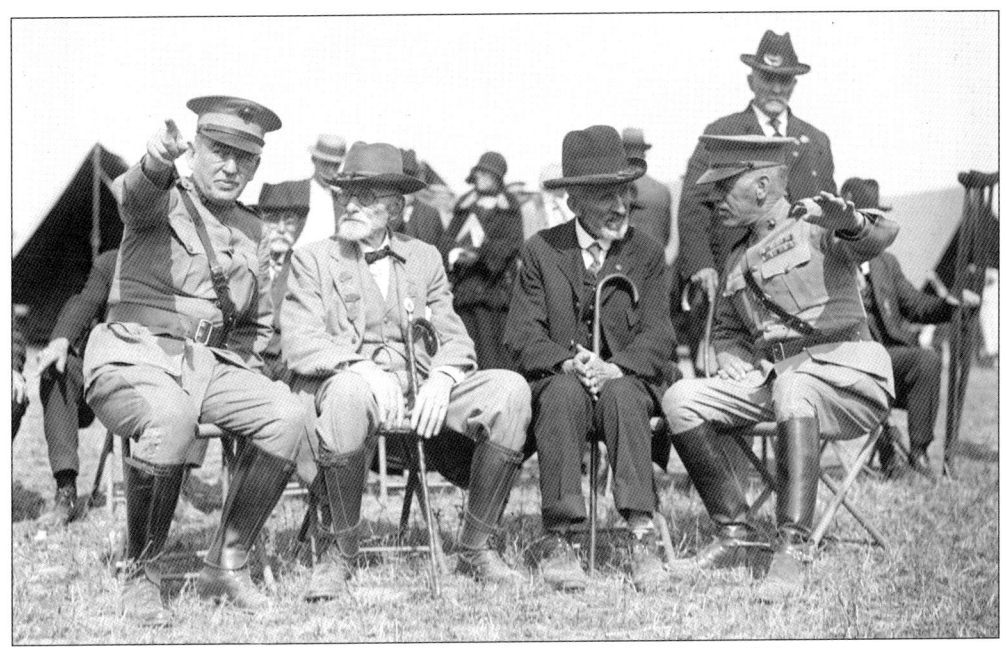

Members of the Grand Army of the Republic—the largest organization of Union army veterans—attended the event. While witnessing the mock battle, one of the veterans was heard to say, "Look at those boys. You'd think there was a dozen or two of them. Why, when our outfit marched into this battle it went shoulder to shoulder, like it was on a parade. No creeping and falling down like those boys." One Confederate veteran attended: 84-year-old Francis Jones. Lejeune (above, left) and Gen. Dion Williams (above, right) sat with the veterans during the program. Jones and his Union counterparts squabbled about who fought for the winning side at Antietam "even as they walked off together to eat lunch after the battle ended," wrote James Rada Jr. in the *Hagerstown Magazine*. (Both, courtesy of the Library of Congress.)

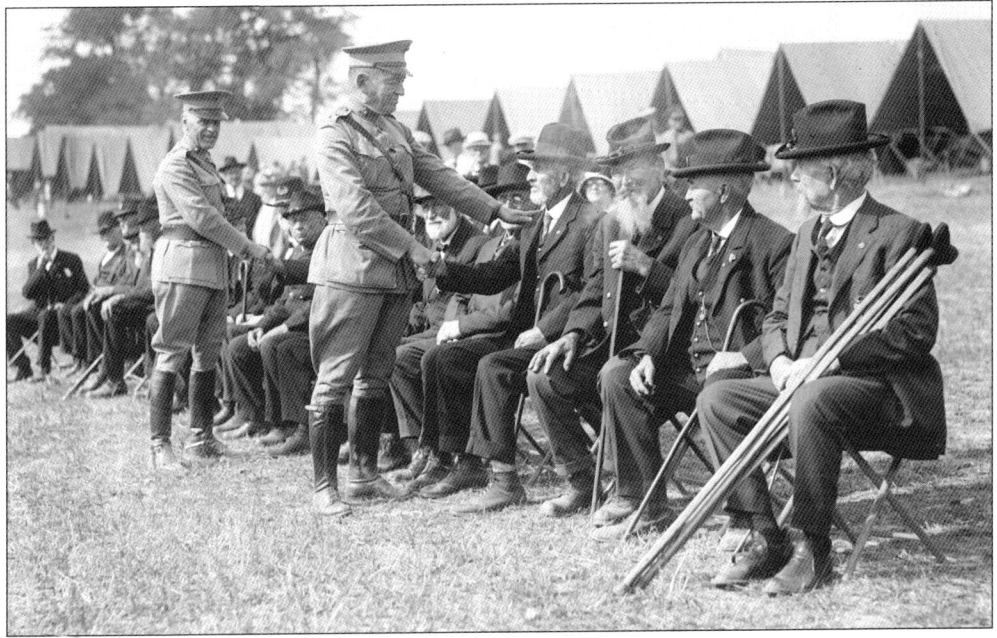

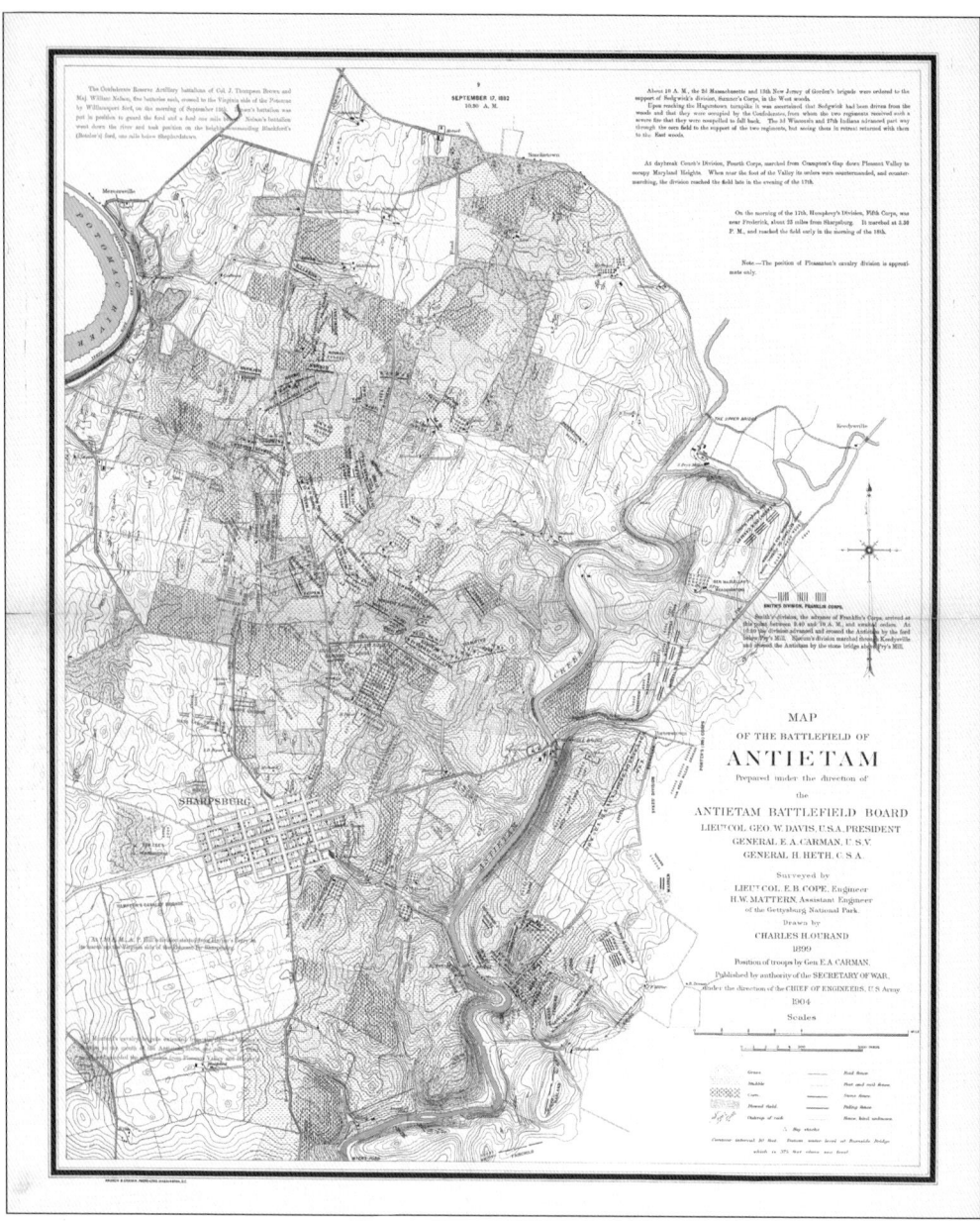

Mapping the Antietam battlefield began as soon as the battle took place. Numerous maps of the battlefield abound, but when it comes to studying the battle itself, no maps are more important than the Carman-Cope maps. Emmor Cope surveyed the Antietam battlefield by direction of the Antietam Battlefield Board while Charles Ourand put Cope's work to paper. Together, they produced 14 detailed troop movement maps of the Antietam battlefield that remain a useful tool to historians today. They completed the second edition of the maps in 1908. Cope was a Pennsylvania Quaker who joined the Union war effort in 1861. He participated in the Maryland Campaign before serving as a topographical engineer for the Army of the Potomac. One of his first assignments in this capacity was to map and survey the Antietam battlefield in early 1863. After the war, Cope became the first superintendent of Gettysburg National Military Park. (Courtesy of the Library of Congress.)

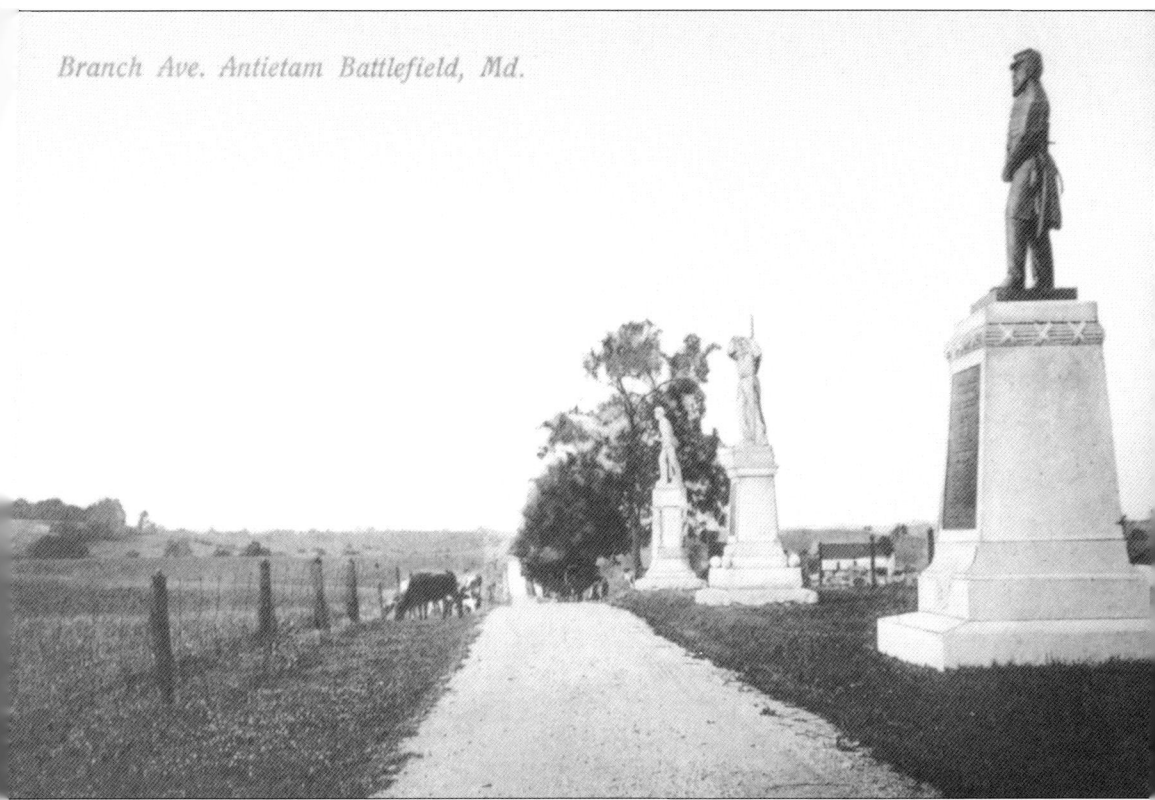

Branch Ave. Antietam Battlefield, Md.

George W. Davis served as the Antietam Battlefield Board's president from 1895 to 1898. Under his leadership, the "Antietam Plan" of battlefield preservation was adopted by the War Department. This plan "preserved narrow strips of land" upon which roadways were built to provide access to the battlefield while the rest of the land remained in private hands. One of these roadways was Branch Avenue, seen here, on the southern end of the battlefield. It was named for Confederate general Lawrence O'Bryan Branch, who was killed in the battle's waning hours. Notice the cattle grazing freely near the monuments, a constant issue that the early battlefield governing bodies continually faced. Superintendent Adams later wrote of this issue inhibiting battlefield visitors: "A large portion of the travel on the avenues is by Automobile, if sometime an accident should occur by a car running into a bunch of cattle, severe criticism of the policy of allowing livestock at large on the avenues would undoubtedly be the result." (Courtesy of the Western Maryland Room, Washington County Free Library.)

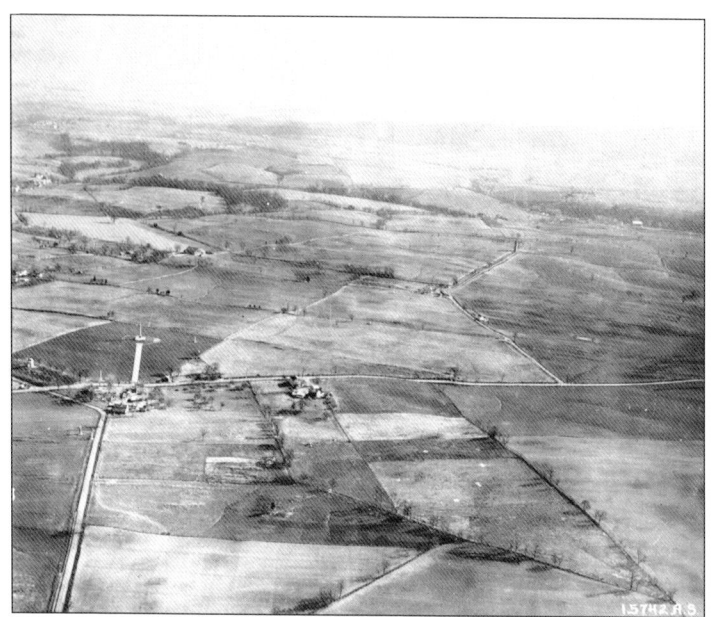

An Army Air Force plane flew over the battlefield on December 2, 1930, to capture its landscape and monuments. These aerial views provide a unique perspective of the battlefield. On the left side can be seen the New York Monument, which once had a path leading to it from the Hagerstown Pike, the Dunker Church site, and the area of today's visitor center. (Courtesy of the National Archives and Records Administration.)

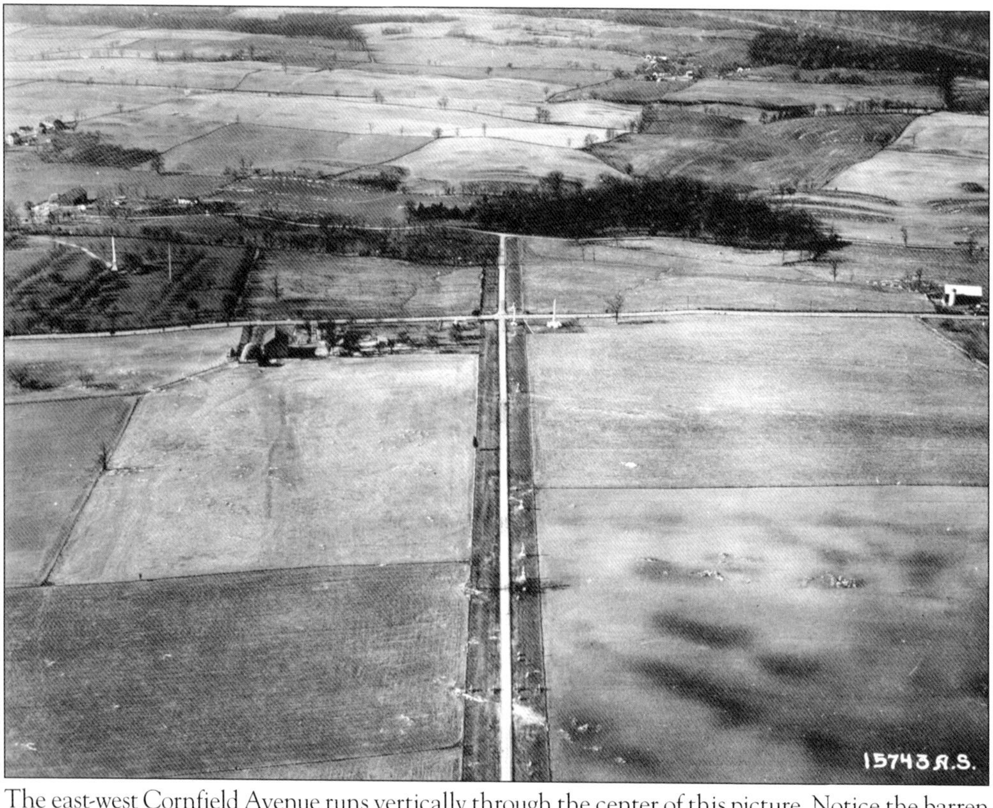

The east-west Cornfield Avenue runs vertically through the center of this picture. Notice the barren West Woods. Also, the Philadelphia Brigade monument pokes out above the surrounding trees while monuments along Cornfield Avenue, specifically the New Jersey and Indiana state monuments, are in the center. (Courtesy of the National Archives and Records Administration.)

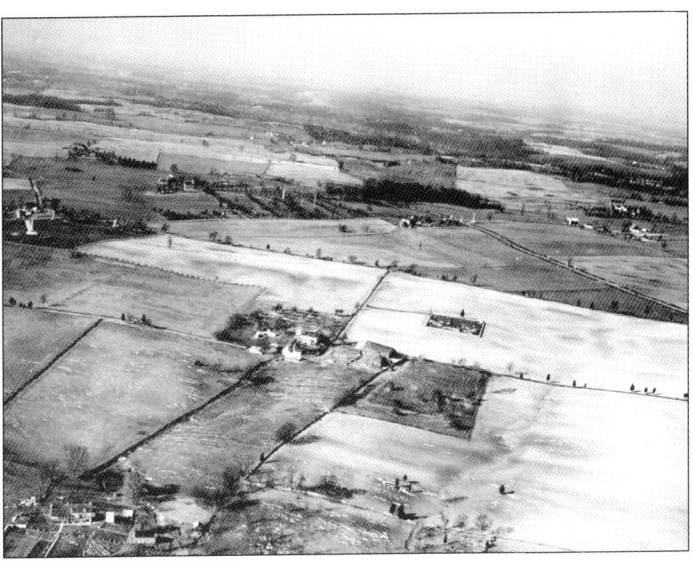

The Mumma farm sits in the center of this photograph from the air while the Roulette farm can be seen in the bottom left. The fenced-in New York State Monument is visible on the left. This view, facing west, also shows the more wooded ground west of the battlefield running toward the nearby Potomac River. (Courtesy of the National Archives and Records Administration.)

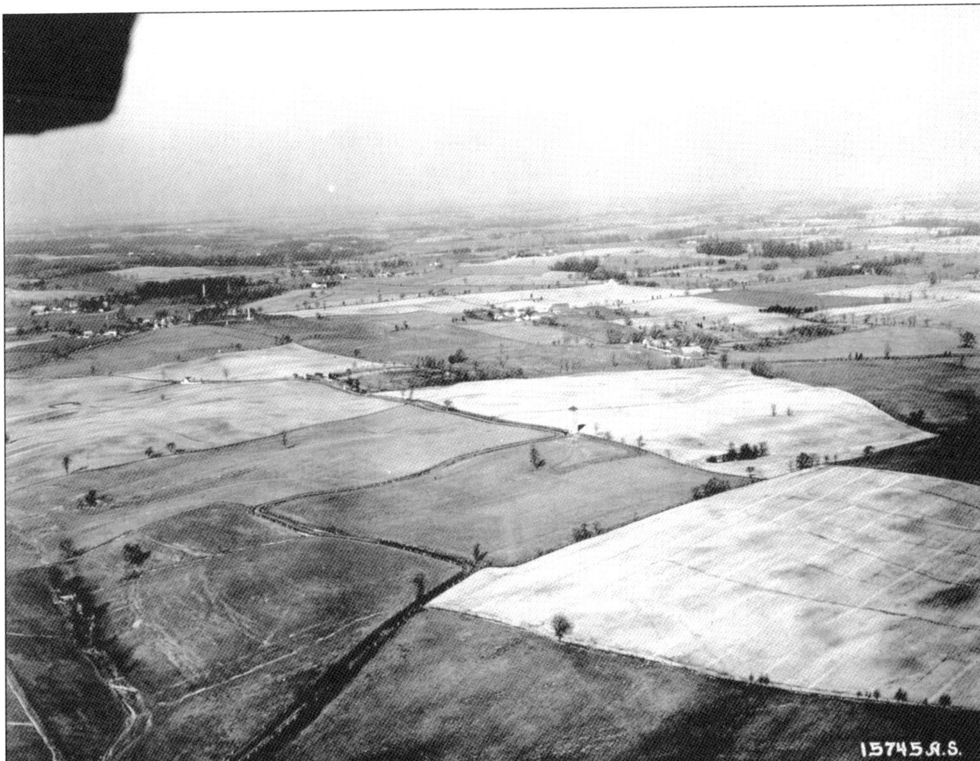

Confederates defended portions of the Bloody Lane that snakes its way through this photograph past the prominent stone observation tower. To the left of the tower, some of the Lohman property developed along the historic roadway can be seen. A part of the plane appears in the upper left. (Courtesy of the National Archives and Records Administration.)

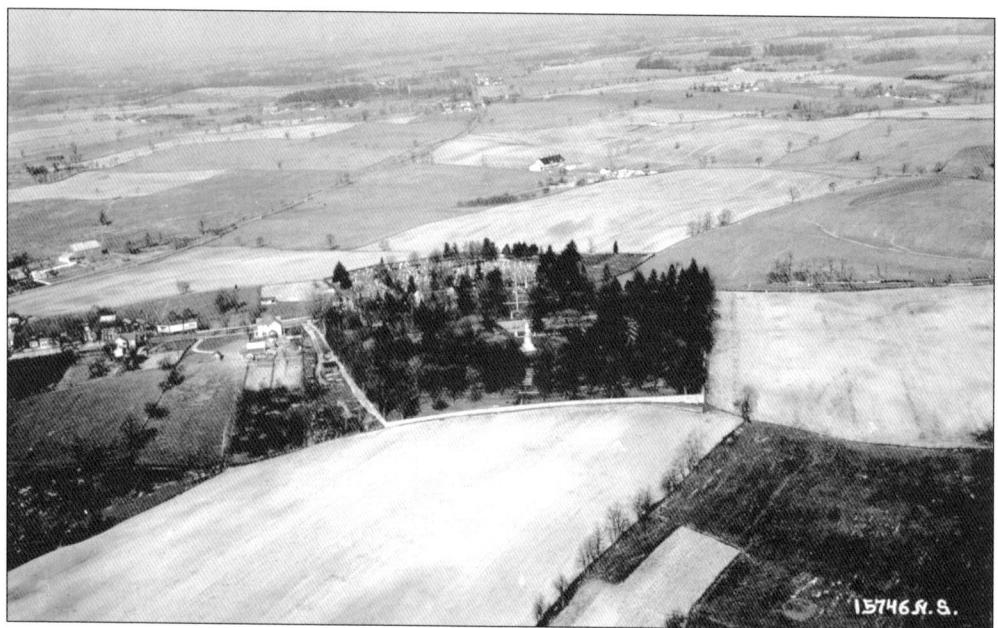

"Old Simon" (the nickname of *The Private Soldier*) appears prominently in the middle of the National Cemetery with his back to the camera. The Piper barn is almost directly above the cemetery. This terrain appears more open than it does today. Tree lines often mark historic fence lines, but those trees lines were sparser in 1930. (Courtesy of the National Archives and Records Administration.)

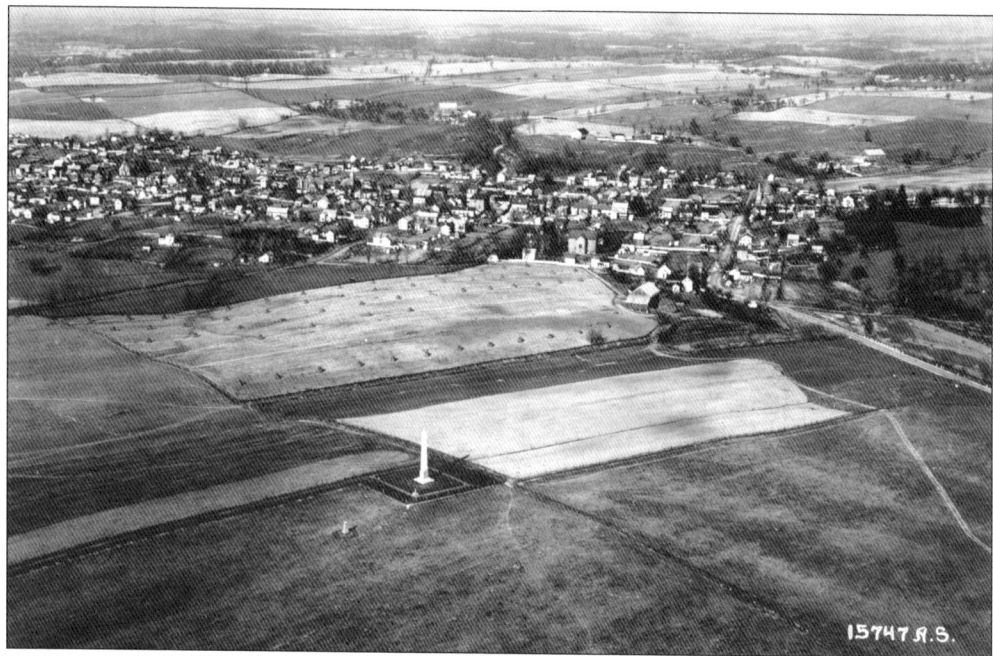

Both the tall 9th New York Monument and the smaller 8th Connecticut Monument show up conspicuously as does a mortuary cannon to Union general Isaac Rodman. The town of Sharpsburg, whose boundary has expanded only slightly since 1862, can be seen in great detail beyond these monuments. (Courtesy of the National Archives and Records Administration.)

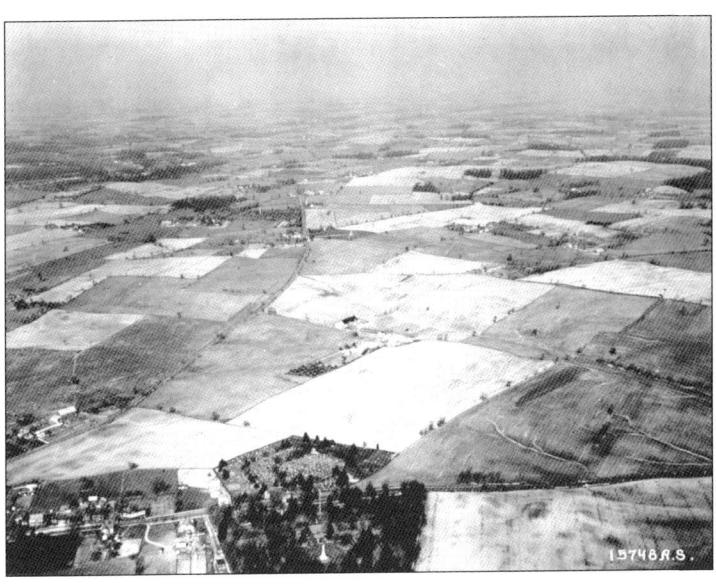

This last view from a higher altitude looks north once again beyond the National Cemetery. Within this image, some of the most iconic sites related to the Battle of Antietam are shown: the Dunker Church Plateau, the West Woods, the Cornfield, and the Bloody Lane, among others. (Courtesy of the National Archives and Records Administration.)

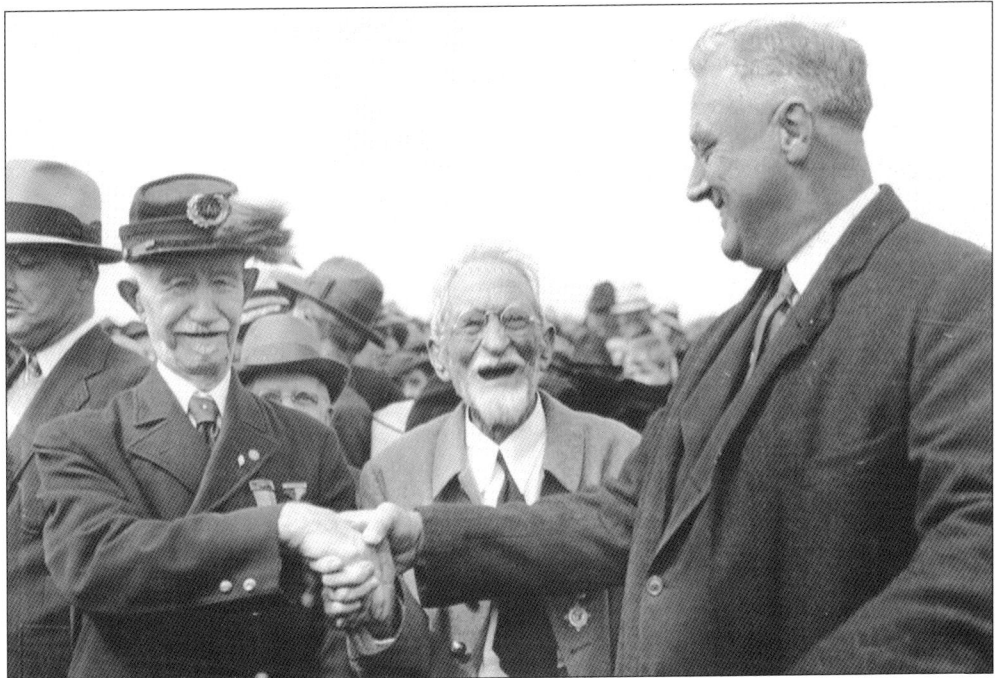

"All roads leading to the battlefield were one continuous line of motor vehicles," wrote Hagerstown's *Daily Mail* of the 75th-anniversary events. Pres. Franklin D. Roosevelt spoke from a stand situated on the Piper farm. He met veterans of the battle, "looked over the scene, had some of the historic landmarks pointed out to him and then left the field," recorded the Baltimore *Sun*. (Courtesy of the National Park Service.)

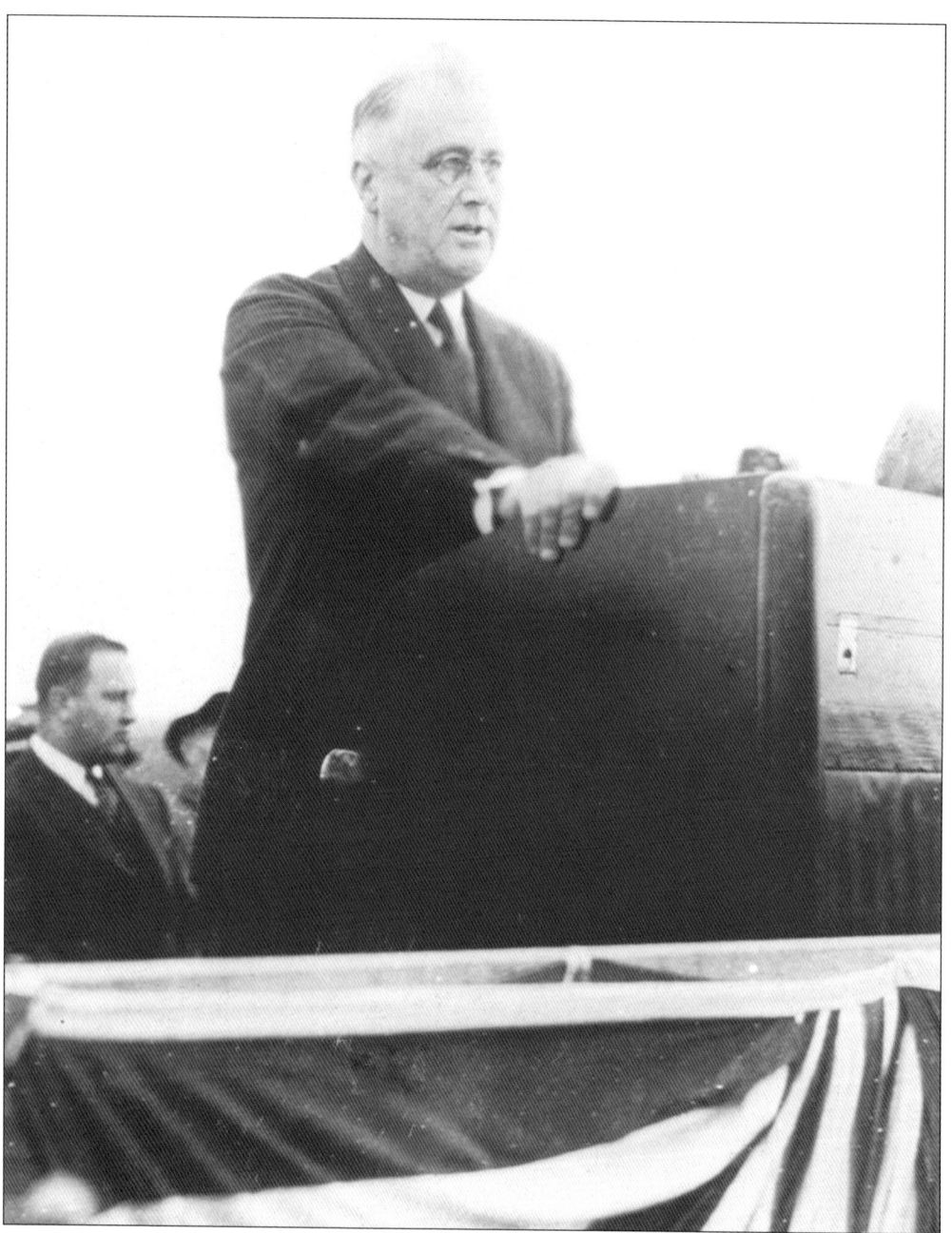

President Roosevelt's speech struck a tone of reconciliation between North and South. "[I]t serves us little to discuss again the rights and the wrongs of the long four-year War Between the States," he said. "We can and we do revere the memory of the brave men who fought on both sides—we can and we do honor those who fell on this and other fields." Roosevelt concluded his speech with the following remarks: "In the presence of the spirits of those who fell on this field—Union soldiers and Confederate soldiers—we can believe that they rejoice with us in the unity of understanding which is so increasingly ours today. They urge us on in all we do to foster that spirit of unity, foster it in the spirit of tolerance, of willingness to help our neighbor, and of faith in the destiny of the United States of America." (Courtesy of the National Park Service.)

Sixty-five known living Antietam veterans attended the 75th-anniversary events at the battlefield. Twenty-one of them sat on stage with President Roosevelt. In the president's speech, he emphasized that "the United States is now thinking and acting with national unity for the first time since the Civil War." Returning veterans reciprocated this theme of reconciliation. A staged reenactment of the battle for the Sunken Road followed Roosevelt's remarks and involved 1,200 National Guard soldiers. The mock battle inaccurately portrayed Confederates on the offensive, thereby affording "both sides an opportunity to show their valor and bravery," wrote battlefield historian Dr. Susan Trail. Approximately 25,000 people attended the National Antietam Celebration in 1937. (Both, courtesy of the National Park Service.)

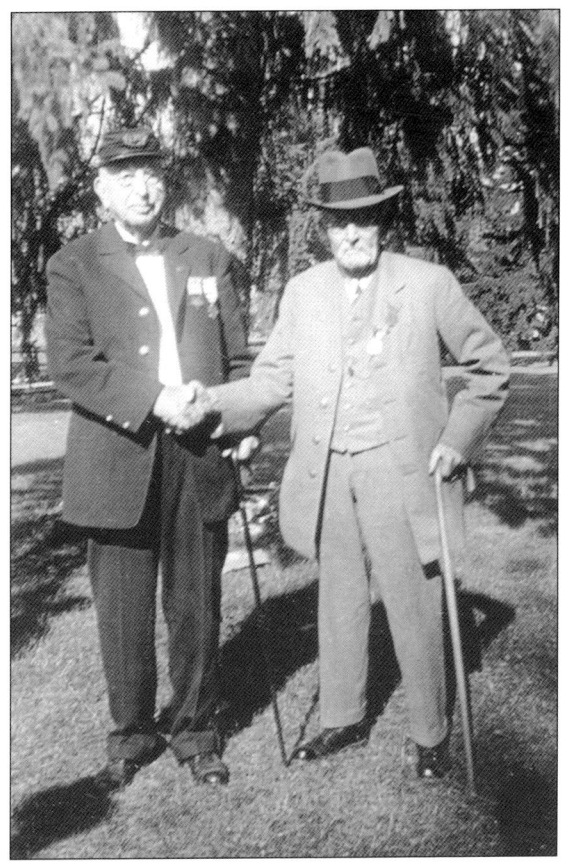

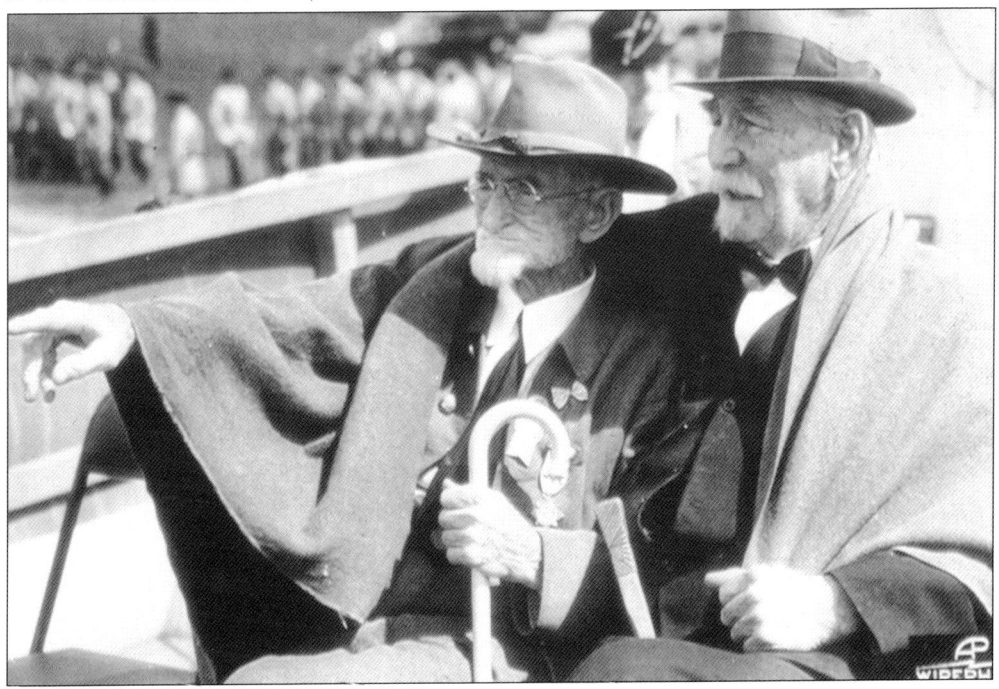

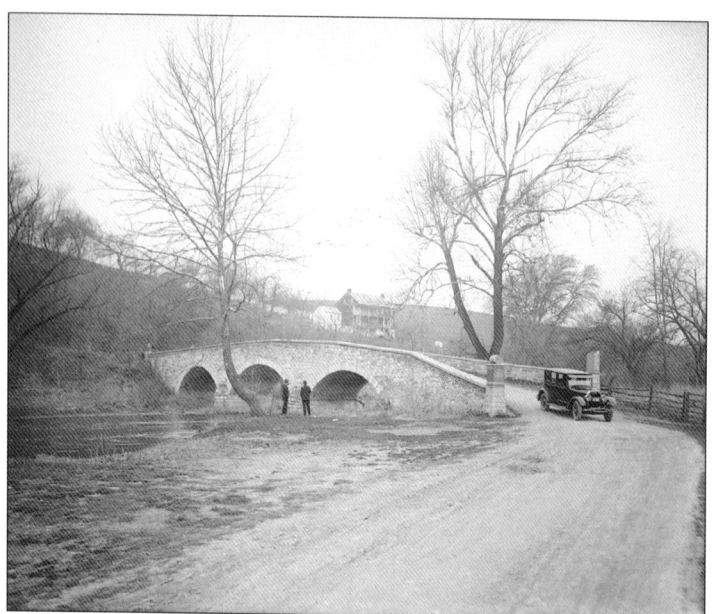

Throughout the Burnside Bridge's history, vehicular traffic crossing the span constantly created problems. In 1942, a truck knocked the 35th Massachusetts monument off the bridge. A similar accident happened twice to the 21st Massachusetts monument the next year. In 1947, a contractor noted that the bridge shook when large vehicles traveled across it. A section of the bridge collapsed in 1953. (Courtesy of the Library of Congress.)

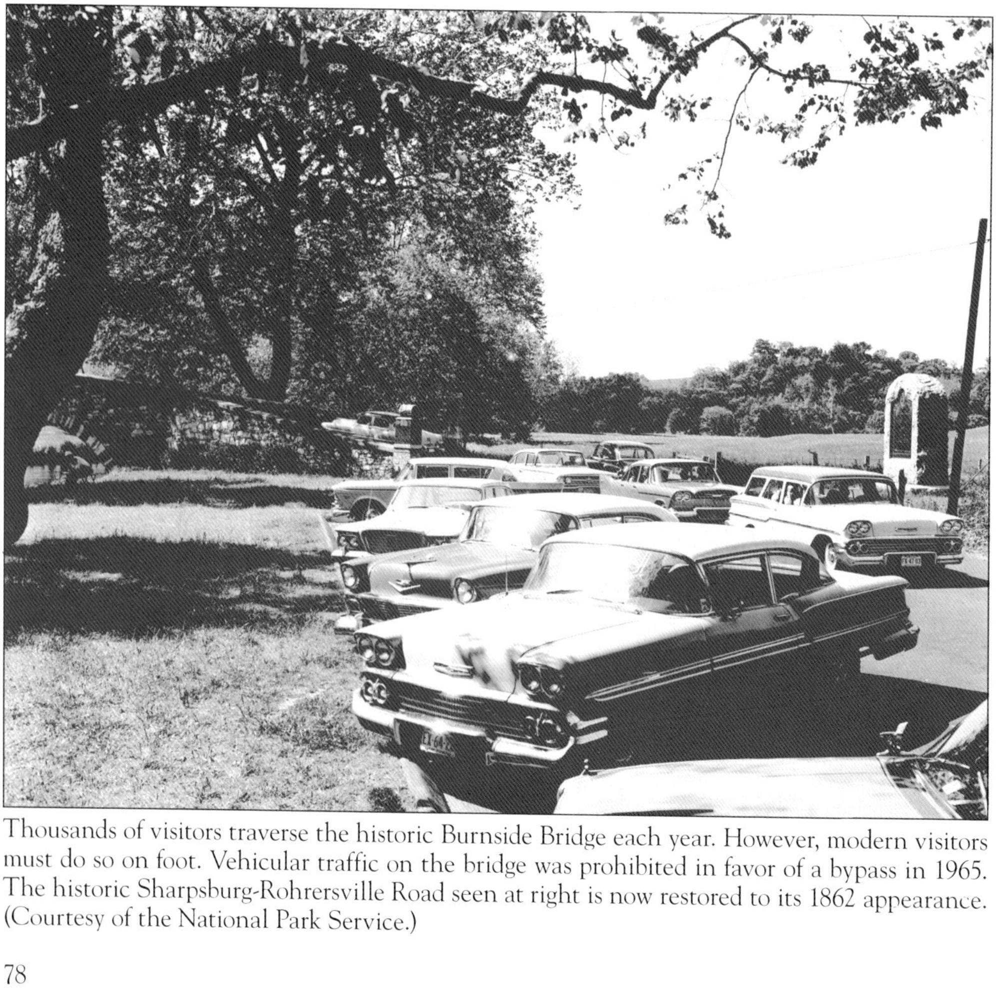

Thousands of visitors traverse the historic Burnside Bridge each year. However, modern visitors must do so on foot. Vehicular traffic on the bridge was prohibited in favor of a bypass in 1965. The historic Sharpsburg-Rohrersville Road seen at right is now restored to its 1862 appearance. (Courtesy of the National Park Service.)

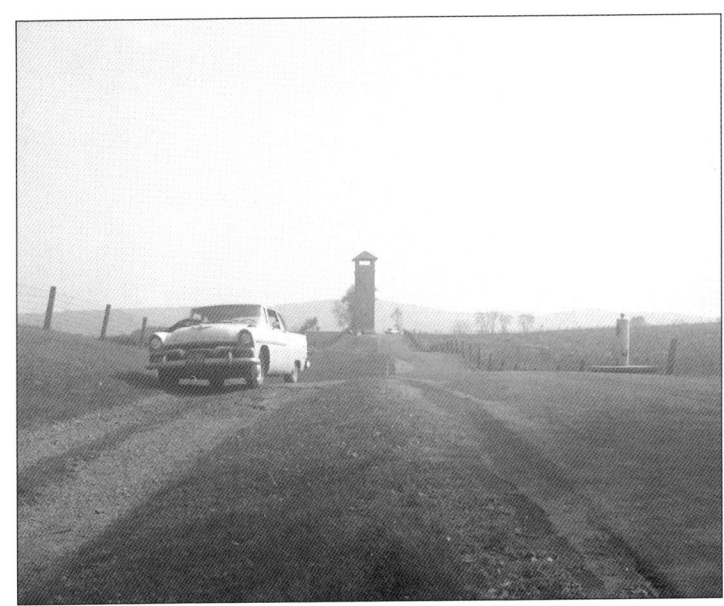

Gen. George B. Anderson's mortuary cannon, completed by October 15, 1897, now rests on the opposite side of Richardson Avenue than it does in this 1954 photograph. This view of the battlefield reflects the constant changes required within the park to meet visitors' needs. In 1954, a total of 71,727 visitors came to Antietam National Battlefield. (Courtesy of the National Park Service.)

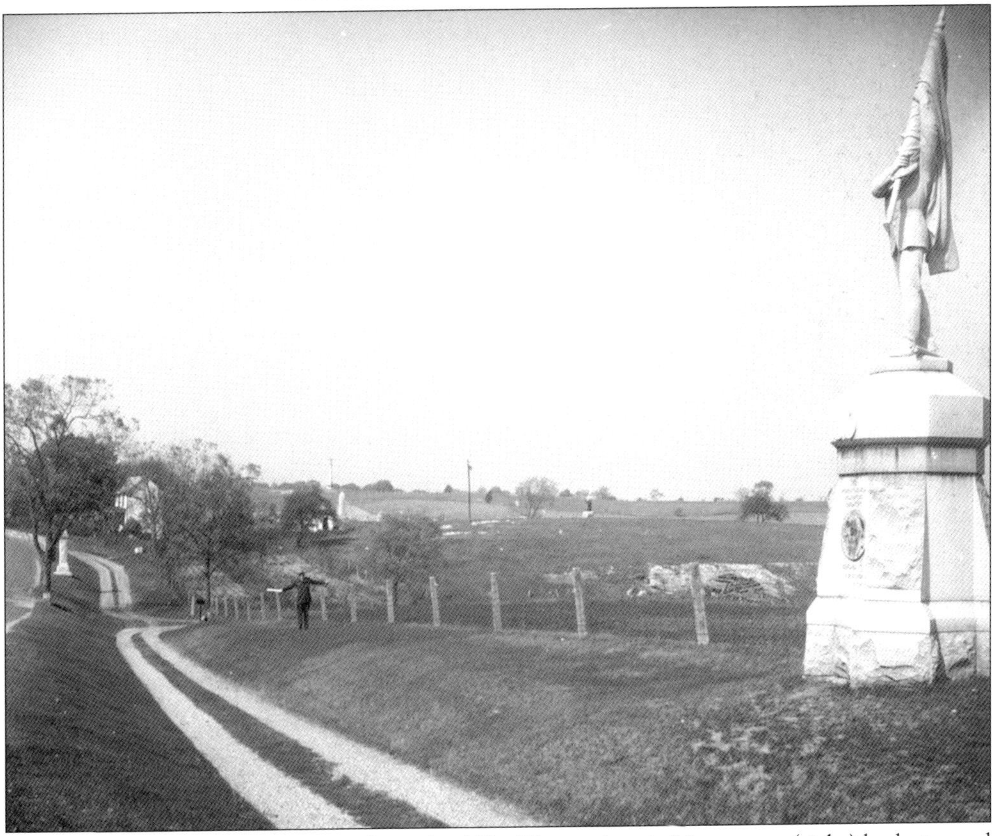

This 1954 view of the Bloody Lane from the 132nd Pennsylvania Monument (right) looks toward the area where today's visitor center stands. Trees obscure the view of the 14th Connecticut and 5th Maryland monuments. Additionally, the house seen at left is long gone. Note the park ranger standing on the lip of the lane. (Courtesy of the National Park Service.)

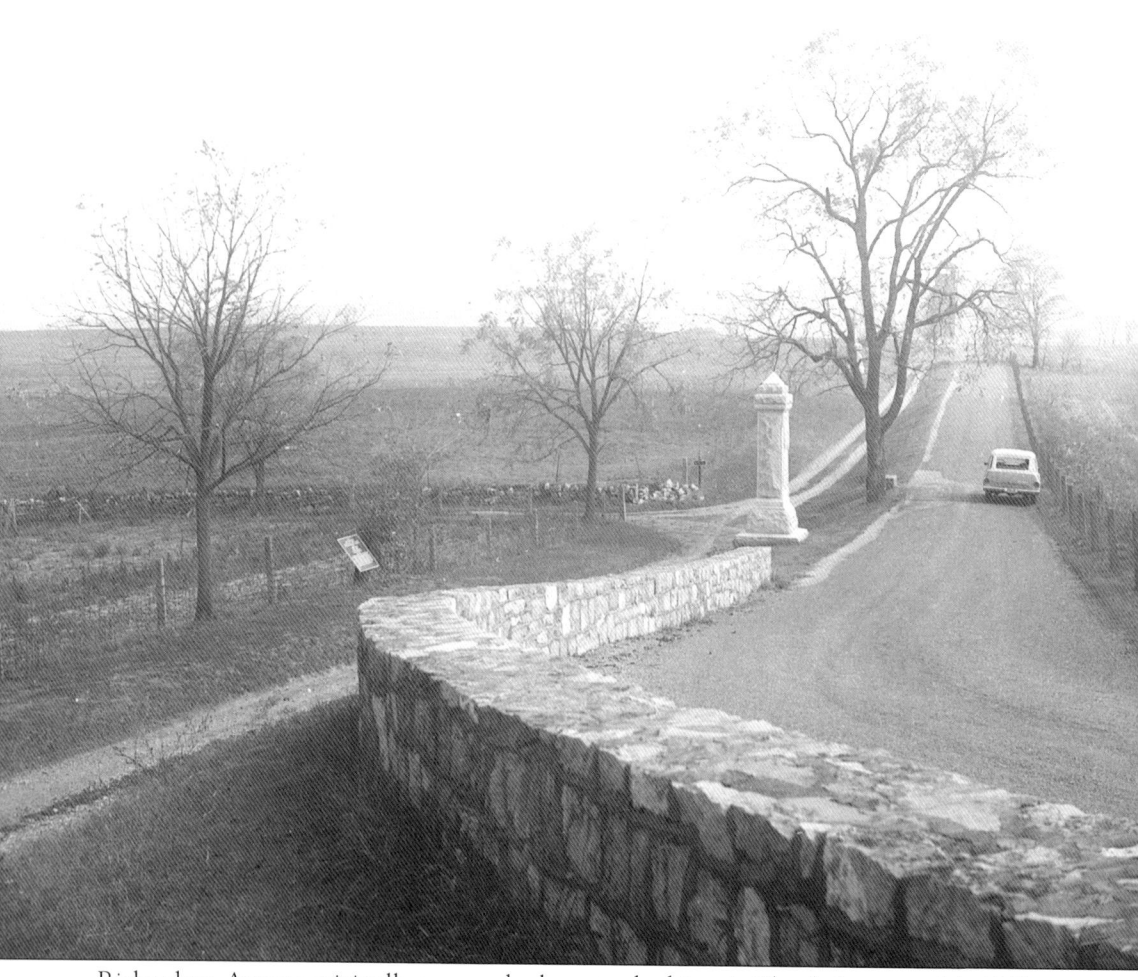

Richardson Avenue originally ran much closer to the historic Bloody Lane, as this 1954 view illustrates. Today, there is a larger parking area for the battlefield driving tour's eighth stop near where the car is parked in this image. The stone wall in the foreground no longer stands. The avenue is named for Union major general Israel B. Richardson. Richardson commanded a division that assaulted the Confederates defending the Sunken Road. "Fighting Dick," as he was known, was a tough fighter though he related to his soldiers well. He likewise knew what he was about on a battlefield, having graduated from the US Military Academy at West Point in 1841. He subsequently served in the US Army until he resigned in 1855. When the Civil War began, Richardson rejoined the ranks. At Antietam, he fell mortally wounded in the fight for the Sunken Road. He died in the Pry House on November 3, 1862. (Courtesy of the National Park Service.)

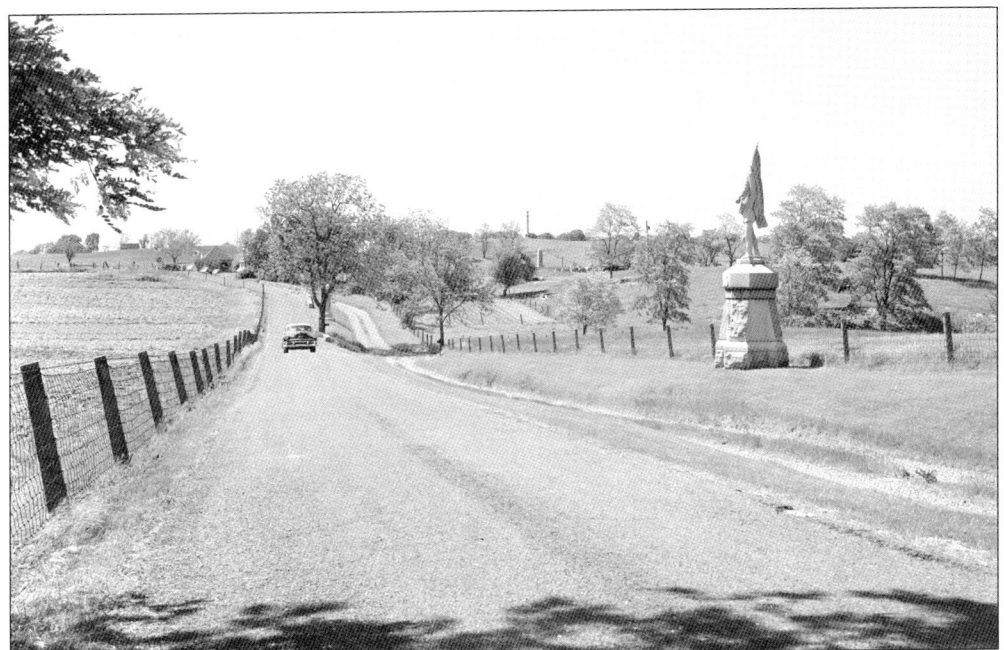

Details of this undated image reveal United States and Confederate flags flying over Lohman's Souvenir Stand with a large Coca-Cola sign nearby. A cow can be seen grazing in the field where the 5th Maryland Monument stands to the right of the 132nd Pennsylvania Monument (with a soldier holding a flag aloft). (Courtesy of the National Park Service.)

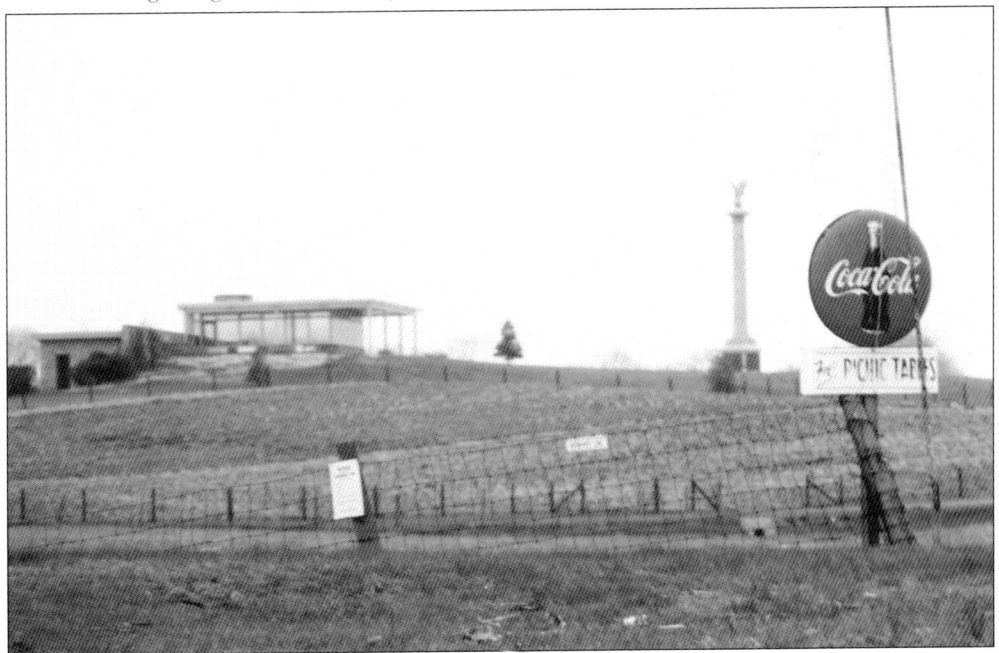

Signs along the fence in the foreground along the Bloody Lane mark Antietam National Battlefield's boundary while large "Coca-Cola" and "Free Picnic Tables" signs at Lohman's Souvenir Stand are overshadowed by both the New York State Monument and the battlefield visitor center. (Courtesy of the National Park Service.)

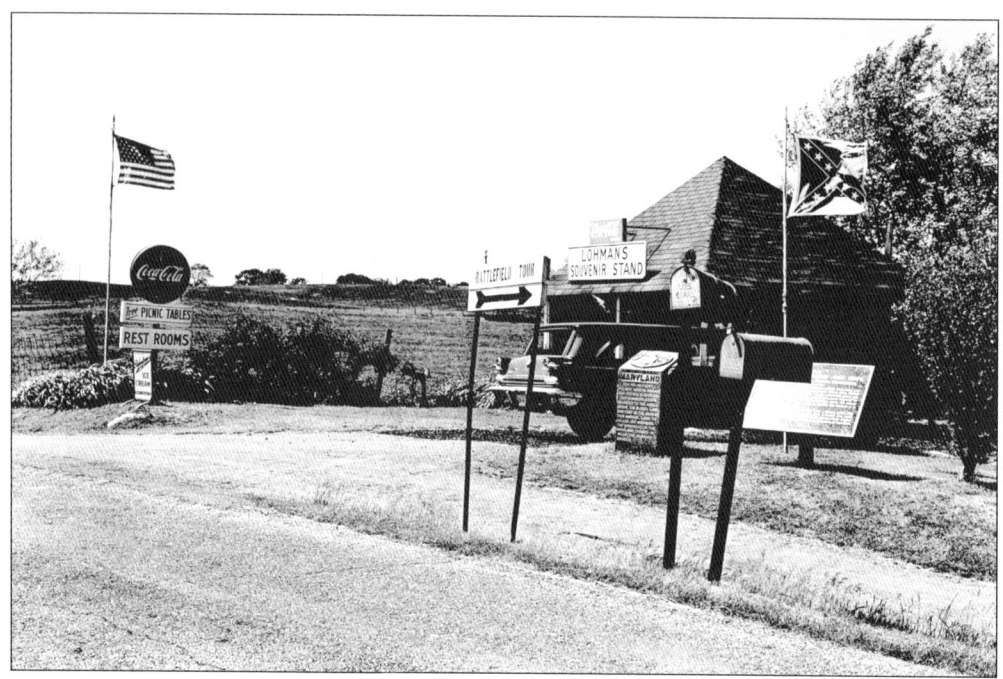

Lohman's Souvenir Stand was a great eyesore along the Bloody Lane. It offered Coca-Cola bottles, Rakestraw's Ice Cream, Antietam battlefield pennants, and more within just a few feet of monuments to the 5th Maryland Infantry and the 130th Pennsylvania Infantry as well as an iron War Department tablet. Superintendent Beckenbaugh called the stand and the rest of the Lohman property "a disgrace to the Bloody Lane section of the Battlefield" in 1936. The Lohman family constructed the concession stand around 1928. It operated until 1973. Today, remains of the building are scant. (Both, courtesy of the National Park Service.)

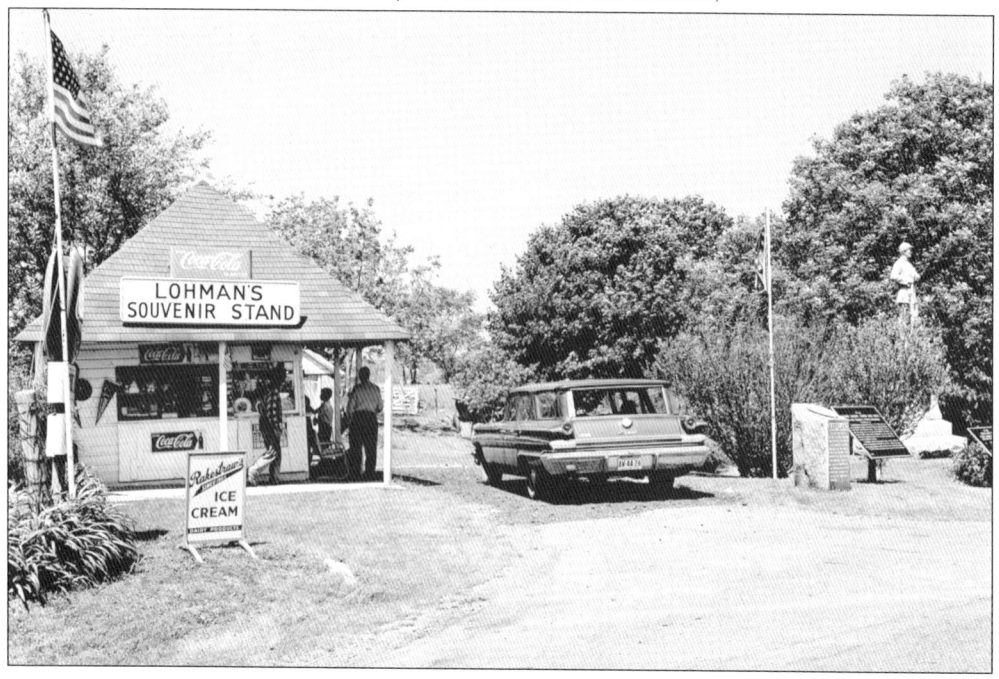

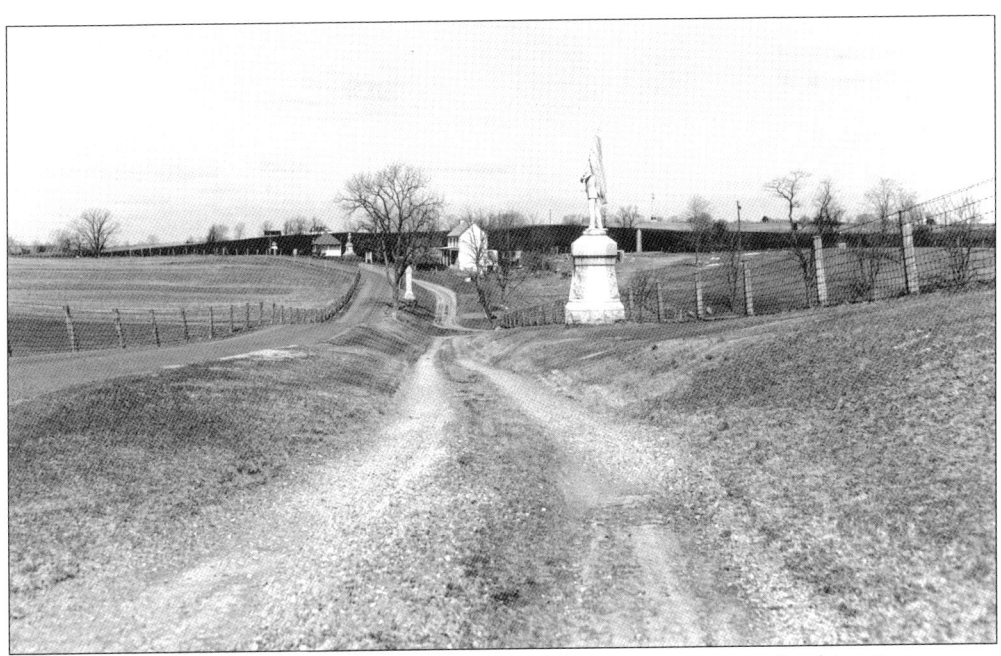

In 1974, park superintendent William Failor requested permission to remove five historic structures on the Lohman property, visible in the background of the 1955 image above. Failor's superiors approved the removal of four of the five buildings but took a more careful consideration regarding the two-story house, constructed sometime between 1862 and 1873. A 1974 National Park Service report concluded, "The house, souvenir shop, privy, garage, and chicken house should be obliterated." Efforts to restore the historic landscape through building demolition and the erection of historic fencing, as seen in the 1971 image below, illustrate growing efforts after the battle's centennial anniversary to restore the battlefield to its 1862 appearance. (Both, courtesy of the National Park Service.)

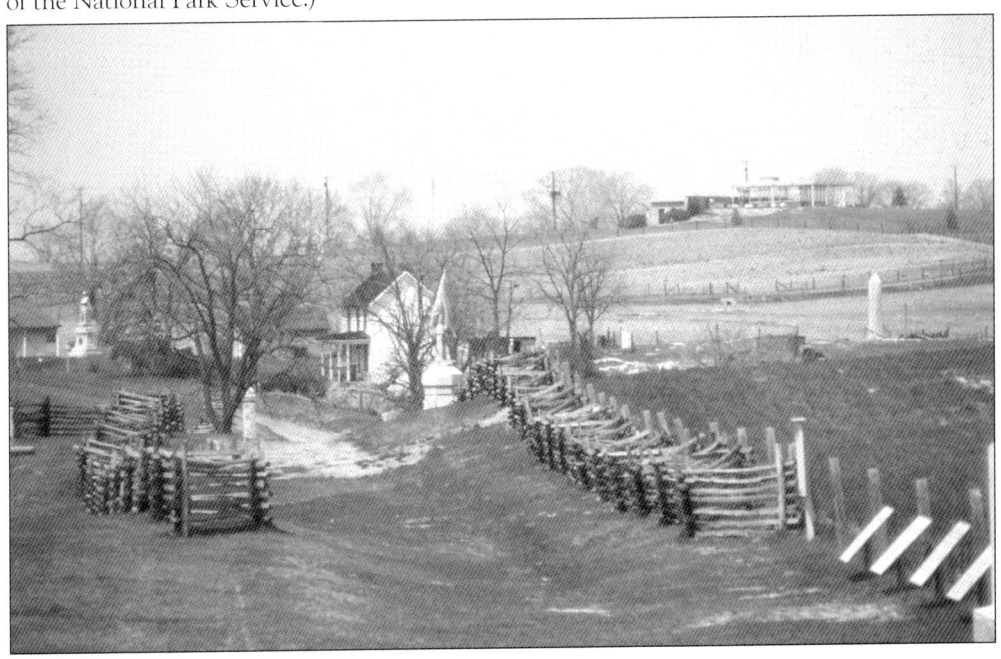

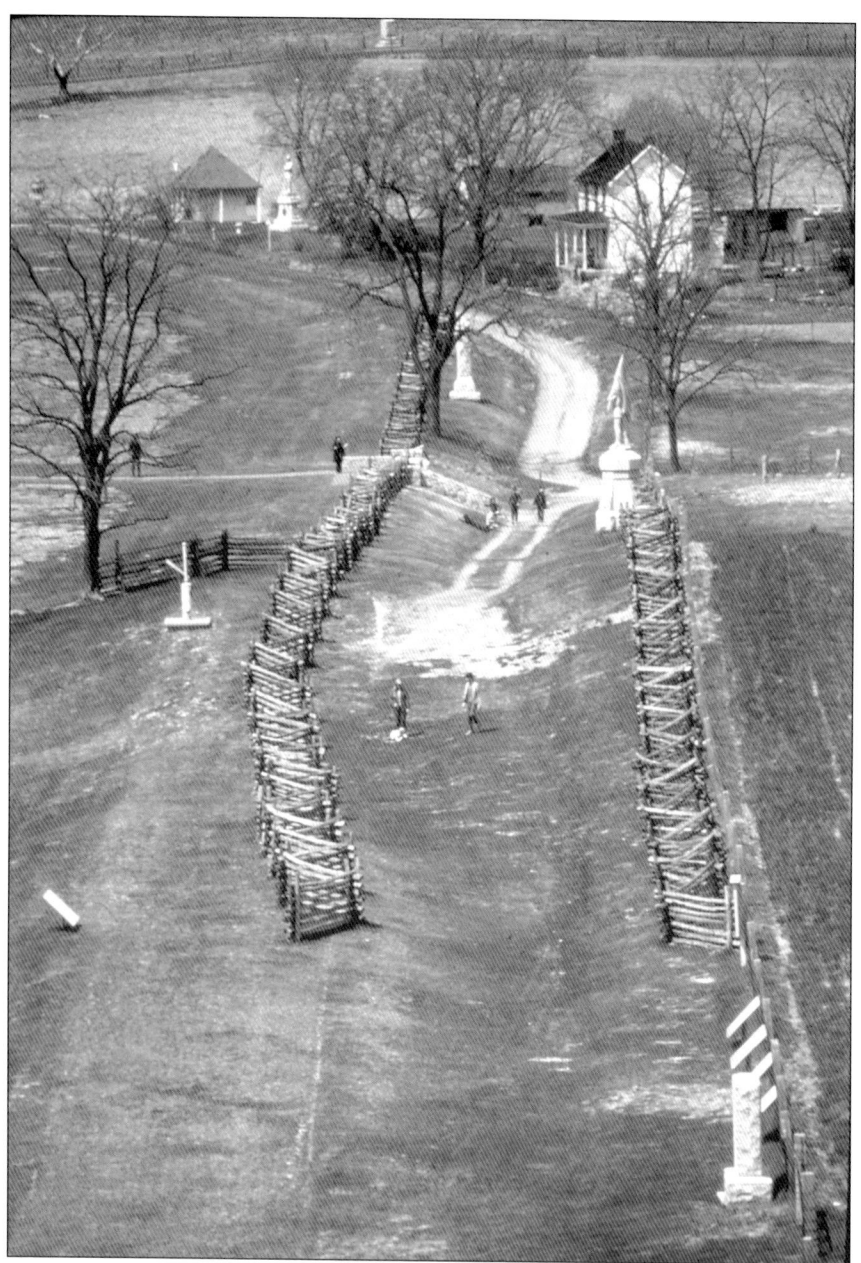

A climb to the top of the 54-foot-tall observation tower gives visitors a bird's-eye view of most of the Antietam battlefield. Directional tablets in the viewing platform, made from a cannon that participated in the battle, orient visitors to the view. O.T. Reilly, one of the first battlefield guides, wrote, "The view from this point alone is worth a visit to the famous Bloody Lane as you can take in the entire right to the left nearly four miles." Due to its height and the fact that it stands above the rest of the landscape, the tower is a constant attraction for visitors. Before the construction of the visitor center and its bathrooms, some tourists, far from a restroom, utilized the tower instead. Additionally, the park's second superintendent once aimed his shotgun at one of the tower's visitors. This, among other infractions, eventually led to him being fired. (Courtesy of the National Park Service.)

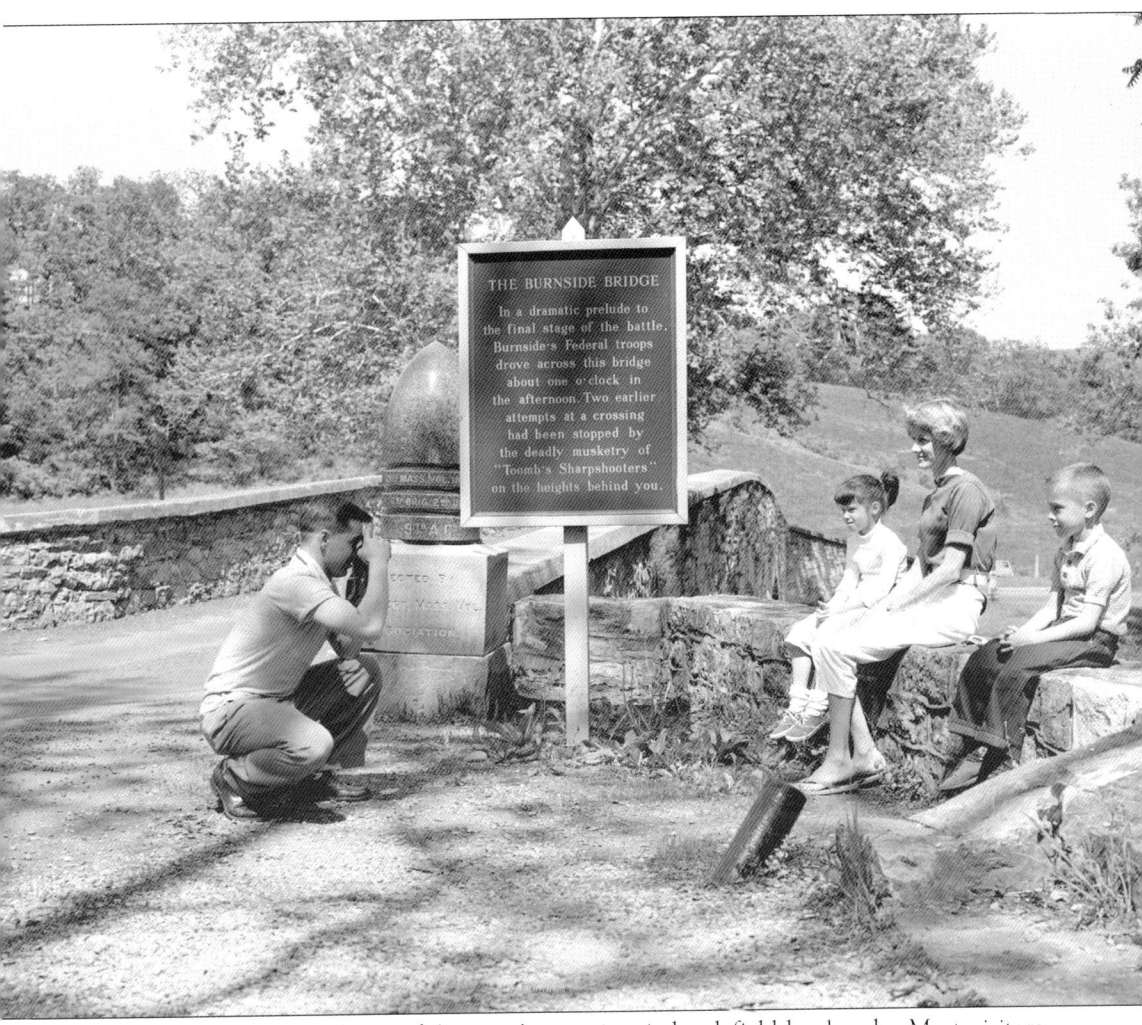

The Burnside Bridge is still one of America's most iconic battlefield landmarks. Most visitors to Antietam National Battlefield have heard of the bridge. Alexander Gardner photographed it extensively in 1862, and it has continued to be the subject of many visitors' pictures. The fact that it took approximately 12,000 Federal soldiers under Ambrose Burnside's command three hours to cross a span guarded by less than 400 Georgians has likewise made the bridge a source of controversy. "Go and look at it," wrote Henry Kyd Douglas, a local Confederate veteran, in 1899 of the Antietam Creek at the bridge, "and tell me if you don't think Burnside and his corps might have executed a hop, skip, and jump and landed on the other side. One thing is certain, they might have waded it that day without wetting their waist belts in any place." In reality, the Antietam was deep enough to force Burnside's men to use the bridge in order to cross the creek. (Courtesy of the National Park Service.)

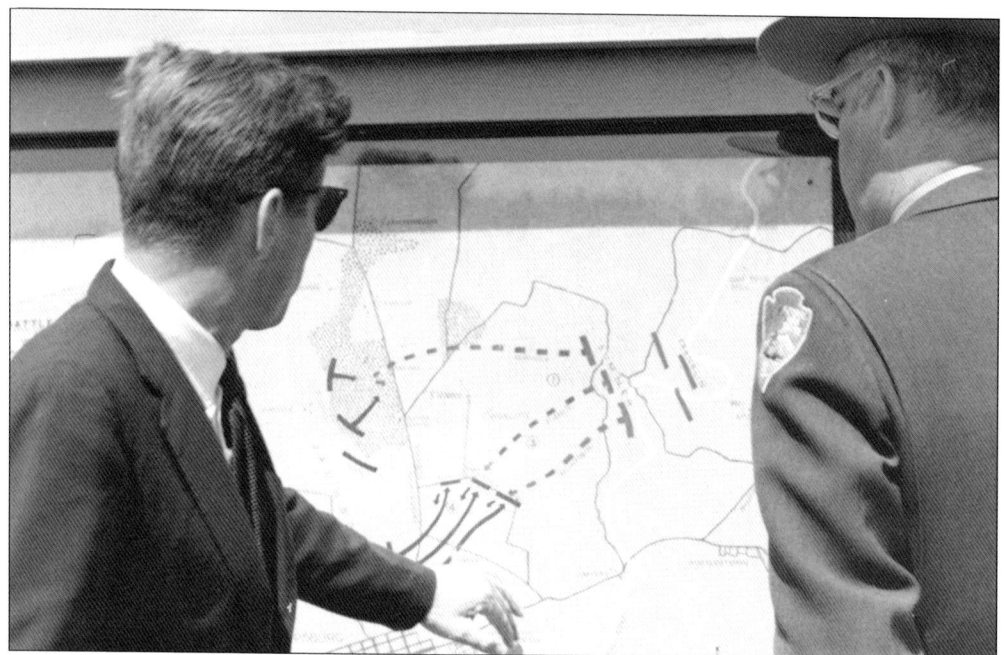

Pres. John F. Kennedy visited Antietam on April 7, 1963. Kennedy was a student of history and took an intense interest in the battlefield. Supt. Robert Lagemann served as the president's guide. "He asked questions about the directions of the Civil War armies which he couldn't have known if he hadn't been familiar with this battle," said Lagemann. (Courtesy of the John F. Kennedy Presidential Library and Museum.)

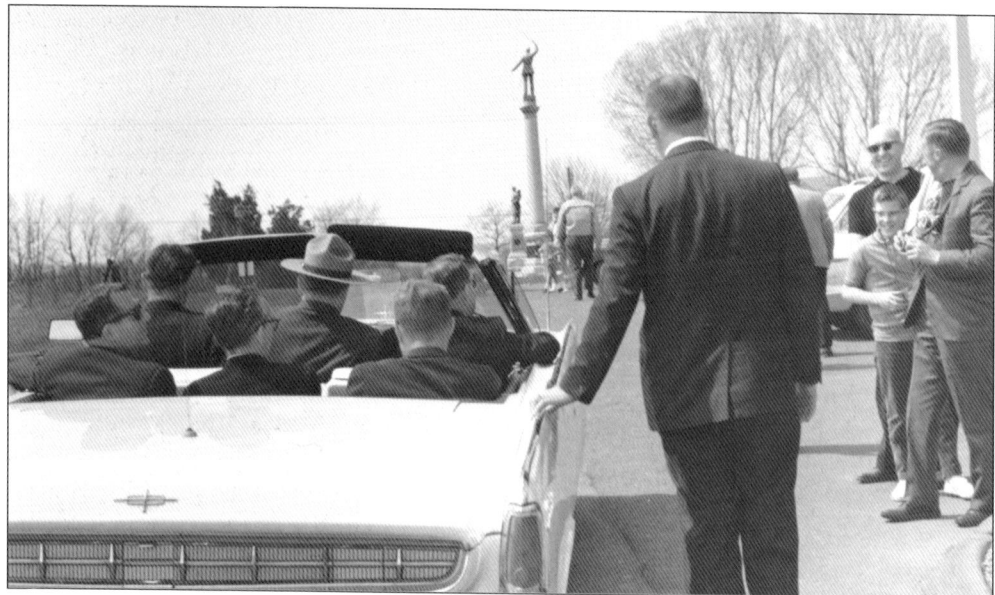

Kennedy's Antietam tour was obviously not advertised. Most of the residents did not know of his visit until after he was back on his way to Camp David via helicopter. However, people already visiting the battlefield saw him, and Kennedy interacted with them. People began to follow the motorcade, adding their own vehicles to the presidential caravan. (Courtesy of the John F. Kennedy Presidential Library and Museum.)

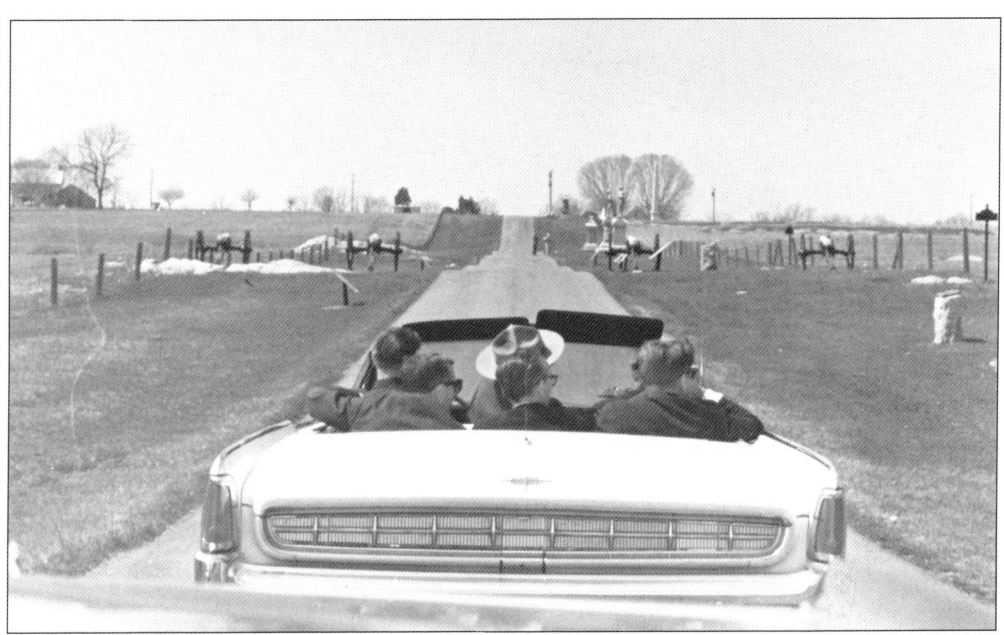

President Kennedy traveled to the battlefield by helicopter, arriving at 11:45 a.m. on April 7. The helicopter landed on the Spong farm near Burnside Bridge before the president and his guests drove around the battlefield in a caravan of cars. They drove down Cornfield Avenue (above) and through the Bloody Lane. The President walked the battlefield at four spots: the Cornfield, Bloody Lane (below), Burnside Bridge, and the New York Monument. The tour lasted 90 minutes. Kennedy, profoundly impressed by the importance of Antietam, said this during his life: "Antietam symbolizes something even more important than combat heroism and military strategy. It marks a diplomatic turning point of world-wide consequence. From this point onward, our Civil War had a new dimension which was important to the whole course of human liberty." (Both, courtesy of the John F. Kennedy Presidential Library and Museum.)

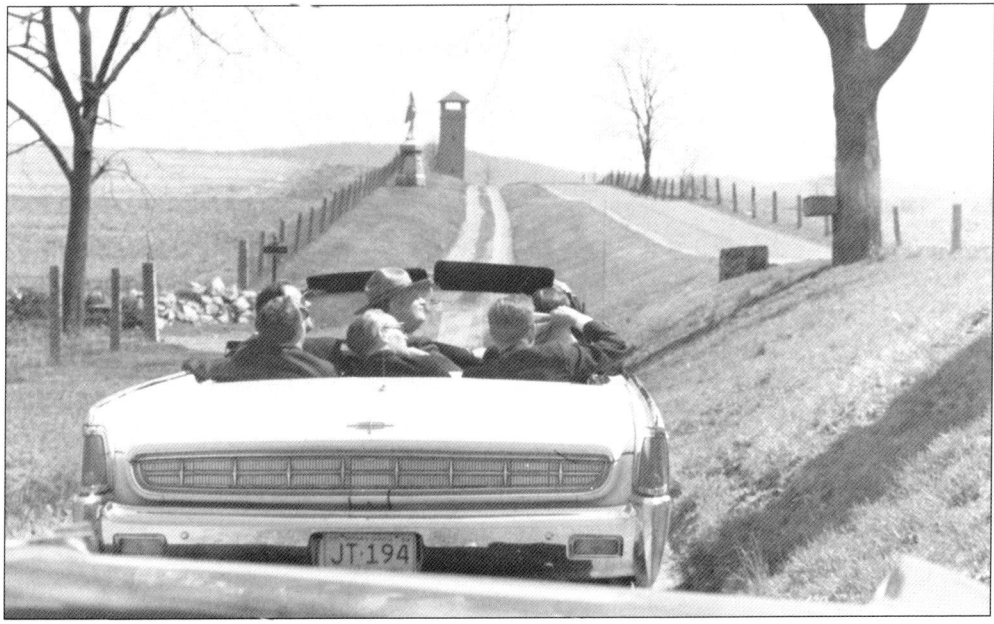

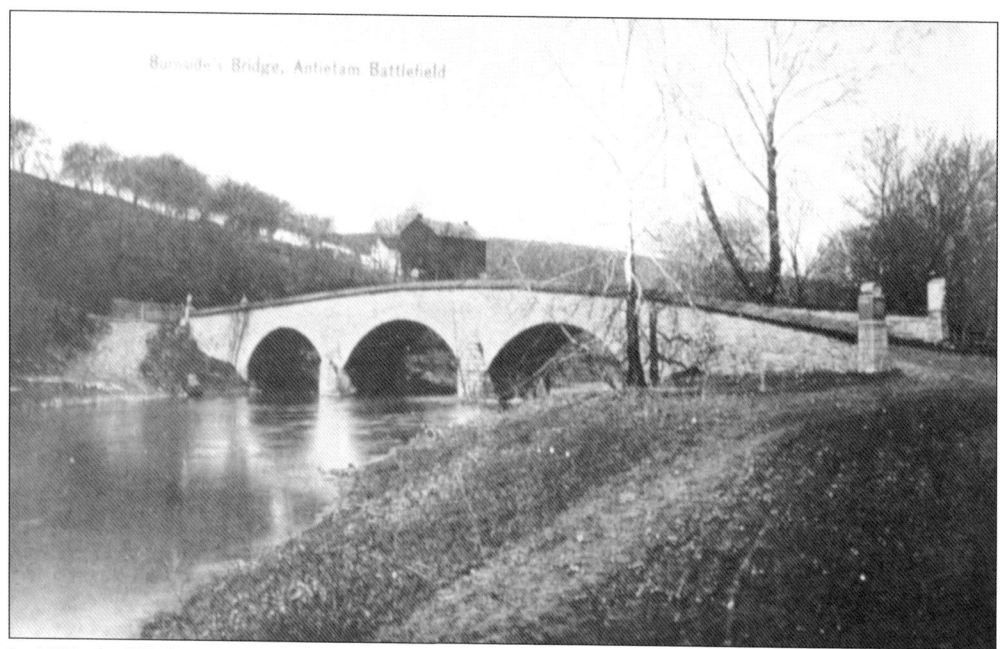

In 1939, the Washington County Historical Society purchased the 136-acre Spong farm, including the house seen in this postcard overlooking the Burnside Bridge. Within the next two years, a National Park Service study concluded the farm's buildings were not relevant to the battle, and they were removed in 1946. (Courtesy of the Western Maryland Room, Washington County Free Library.)

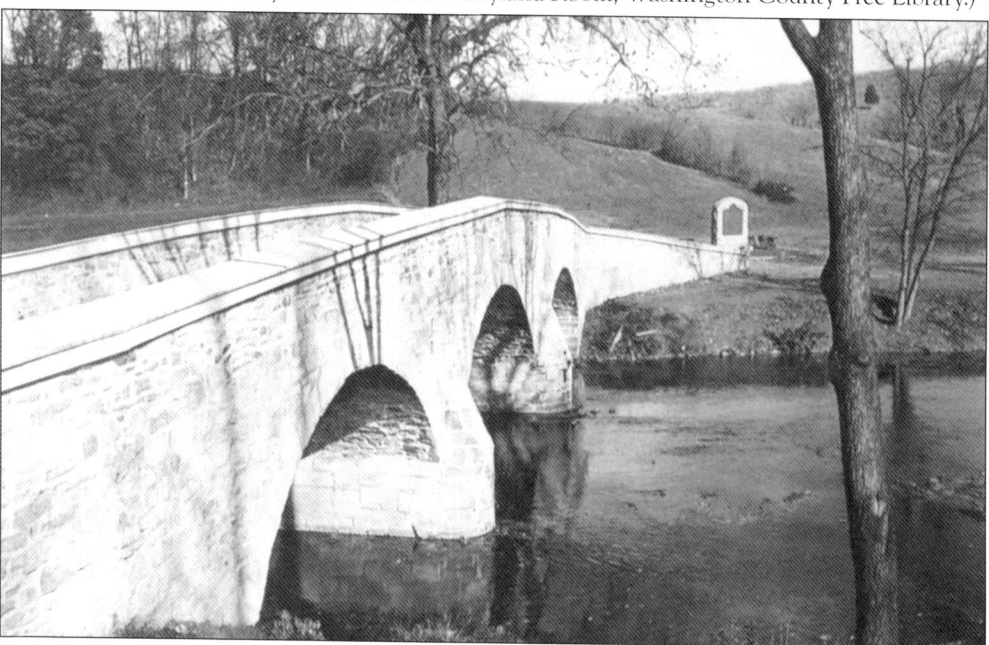

As early as 1963, the National Park Service began prohibiting vehicles from using the Burnside Bridge to cross Antietam Creek. It was in that year that the agency moved each of the four monuments adorning the bridge to the creek's east bank. By 1966, construction finished on the modern bypass, diverting traffic and permanently restoring the bridge to its historic appearance in September 1862. (Courtesy of the Western Maryland Room, Washington County Free Library.)

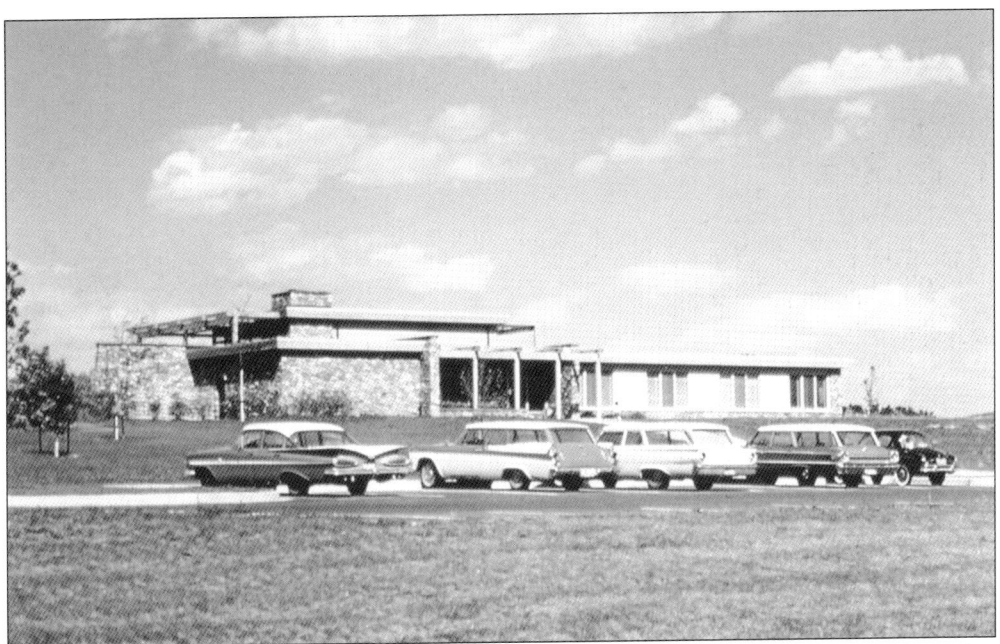

Conrad Wirth, director of the National Park Service, devised Mission 66 in the early 1950s. This initiative sought to enhance the park service's visitor services. The new visitor center at Antietam sat across the Hagerstown Pike from the historic Dunker Church, where visitors can receive an excellent view of much of the battlefield. The new visitor center opened its doors in 1963. (Courtesy of the National Park Service.)

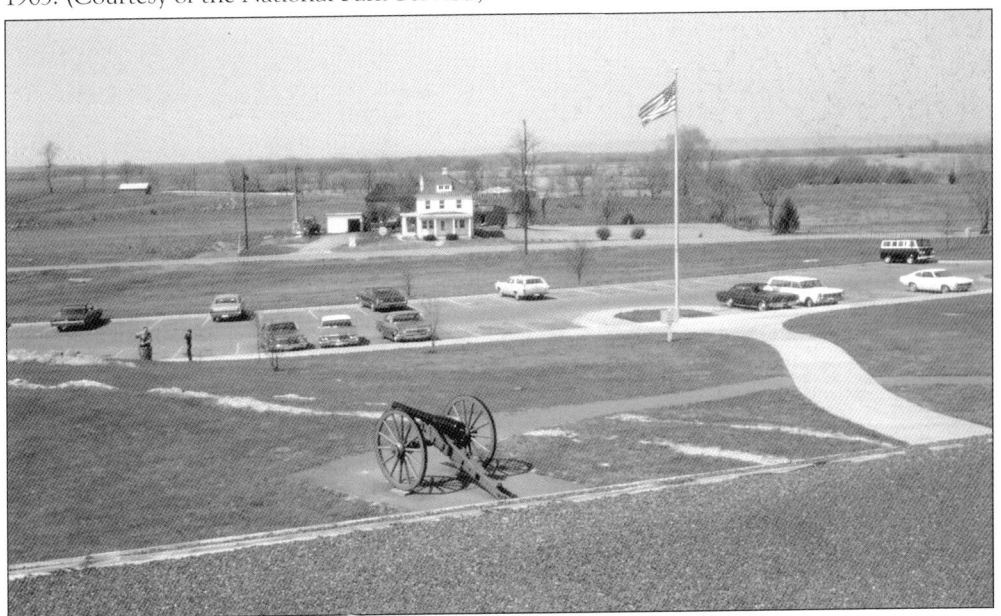

A similar view today, compared with this 1971 image from atop the visitor center, would show a number of battlefield preservation and restoration improvements. Portions of the open field on the right have been replanted to reflect the historic West Woods. As of 2018, the house at center is owned by the American Battlefield Trust, the nation's largest battlefield preservation organization. (Courtesy of the National Park Service.)

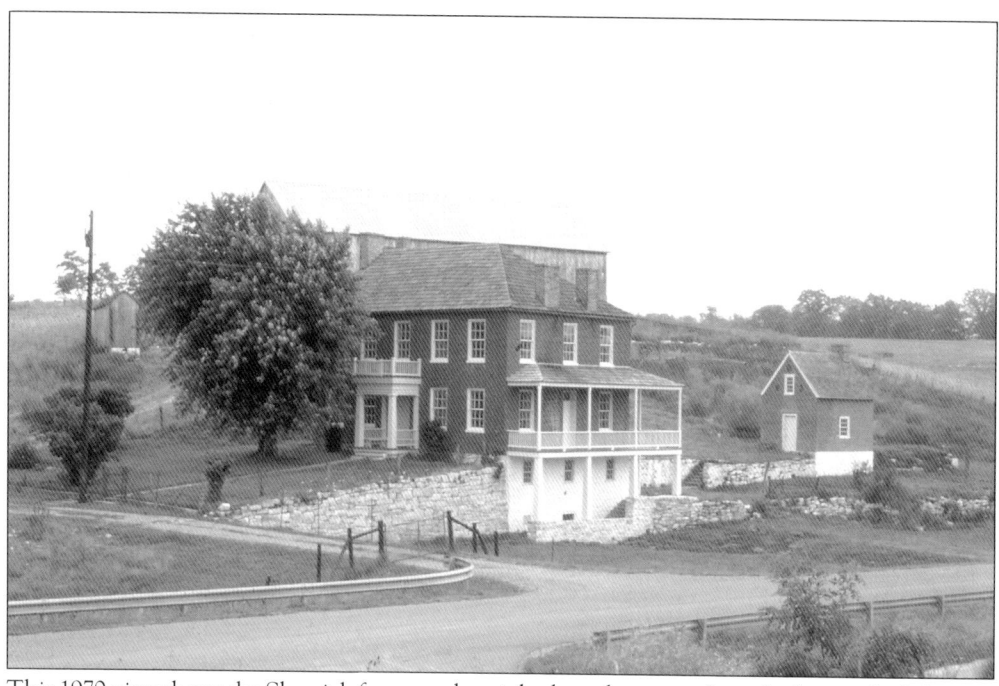

This 1970 view shows the Sherrick farm much as it looks today, apart from the barn, which burned from a lightning strike in 1985. The Sherrick family did not inhabit the farm in September 1862, and it is unknown where they lived at that time. Following the battle, the Mumma family, whose home burned during the battle, occupied the house until June 1863. (Courtesy of the National Park Service.)

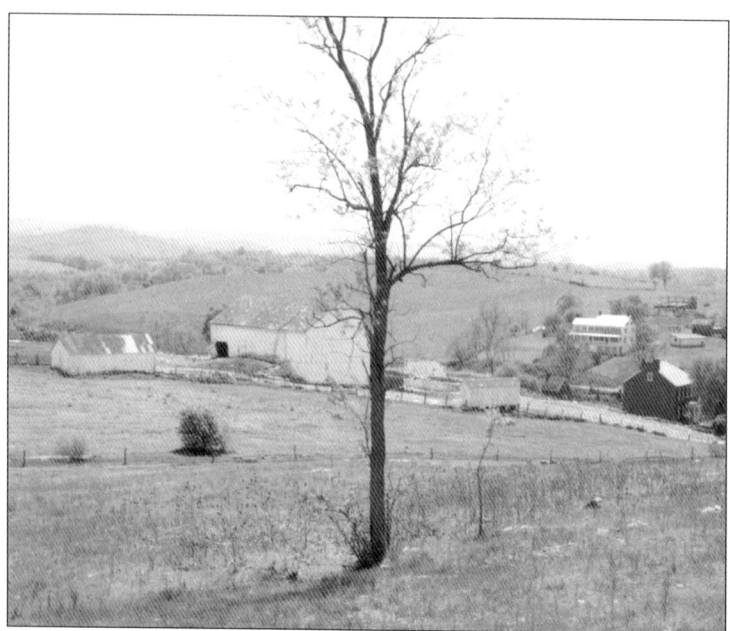

Both the Sherrick and Otto farms witnessed intense fighting during the afternoon of September 17, 1862. The cleared land around the farm buildings underscores the land's agricultural purposes. No longer operating farms, trees have swallowed much of the land to the left of the Otto farmhouse. This view better represents what this section of the field would have looked like at the time of the battle. (Courtesy of the National Park Service.)

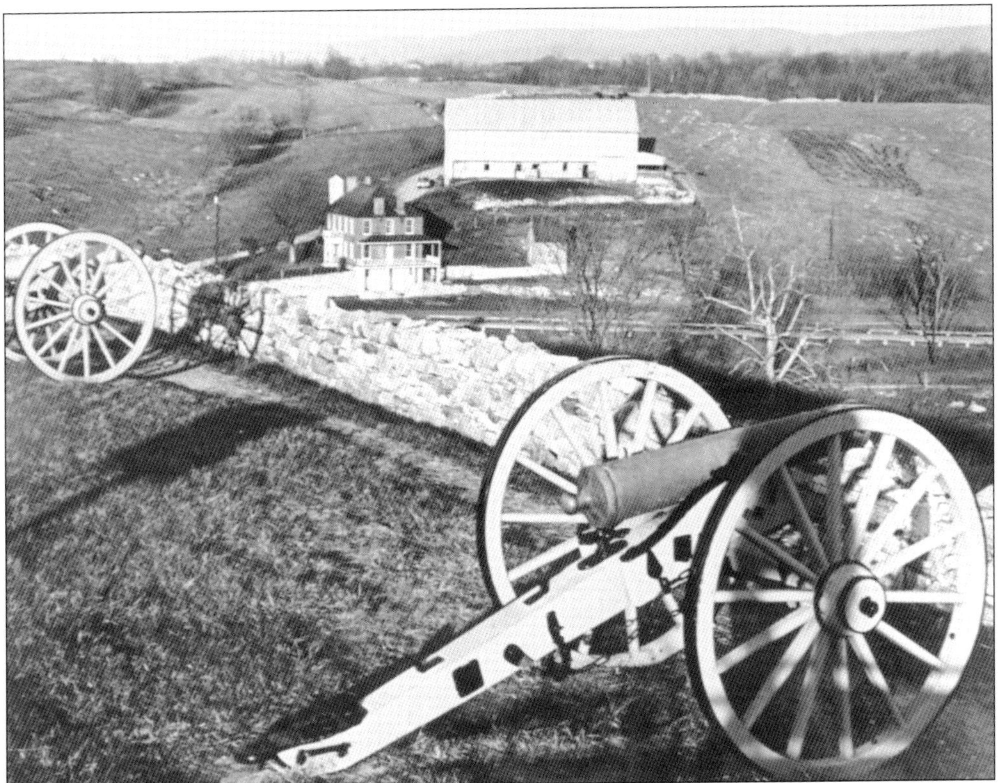

In 1965, the National Park Service continued to add more cannon to the battlefield landscape to further enhance visitors' experience and understanding of the battle. "The presence of numerous cannons has enhanced the martial aspect of the former dark and bloody battleground," Supt. Harold Lessem wrote. The 18 guns added in 1965 upped the total number on the field to 39. Superintendent Lessem also reported that all of the guns were original, though the reproduction gun carriages were manufactured at the District of Columbia Reformatory in Lorton, Virginia. These guns, seen along Branch Avenue, denote the position of Capt. James Brown's Virginia battery of four guns. (Both, courtesy of the Western Maryland Room, Washington County Free Library.)

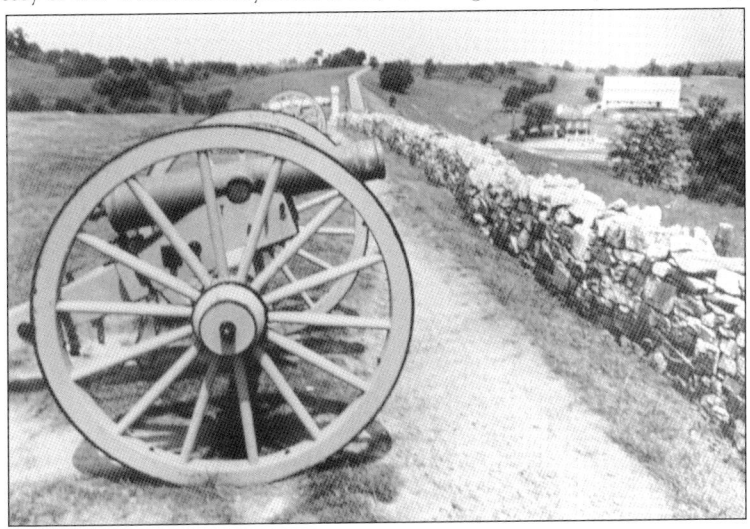

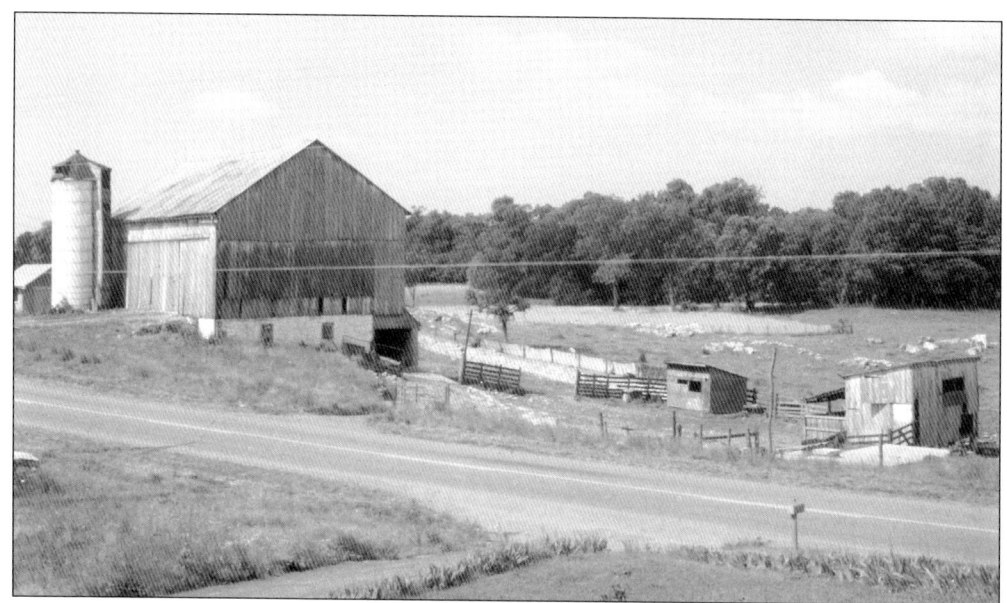

Some of Antietam's heaviest fighting swirled through and around the D.R. Miller farm. Wounded soldiers sought the house and barn (pictured) for shelter. However, for the next 20 years after the battle ended, the Miller family continued to farm the property. Incredibly, the farm remained in private hands until the National Park Service received it through a donation in 1990. (Courtesy of the National Park Service.)

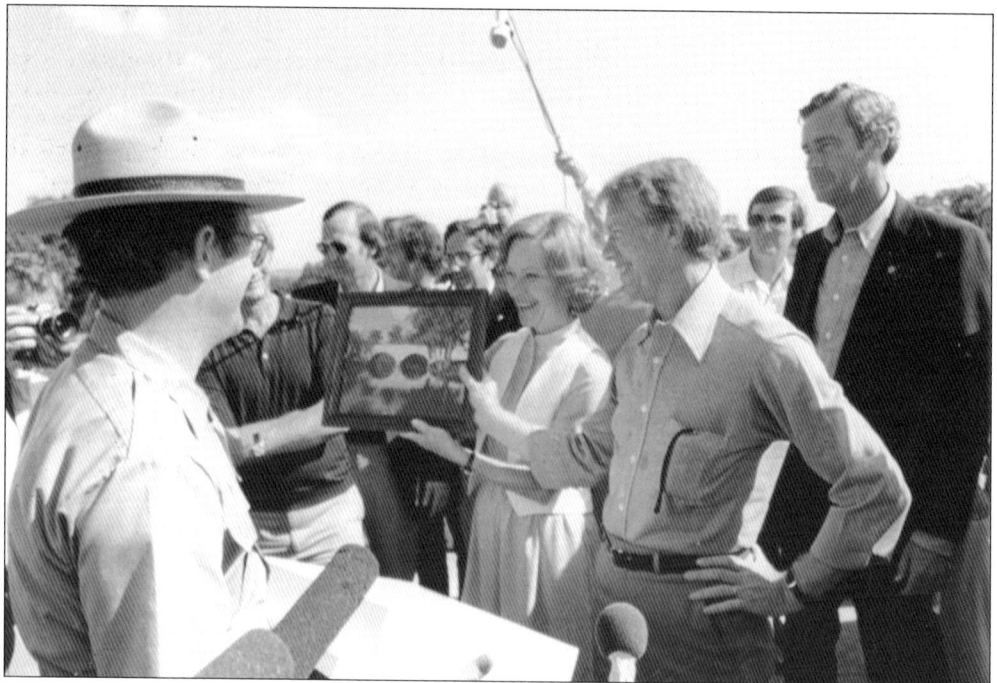

Pres. Jimmy Carter and his wife, Rosalyn, toured the Antietam battlefield on July 6, 1978. Historian Shelby Foote led the tour. Shown here is park superintendent Virgil Leimer presenting the Carters with a framed image of the Burnside Bridge. President Carter made a brief speech commending the National Park Service before departing. (Courtesy of the National Park Service.)

Four

THE MEMORIAL

Whether the Battle of Antietam is viewed through the ghastly lens of America's bloodiest day or the brighter lens as being the event that triggered the Emancipation Proclamation, Antietam National Battlefield is a memorial to those who died in the struggle and for those who fought for the advancement of the United States.

Beginning on the 25th anniversary of the battle, veterans returned to the cemetery and battlefield to dedicate monuments to their fallen friends. "It is to the precious memory of those gallant comrades who fell by our side on that eventful day in defence [sic] of our country . . . that this monument has been erected," said veteran William Wallace at the dedication of the 125th Pennsylvania Monument. But the veterans did not just do this for the fallen but also for the future, "to perpetuate through coming generations for all time, a recognition of their heroic devotion and sacrifice unto death."

Today, 99 monuments populate the Antietam battlefield, a vast majority of which stand on National Park Service property. Most stand to honor Union veterans of the war. Twelve monuments honor Confederate units or commanders while two memorialize private citizens. But the entire preserved battlefield is a memorial along with the 300-plus iron War Department tablets. And the name "Antietam" has been used to designate roads, schools, businesses, and even military vessels.

This place of horror now represents to many a place of peace watched over by stone soldiers. "Future generations looking at the markers will swell with pride as they read of the heroic character of their ancestors, and they will also have more appreciation of peace," wrote Confederate veteran James Dinkins. Rev. Theodore Flood said, "The scenes all about us after these forty years have past speak of peace." Though Antietam National Battlefield is now a place of peace, where history enthusiasts learn while others use the park's green space for recreational use, its passive appearance might make one "suppose that no such bloody conflict had ever taken place on this soil, but history will tell another story," said Flood. Antietam as a memorial tells that story.

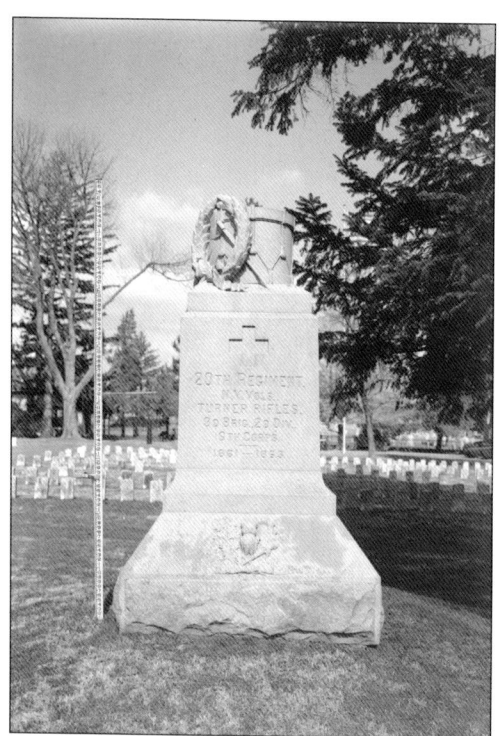

Veterans of the 20th New York Infantry dedicated the first regimental monument on the Antietam battlefield on the 25th anniversary of the battle. Because the federal government already operated the National Cemetery, the regiment placed their monument within its confines. They later placed a second monument on their firing line near the Dunker Church. (Courtesy of the Library of Congress.)

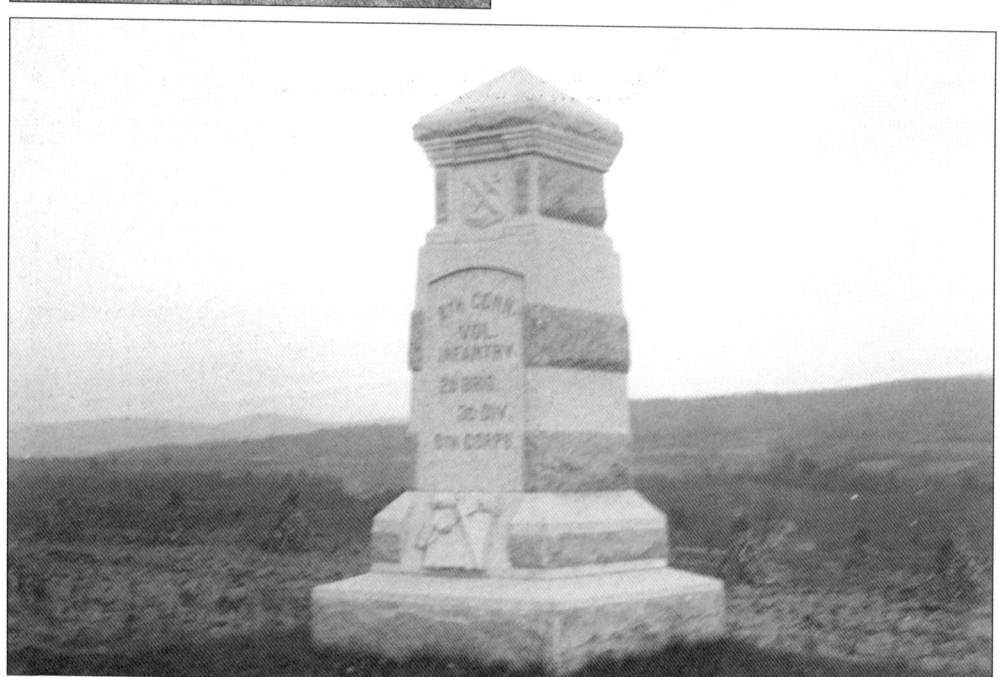

On the southern end of the battlefield, the 8th Connecticut Infantry participated in some of the hardest fighting south of Sharpsburg. The regiment entered the fight with 400 soldiers and lost 194 killed, wounded, missing, and captured in their push toward the Harpers Ferry Road. Veterans of the unit dedicated this monument on October 8, 1894. (Courtesy of the Western Maryland Room, Washington County Free Library.)

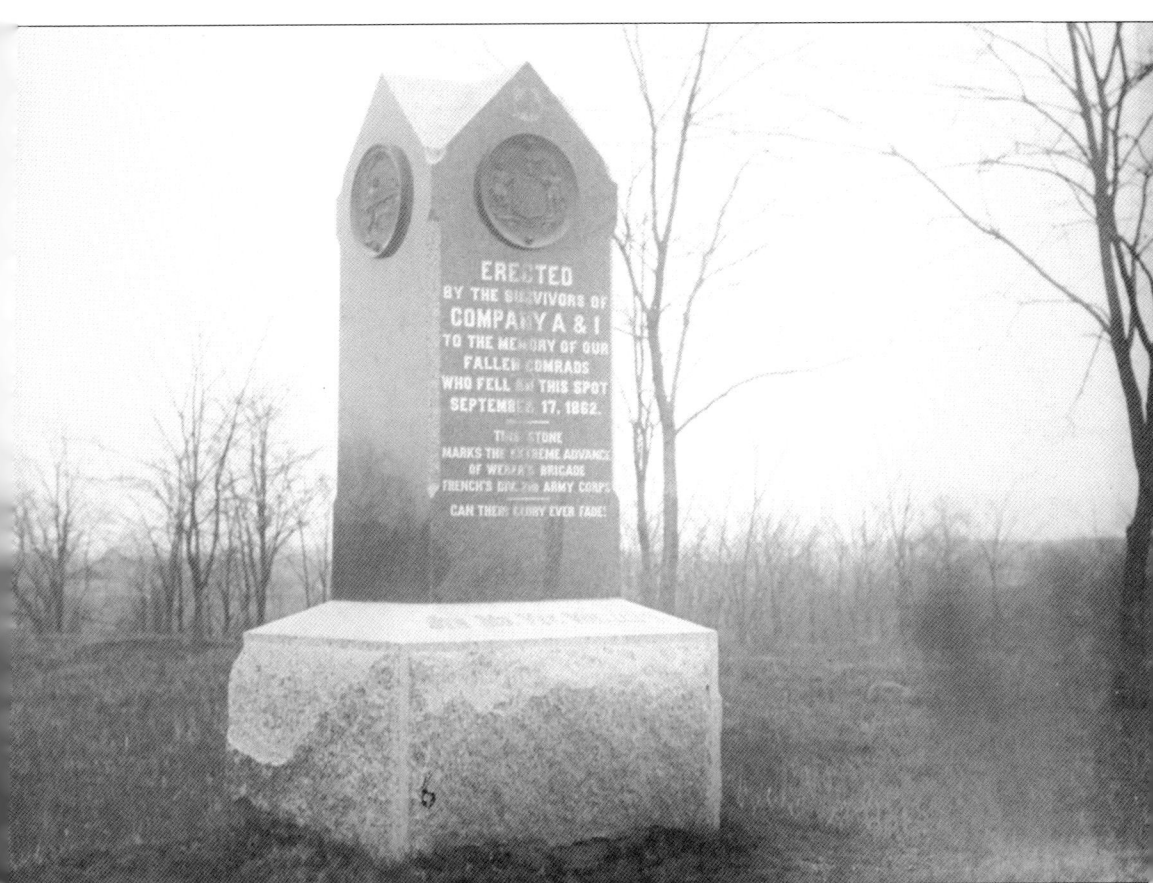

The 5th Maryland Infantry Regiment has two monuments on the battlefield, though this one was specifically established by the survivors of Companies A and I. They dedicated the monument on the 28th anniversary of the battle. Charles A. Foster, a member of Company A, designed the granite monument. Both companies were raised in Cecil County, Maryland, and the rest of the regiment came from the Baltimore area. The 5th Maryland was among the first units to assault the Confederates defending the Sunken Road. As they advanced, they aligned on their colors, held aloft by "a very heavy built German, over six feet in height and weighing nearly 300 pounds, very deliberate in movement," wrote Ezra Carman in his history of the battle. During the action at the Sunken Road, the 5th Maryland lost 163 of 500 soldiers. (Courtesy of the Western Maryland Room, Washington County Free Library.)

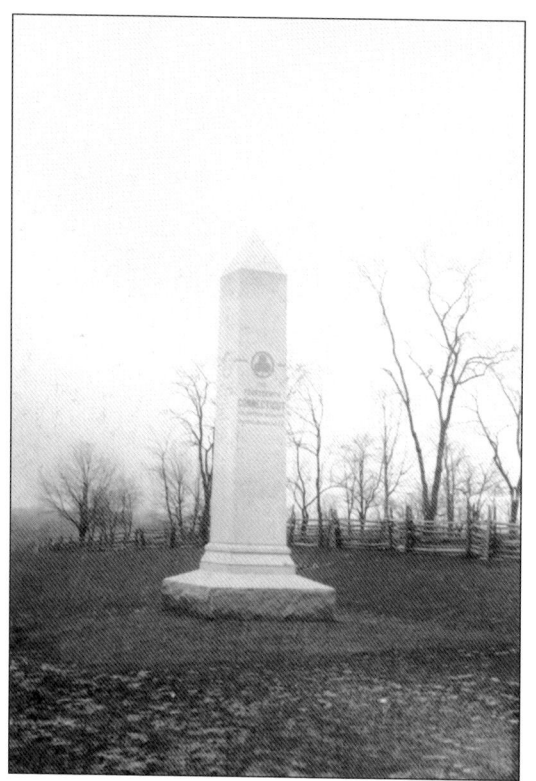

All four of the Connecticut monuments were dedicated on October 8, 1894. The 14th Connecticut's monument near the Bloody Lane was the first to be unveiled that day. This regiment received its baptism of fire at Antietam. It had only been mustered into the service of the US Army on August 23, 1862, just weeks earlier. (Courtesy of the Western Maryland Room, Washington County Free Library.)

Color sergeant George Simpson of the 125th Pennsylvania Infantry holds a unique place in the history of Antietam National Battlefield: he is the only soldier depicted on a monument (this is the 125th Pennsylvania's monument) to be buried in Antietam National Cemetery. He rests in the Pennsylvania section, Grave 3953. He carried the regimental flag on September 17 and was killed in action. (Courtesy of the Library of Congress.)

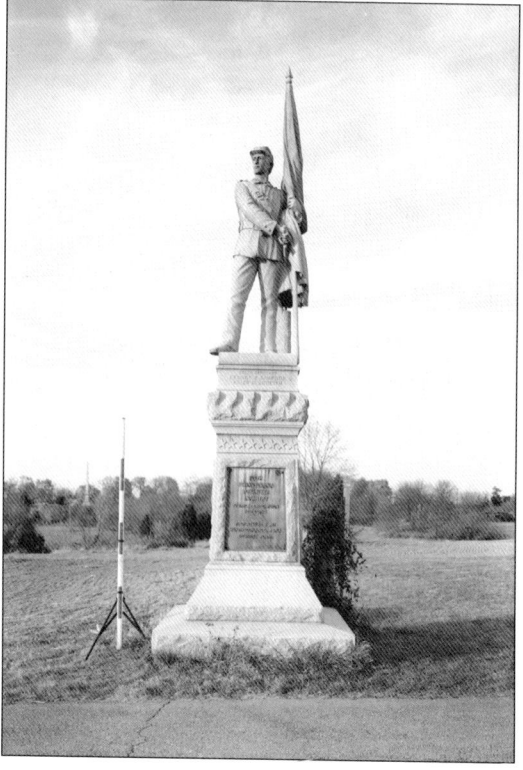

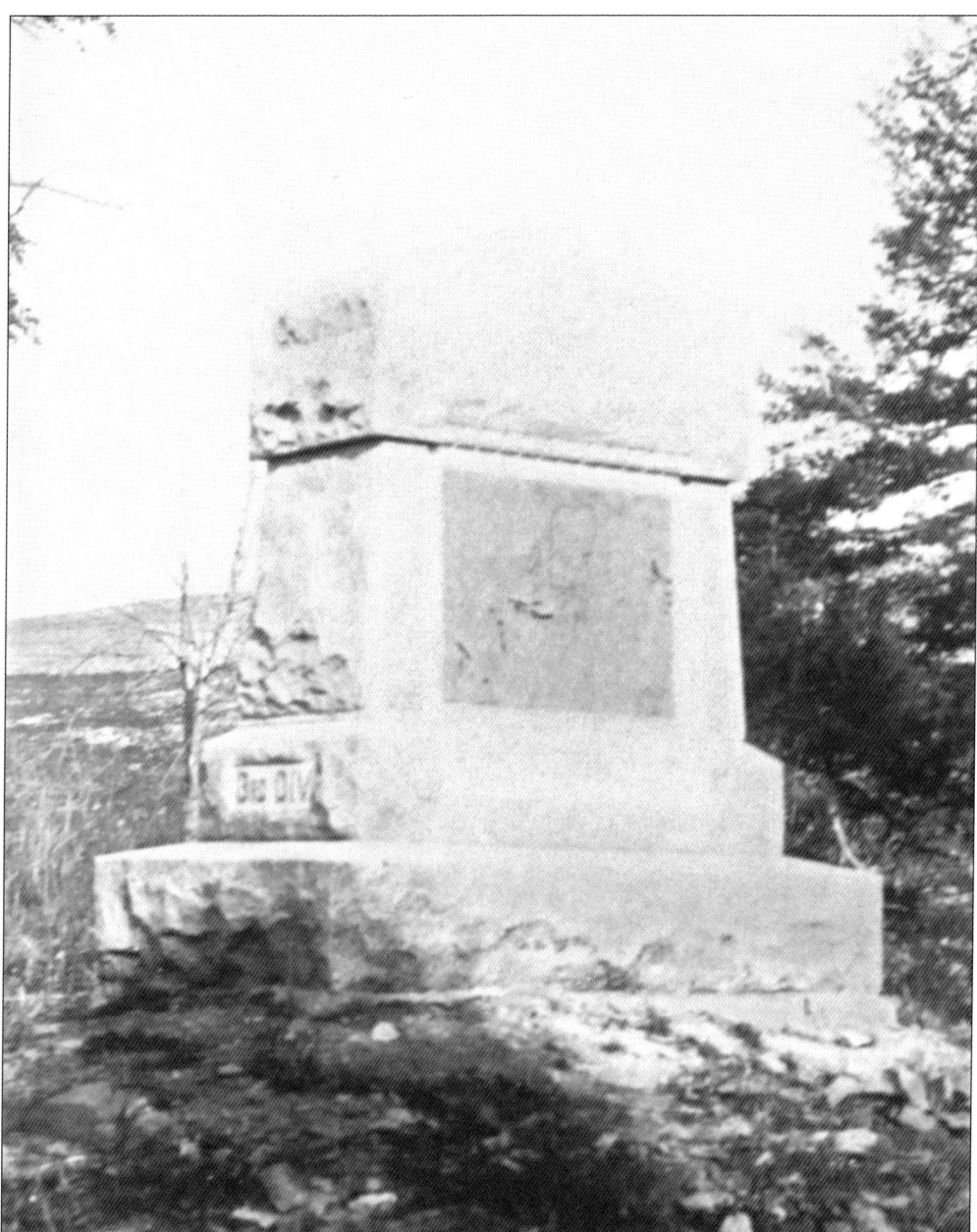

Connecticut veterans erected this monument to the 11th Connecticut in a 10-acre parcel of the Sherrick Cornfield alongside the 16th Connecticut's monument. The plot of land was known as Connecticut Park. However, the 11th never fought in this position. Instead, their major fighting took place at the Burnside Bridge. A lack of funds prevented the Connecticut men from putting their monument closer to the bridge. "It was a question with the [monument] committee as to this being the most desirable location," reported the *National Tribune*. After the veterans purchased a small plot closer to the bridge, they moved the monument to that location in December 1895. The monument features a bas-relief depicting their ill-fated attack against Confederate positions overlooking the bridge. During the fight, the 11th lost 139 men, including its commanding officer, Col. Henry Kingsbury. (Courtesy of the Western Maryland Room, Washington County Free Library.)

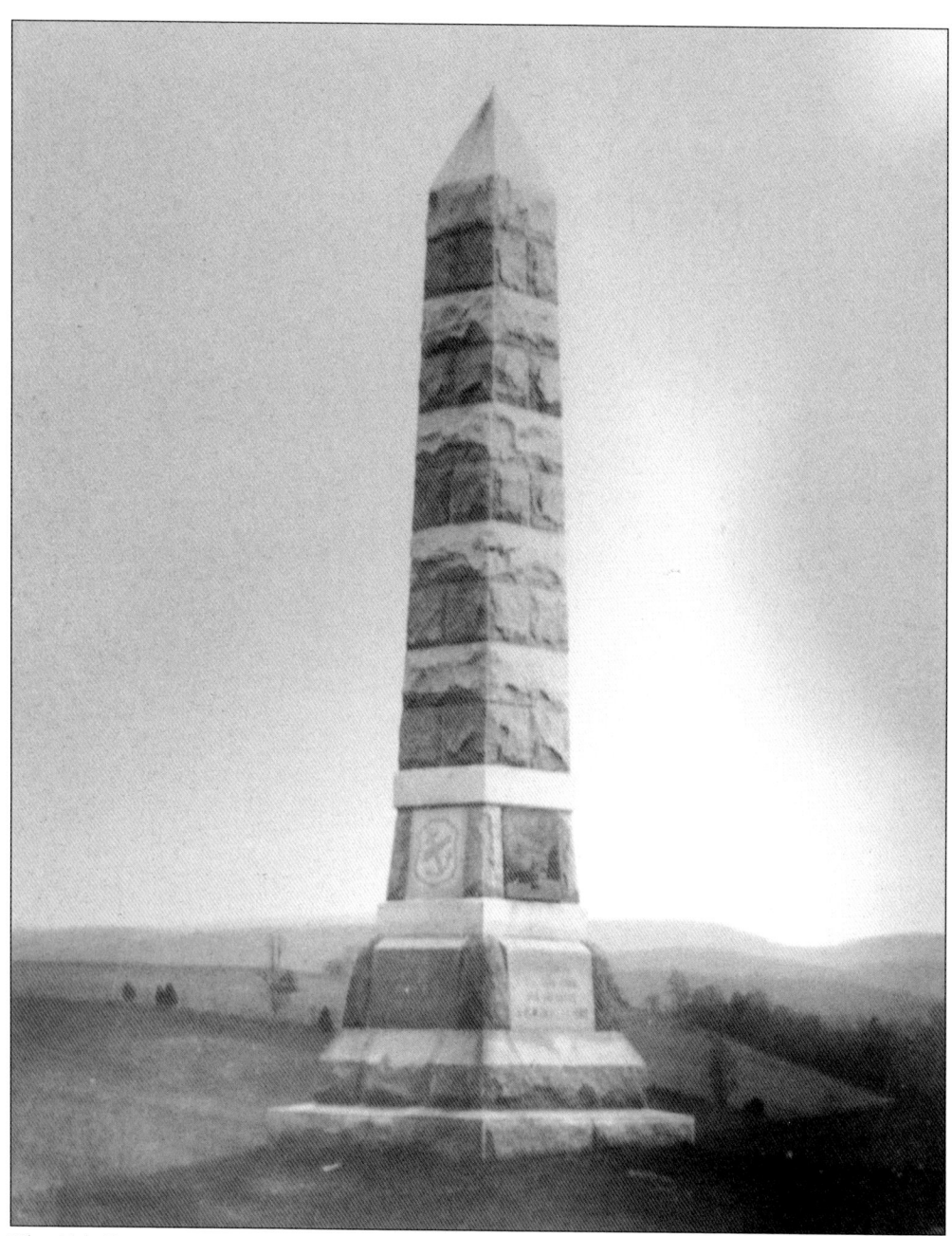

The 16th Connecticut came under fire for the first time during the Civil War on September 17, 1862. In fact, the regiment was only mustered into service on August 24, 1862. It faced the onslaught of a Confederate counterattack late on the afternoon of the battle in the Sherrick Cornfield. James Caldwell, a Confederate involved in the fight, wrote of the action, "So dense was the corn that the lines sometimes approached within thirty to forty yards of each other before [firing]." The regiment suffered dearly. Of 940 men engaged, 43 were killed, 164 wounded, and 20 captured, while 19 fled the field. The 16th Connecticut later suffered another terrible fate in the war, being captured en masse at Plymouth, North Carolina. They erected their monument at their position in the Sherrick Cornfield. (Courtesy of the Western Maryland Room, Washington County Free Library.)

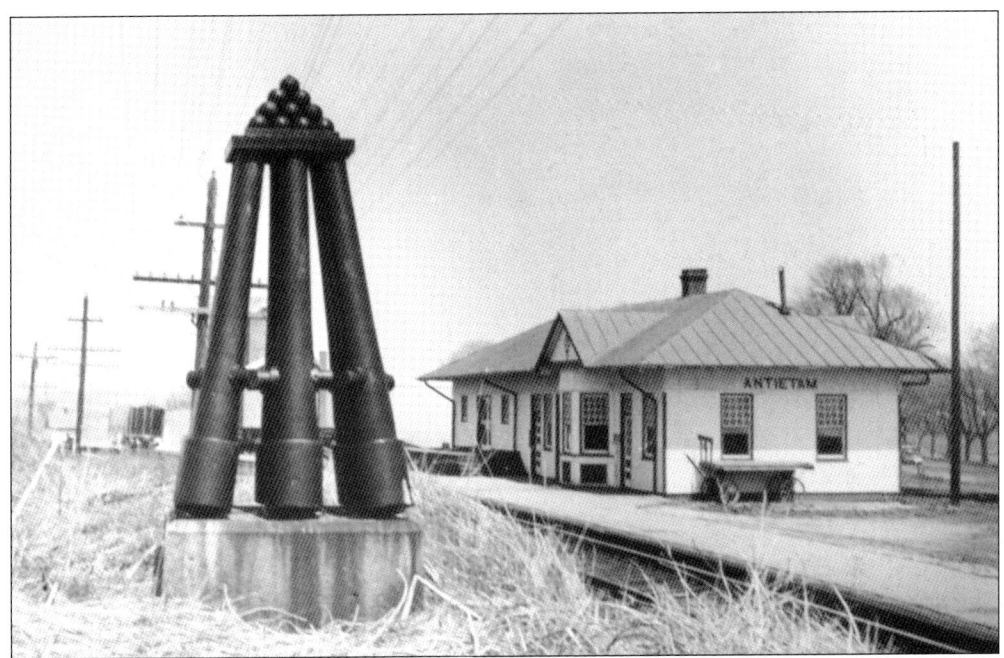

Sharpsburg did not have rail service during the Battle of Antietam. The iron horse did not reach the town until 1881. The Shenandoah Valley Railroad helped bring more people to the Antietam battlefield and even arranged battlefield tours for its passengers. The company had a photographer capture iconic places on the battlefield for advertising use. Sometime in the 1890s, the railroad erected this monument along its tracks on the west end of town, publicizing the battlefield. It is unclear exactly when the monument, which came into the National Park Service's possession in 1942, was dismantled, though it was likely in the 1960s. Only the base of the monument exists today. (Both, courtesy of the Western Maryland Room, Washington County Free Library.)

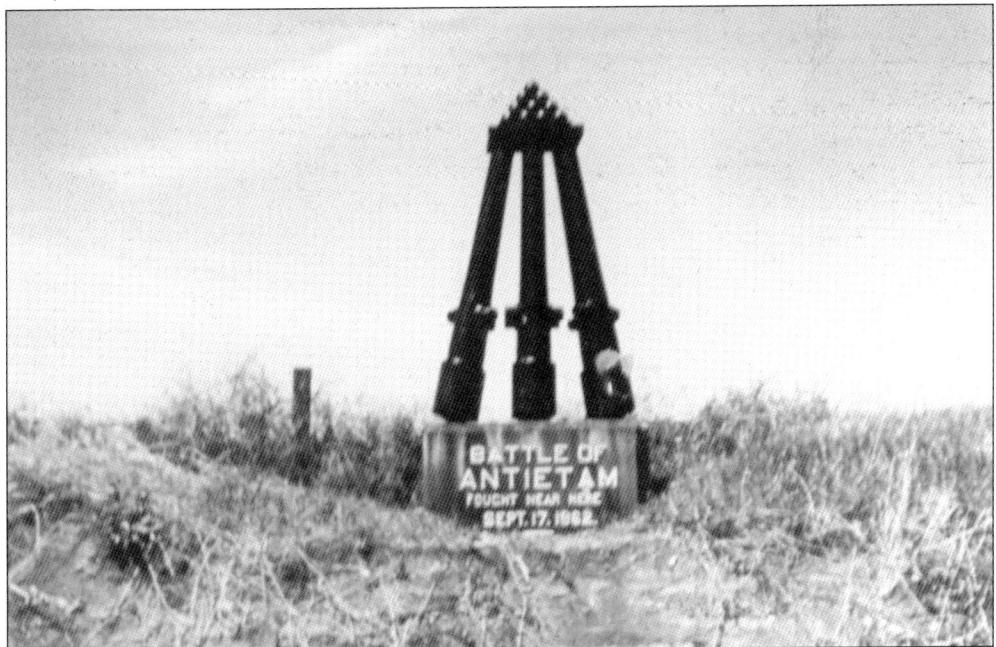

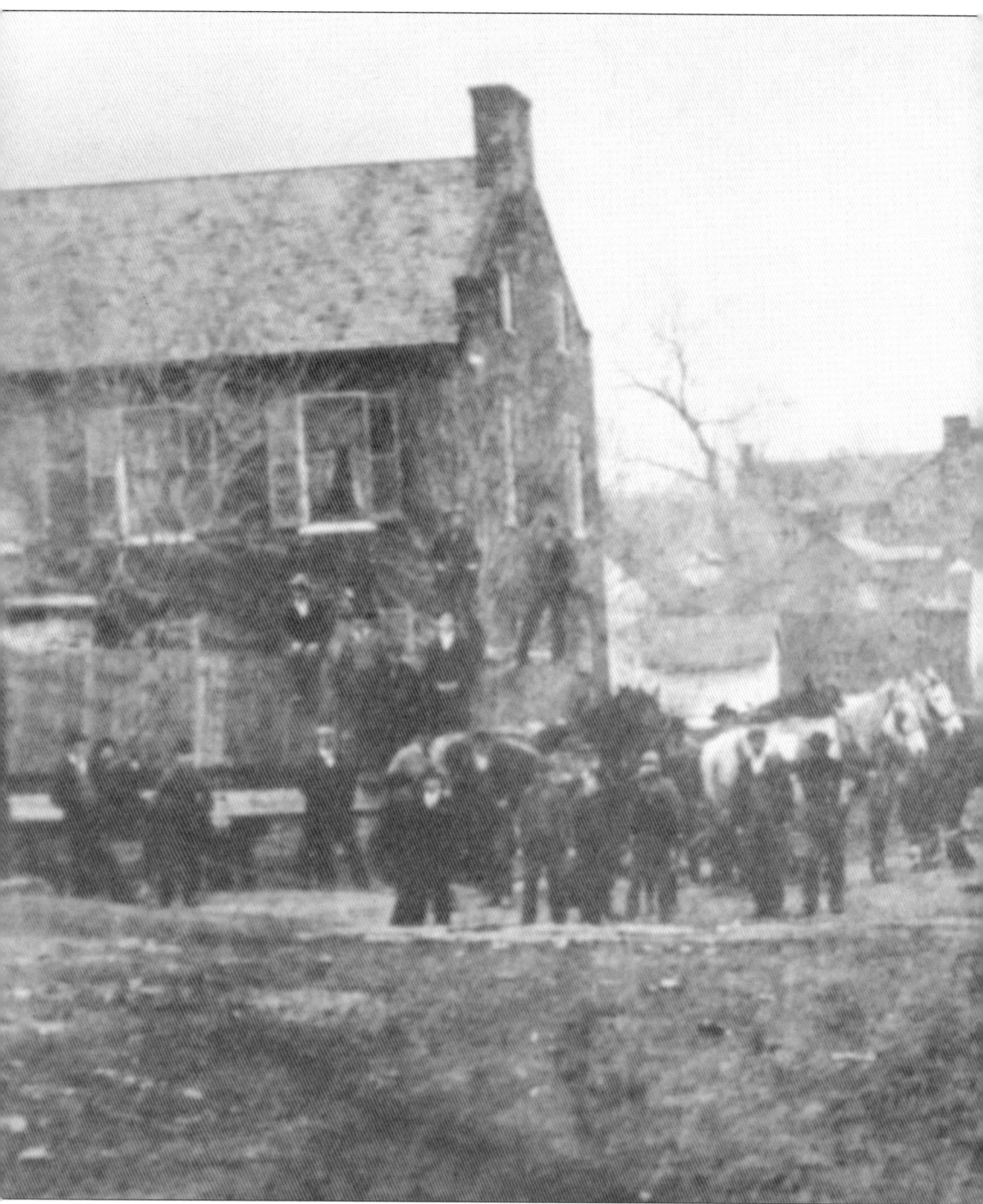

This 1896 view shows the Philadelphia Brigade Monument being hauled through Sharpsburg's main intersection on its way to Philadelphia Brigade Park. In the process of moving the 38-ton obelisk through town, the wagon broke under its weight. "A new and stronger wagon is being made," reported the *Shepherdstown Register*. The Philadelphia Brigade Monument was the product of negotiating between the Philadelphia Brigade Association and the Antietam Battlefield Board.

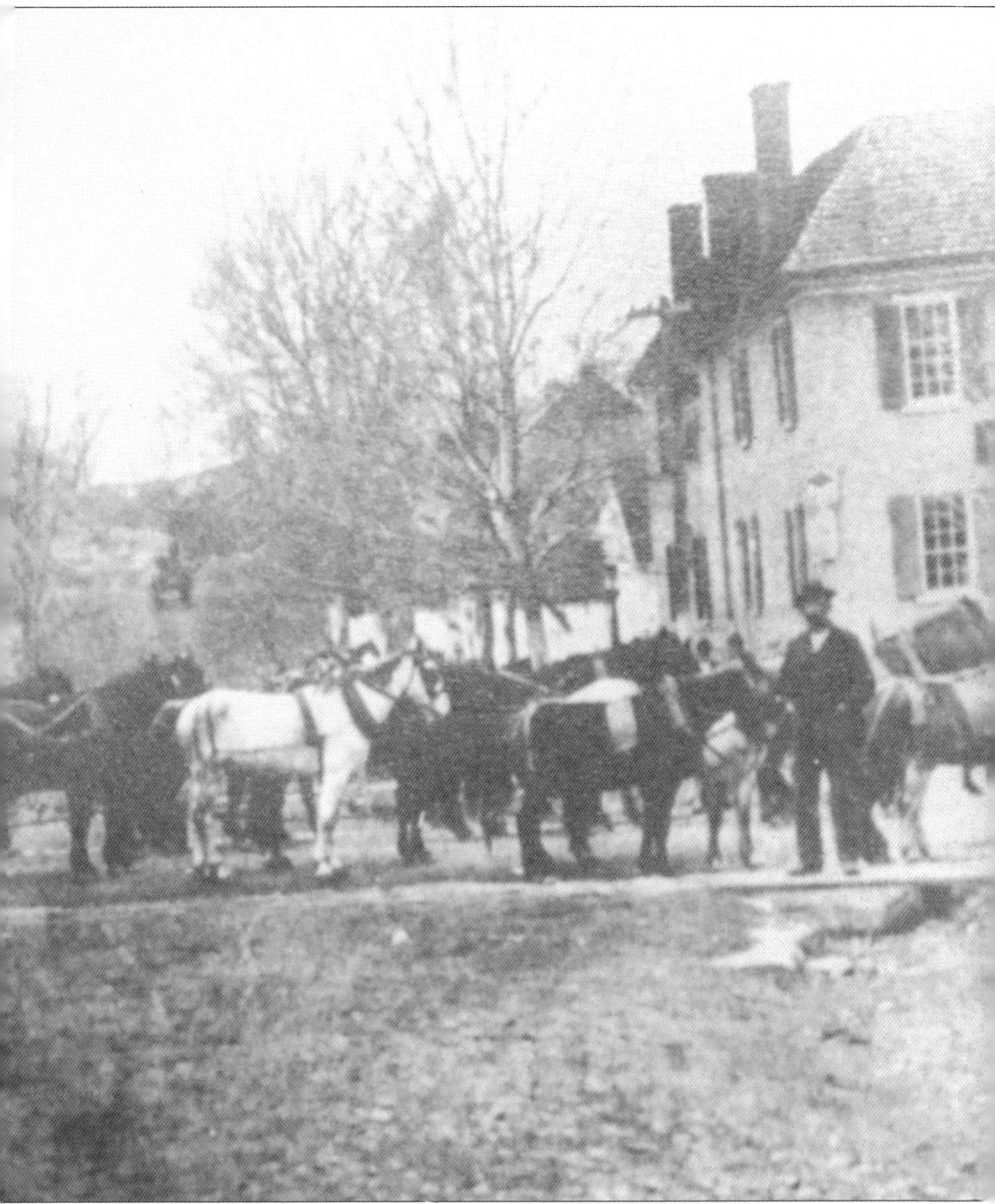

George B. Davis dissuaded the veterans from erecting more than one monument and instead erecting a single one in the West Woods. The association raised its own funds for the monument but also received $5,000 from Pennsylvania's legislature for the venture. (Courtesy of the Western Maryland Room, Washington County Free Library.)

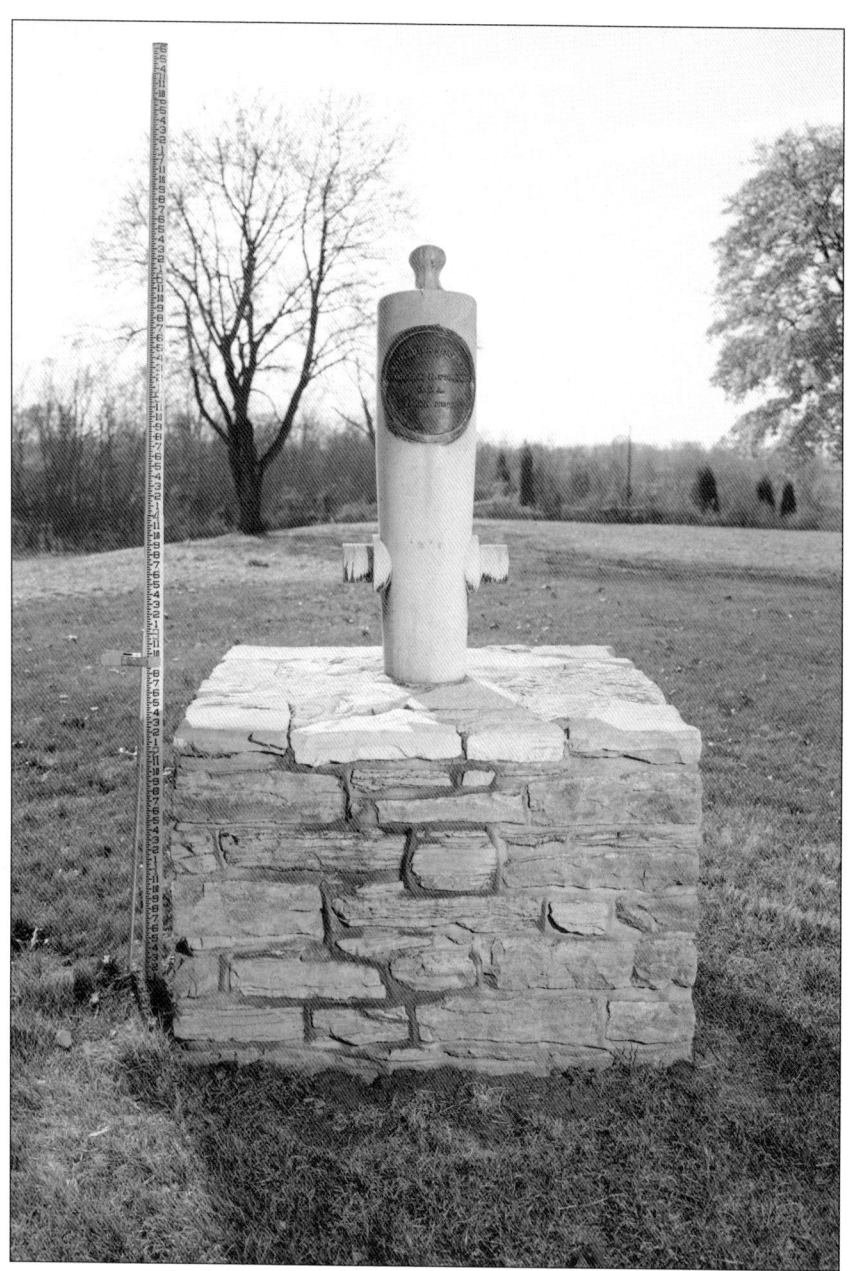

Six mortuary cannons dot the Antietam battlefield. The War Department erected them in 1896 to mark the locations of the death or mortal wounding of six generals at Antietam. Union brigadier general Joseph Mansfield fell in the East Woods and died on September 18 while Confederate general William Starke was shot in the West Woods and died on September 17. In the Sunken Road area, Confederate brigade commander George B. Anderson died from complications of his Antietam wound on October 16 and Federal general Israel Richardson suffered the same fate on November 3. South of Sharpsburg, Union general Isaac Rodman was mortally wounded (he died on September 30) and Confederate general Lawrence O'Bryan Branch died almost instantly. This particular mortuary cannon marks the approximate location where William Starke was struck by three enemy bullets. (Courtesy of the Library of Congress.)

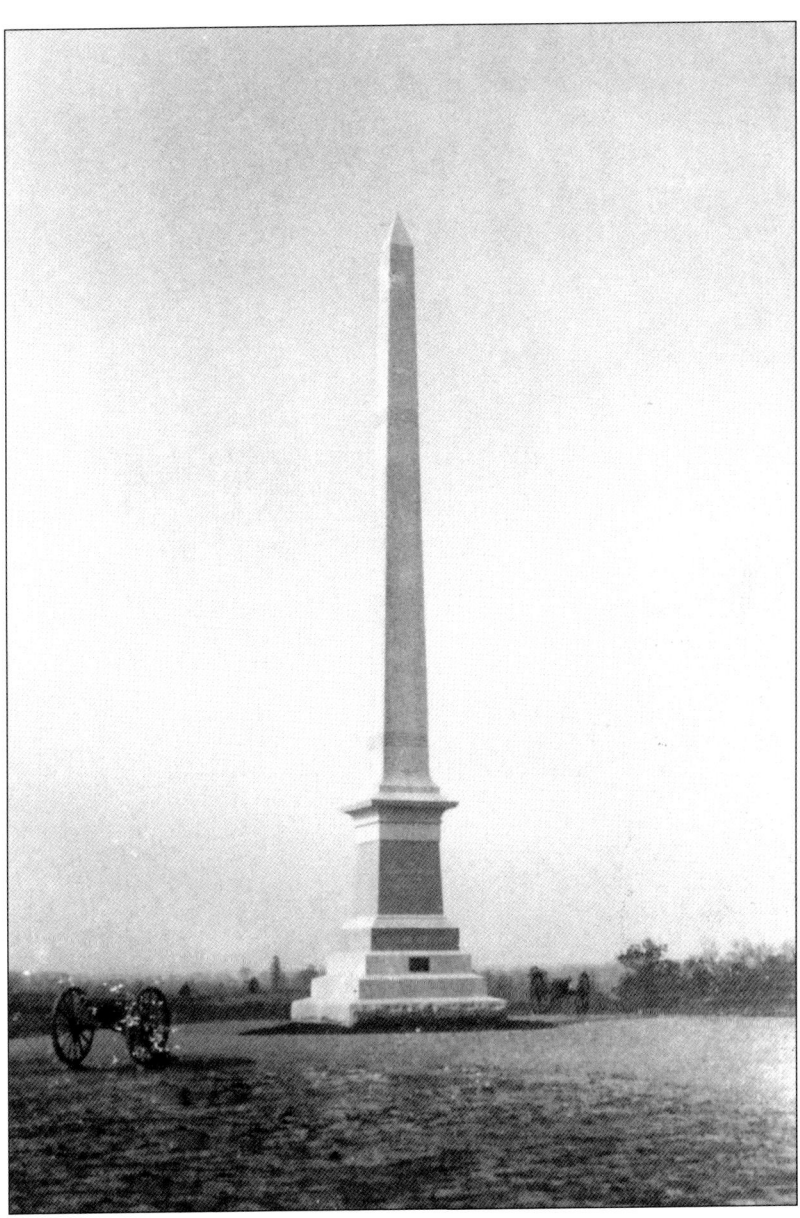

The Philadelphia Brigade Association originally intended to erect monuments to each of its four Pennsylvania regiments that fought at Antietam. Instead, they settled for one monument in the West Woods. They purchased 11 acres for the monument's site, and the veterans unveiled Antietam's tallest monument—73 feet—on September 17, 1896. The association turned the plot of land over to the City of Philadelphia in 1903. George Poffenberger, the man who sold the land to the association, became its caretaker, though he was apparently not the man for the job. One examiner discovered "a locked gate [at the park's entrance], many benches scattered about, helter skelter, and an unsightly wire fence," which penned in Poffenberger's sheep. He reportedly used the animals in lieu of a lawnmower. Disgusted by the state of the park, Hagerstown's chamber of commerce became involved, suggesting to Philadelphia as early as 1932 to deed their park to the National Park Service. The two entities completed the transaction in September 1940. (Courtesy of the Western Maryland Room, Washington County Free Library.)

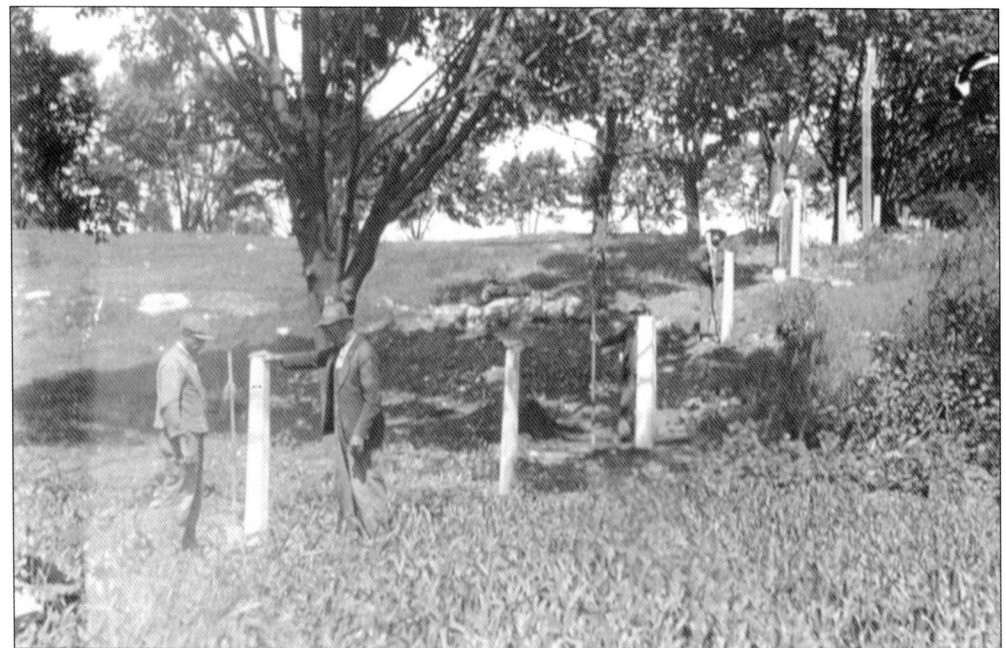

While Philadelphia Brigade Park remained separate from the rest of Antietam National Battlefield, cement fence posts marked the boundaries of the 11-acre park. Here, workers from the 1930s are seen erecting these posts along the park's edge. Some of these same posts can still be found in the West Woods today. (Courtesy of the National Park Service.)

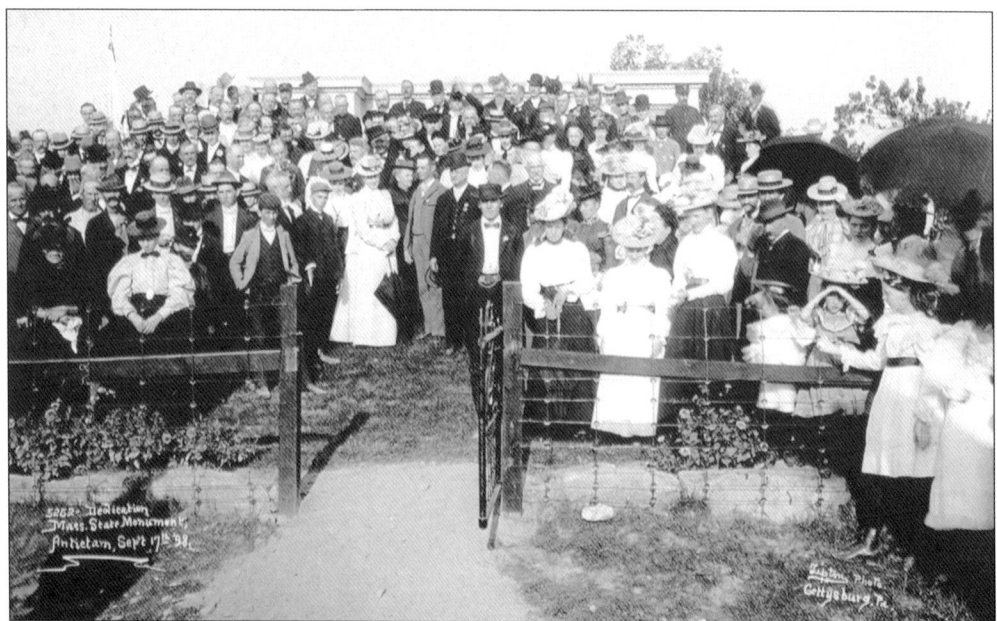

Massachusetts began the process to erect monuments to its units in 1896. However, the fact that the Massachusetts Antietam Commission would have to purchase the land required to erect monuments persuaded them that erecting one monument to all of the state's units would be easier. Massachusetts veterans and citizens dedicated their monument near the Cornfield on September 17, 1898. (Courtesy of the National Park Service.)

Albert A. Pope, a lieutenant in the 35th Massachusetts at Antietam, dedicated this monument to his fallen comrades in 1898. It originally sat on the northwest corner of the Burnside Bridge but now rests on the east bank of Antietam Creek near the bridge. After the war, Pope helped establish the Massachusetts Bicycle Club and is considered to be the father of the American bicycle industry. (Courtesy of the Western Maryland Room, Washington County Free Library.)

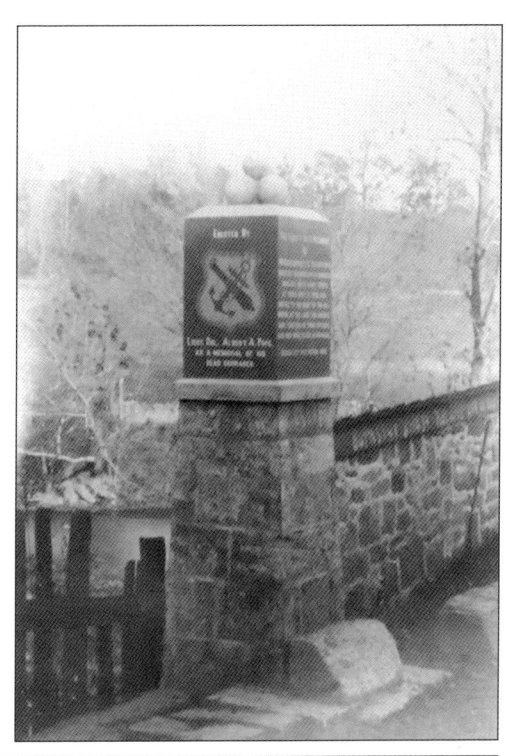

The 45th Pennsylvania Monument, dedicated on September 17, 1904, stands in front of the wartime Sherrick farm. This ceremony followed the dedication of the neighboring 100th Pennsylvania Monument. John Curtin, the regiment's commander at Antietam and the son of Pennsylvania wartime governor Andrew Curtin, supervised the program. (Courtesy of the National Park Service.)

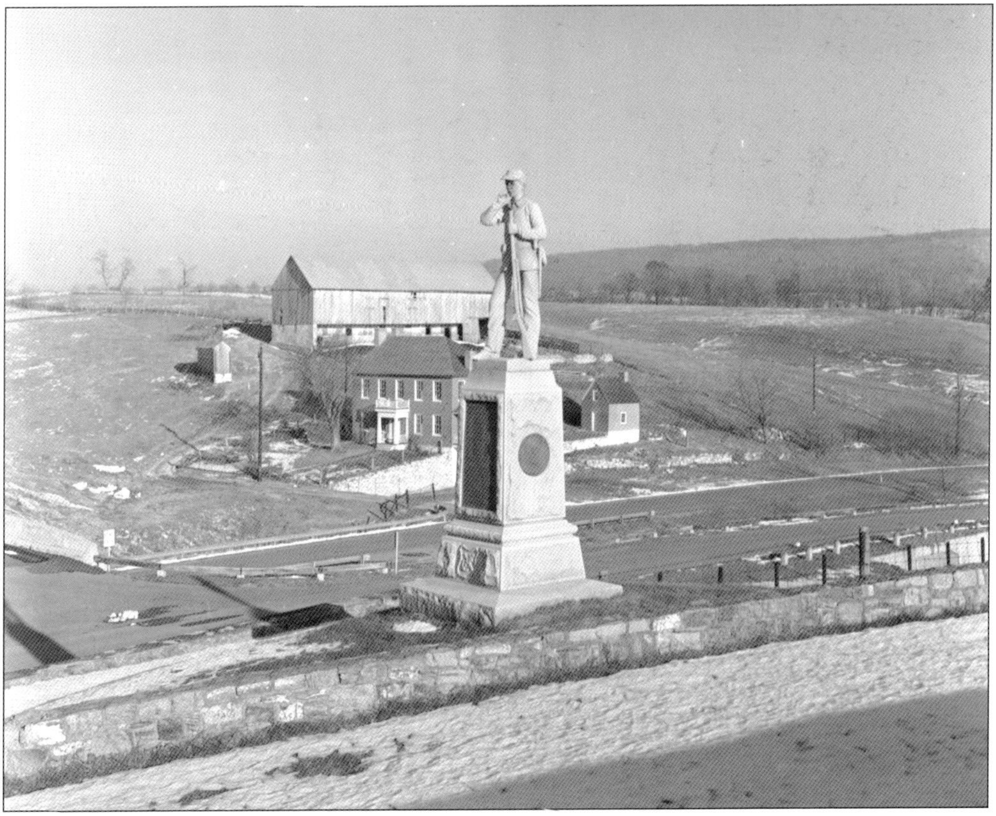

MANY SHAFTS RISE AT ANTIETAM TO HONOR PENNSYLVANIA CORPS

Granite Statues Strew Famous Battlefield as Tribute to Brave Soldiers.

SIMPLE ONE THE BEST

Memorial of Ninetieth Survivors to Dead Comrades Great, Though Humble.

"This Was a Hot Place."

Upon the battle-scarred, weather-beaten trunk of a sturdy oak that stood in the very thickest of the four-day battle of Antietam forty-four years ago this is recorded—a veteran's verdict graphic as the more forceful one of General Sherman.

Beside the tree is a monument that, like the comment, is great in its simplicity—so simple that at first glance it seems to be no monument at all—three muskets, locked by bayonets, in the centre hanging an old camp kettle.

It is the memorial of the survivors of the Ninetieth Pennsylvania Infantry to those with whom they messed for the last time upon that bloodstained field nearly half a century ago. After the many charges, it is said, it was impossible to walk upon this portion of the field without treading upon the bodies of the Blue and the Gray, and more than 1000 Confederates are buried near this gnarled

Veterans of the 90th Pennsylvania sent this monument in 1900 to the Antietam Battlefield Board to be placed near where they fought. The board placed it on the same rock ledge where the regiment planted its colors during their desperate fight on September 17, 1862. It consisted of "three lacquered muskets," according to the *Frederick News*, locked by bayonets with a camp bucket dangling in between them. The inscription on the bucket reads, "Here Fought the 90th Penna. of Philada, Sep. 17th, 1862, A Hot Place." Around 1930, the original monument was dismantled due to its poor condition and for fear of thieves taking the artifacts. A replacement was crafted and rededicated on September 17, 2004. Of the 20 Medal of Honor recipients from the Battle of Antietam, two fought in the 90th Pennsylvania. (Both, courtesy of MOLLUS, US Army Heritage and Education Center, Carlisle, Pennsylvania.)

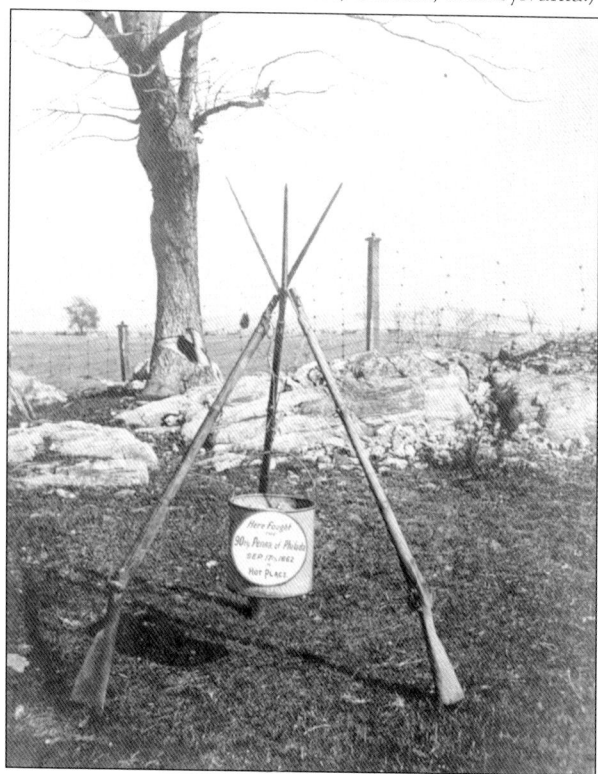

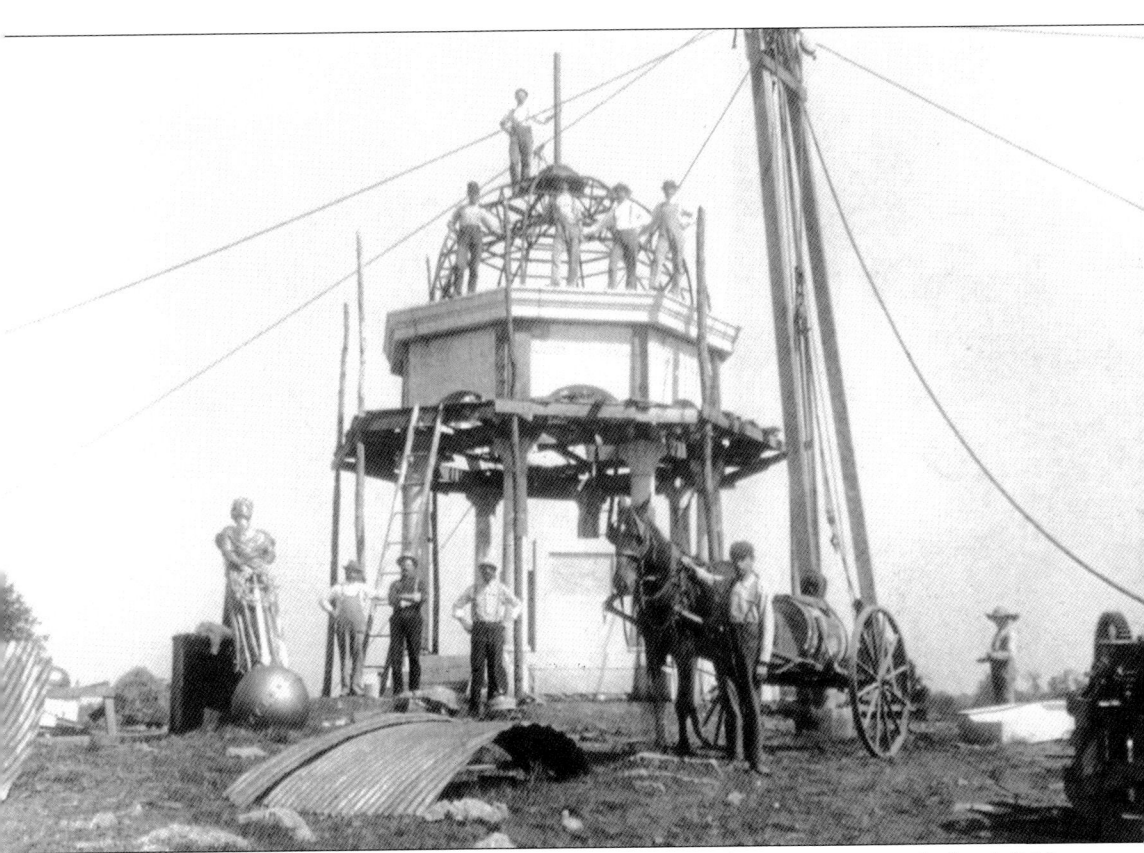

Maryland's role as a border state ensured the unique distinction of its monument on the battlefield as the only one dedicated to soldiers of both the Union and Confederate armies. Two Maryland units fought in the Confederate army during the Maryland Campaign, while five fought for the Union. The monument bears the simple inscription, "Erected by the State of Maryland to her Sons, Who on this field offered their lives in maintenance of their Principles." This view shows the monument under construction before it was dedicated on May 30, 1900. Pres. William McKinley spoke at the ceremony, as did a host of other prominent Antietam veterans, such as Federals John R. Brooke, Orlando Willcox, and Jacob Duryee, and former Confederate general James Longstreet. George B. McClellan Jr., the Union general's son, likewise attended and momentarily spoke. (Courtesy of the National Park Service.)

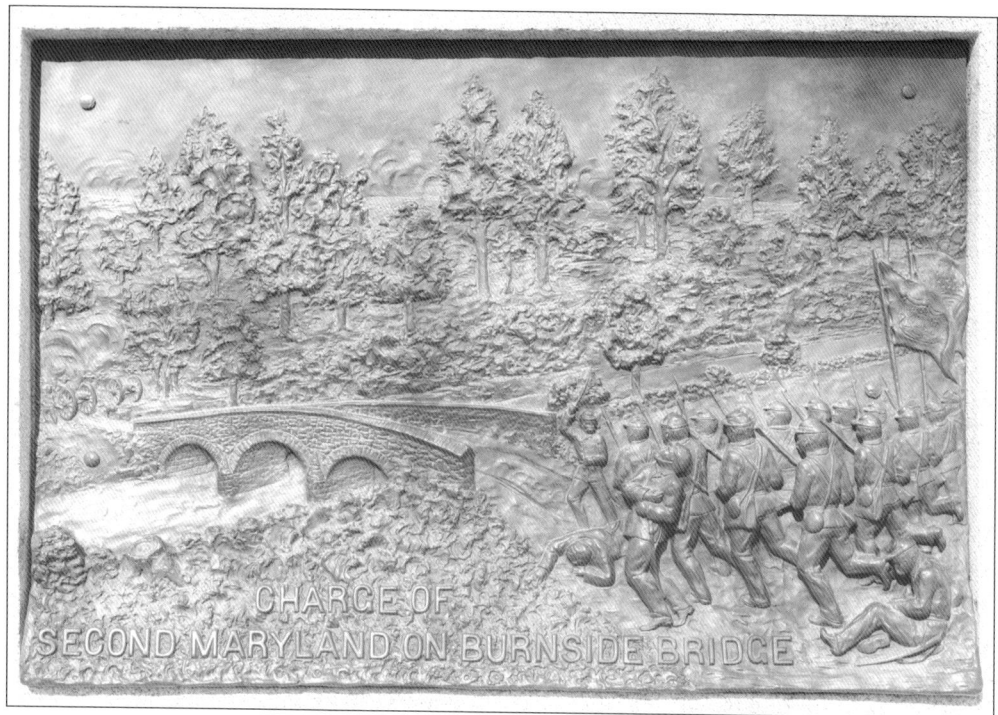

A series of beautiful bas-reliefs adorn the Maryland Monument. The relief shown here depicts the charge of the 2nd Maryland Infantry (US) against the Burnside Bridge on the late morning of the battle. The regiment was raised in Baltimore in 1861 and served in numerous engagements until the end of the war. At Antietam, it charged up the Sharpsburg-Rohrersville Road along with the 6th New Hampshire. Both regiments were cut apart in the attack, and of the 2nd, 17 men were killed, 47 wounded, and 3 missing out of the 162 it took into action without capturing the bridge. (Both, courtesy of the Library of Congress.)

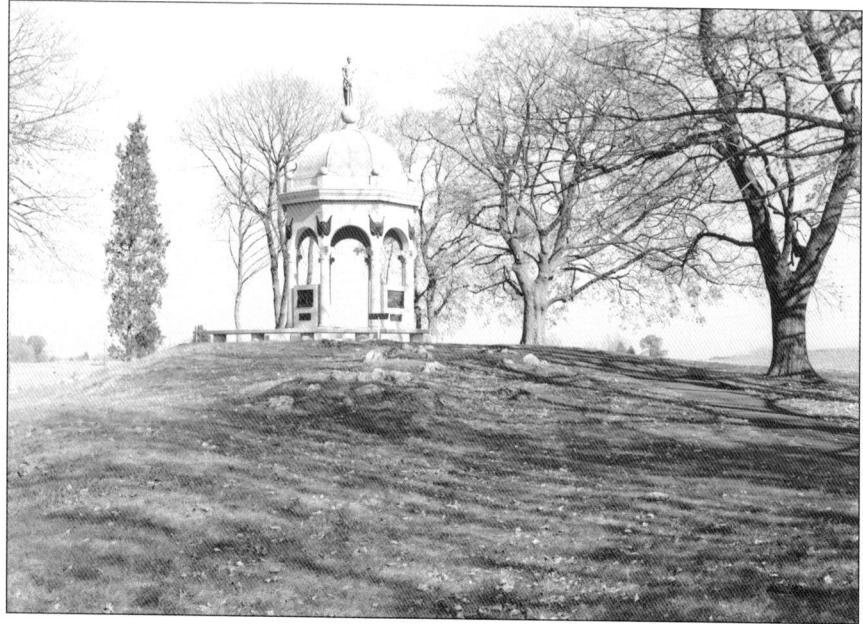

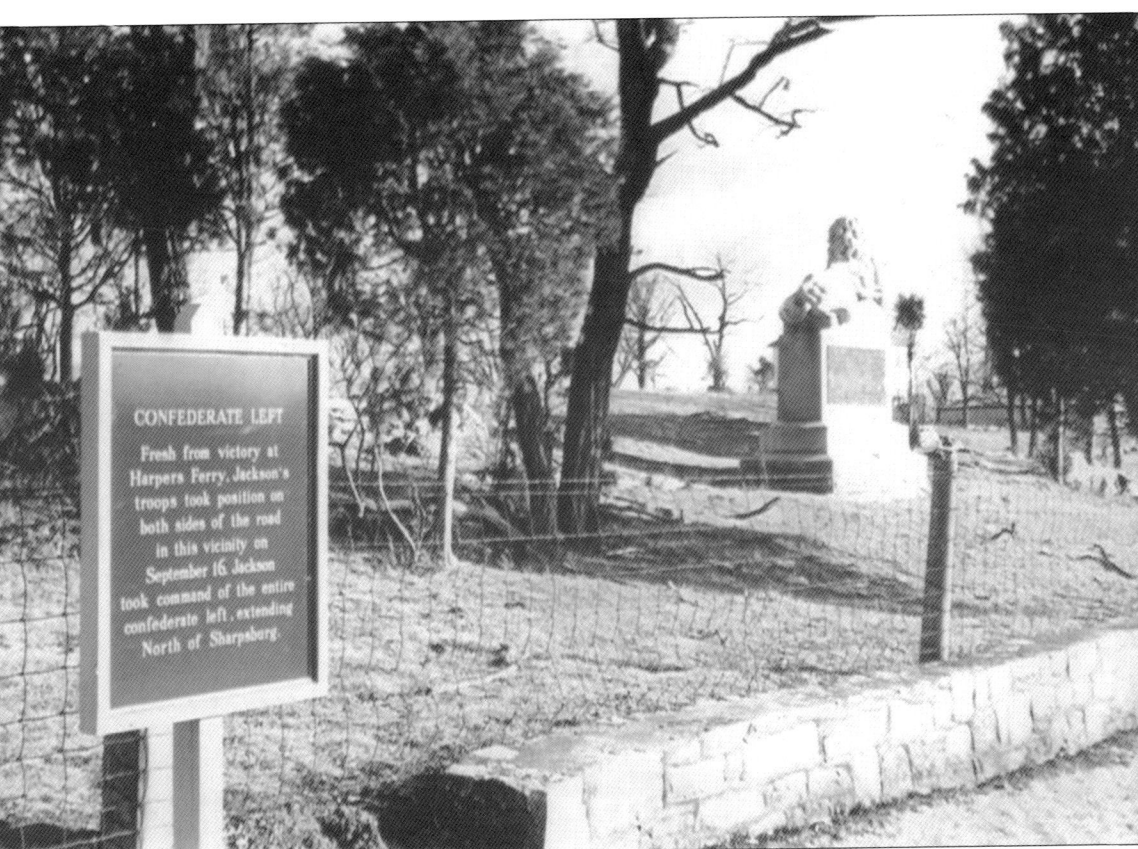

The 15th Massachusetts Infantry's monument sits at the regiment's position on the west fringe of the West Woods, though farmers chopped down the trees between the Civil War and the National Park Service's later reforestation efforts, which began in March 1995. This Massachusetts regiment lost 318 of its 606 men engaged in approximately 20 minutes of combat. No other regiment at Antietam, Union or Confederate, lost a greater number of men than the 15th Massachusetts. Word trickled back to Massachusetts of the regiment's fate, causing the editor of the *Webster Times* to report to its readers, "We fear that the hearts of many in this village are soon to be made sad at the loss of near ones on that terrible day." Their monument was dedicated on September 17, 1900, and is one of the more unique ones found on the battlefield. (Courtesy of the National Park Service.)

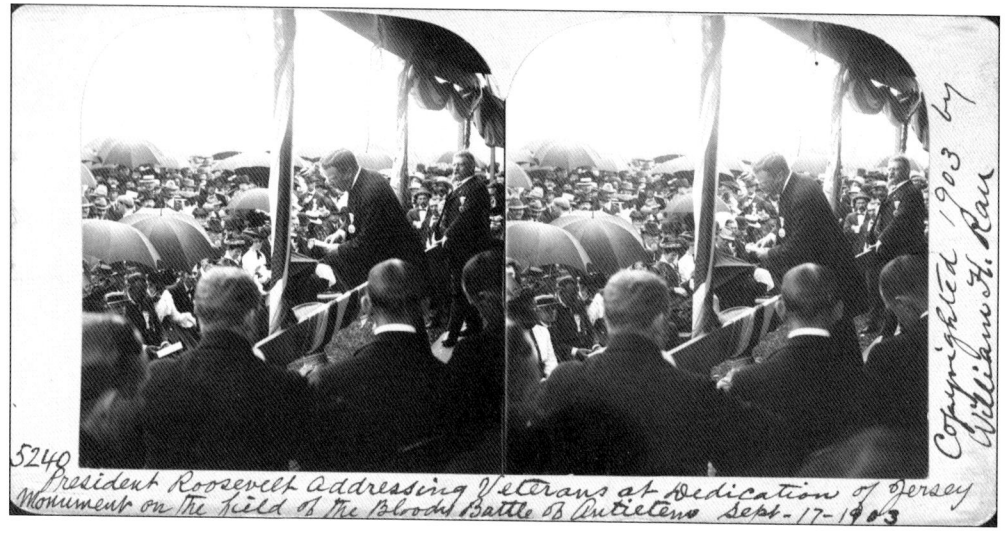

Pres. Theodore Roosevelt dedicated the New Jersey State Monument near the Cornfield on September 17, 1903. Numerous veterans attended the ceremony despite the poor weather, as evidenced by the countless umbrellas seen in these two images. "It was because you, the men who wear the button of the Grand Army, triumphed in those dark years, that every American now holds his head high, proud in the knowledge that he belongs to a nation whose glorious past and great present will be succeeded by an even mightier future," the president stated emphatically to the scores of veterans in the crowd. (Both, courtesy of the Library of Congress.)

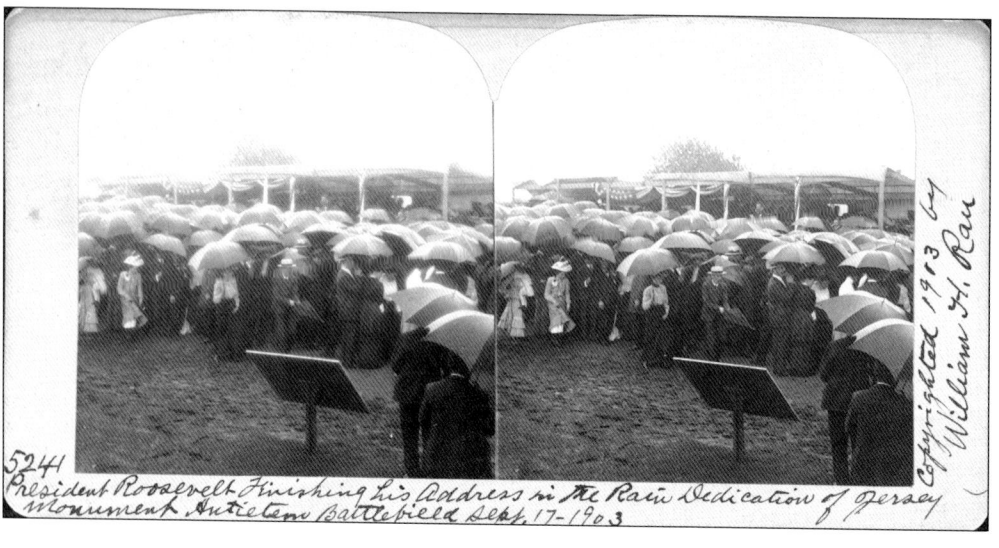

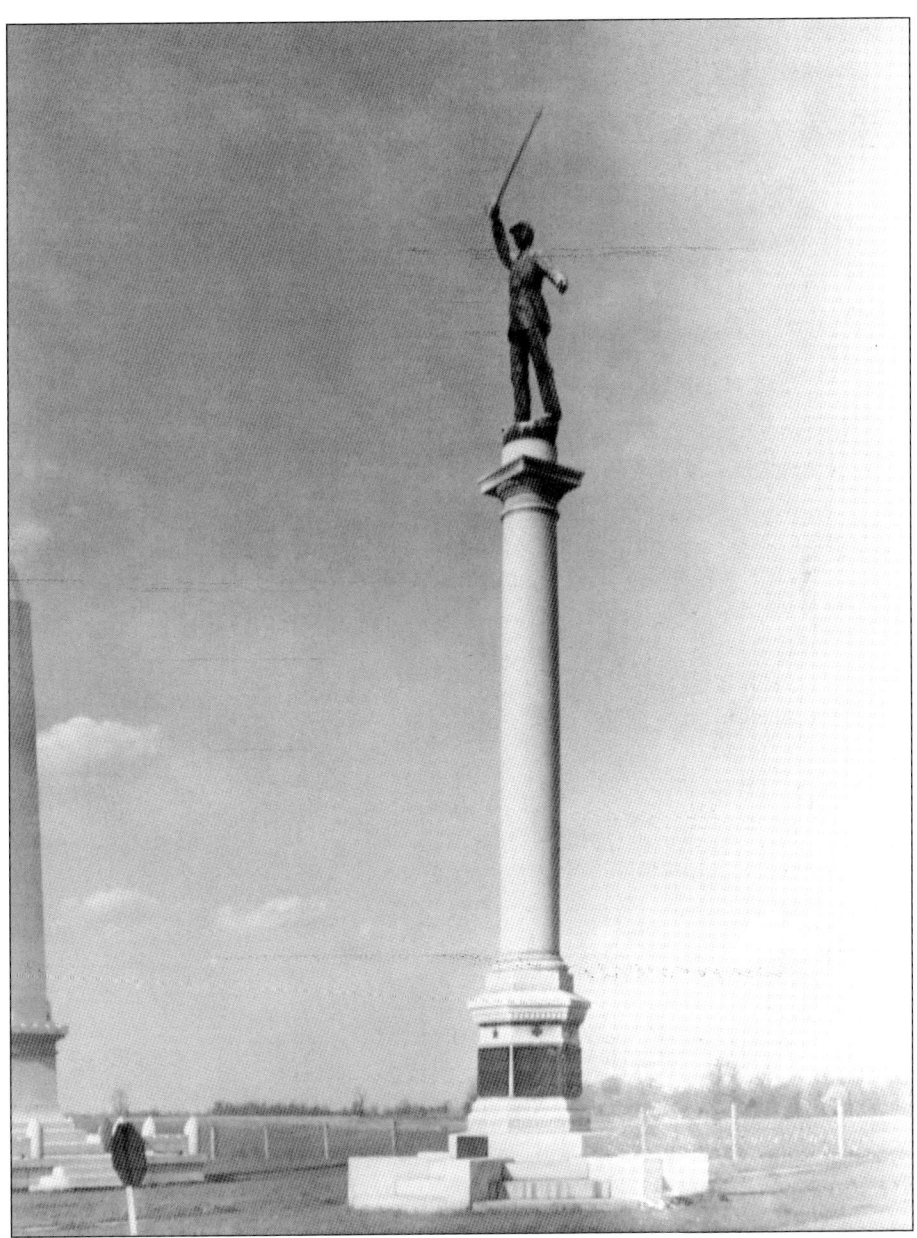

Thirty-year-old Capt. Hugh Irish, 13th New Jersey, adorns the top of the state's monument. Irish was the state's senior officer killed at Antietam. The monument stands near the location of Irish's death. Herber Wells of the regiment recalled his death shortly afterward: "Well the Captain led the way bravely over the fence, his cry being 'Rally, Boys, Rally,' to his men who followed him closely. I was at the head of the company endeavoring to 'dress' them to the left when looking around I saw the Captain fall. I immediately rushed towards him and supported his head, asking him at the time if he was badly hurt. He could say no more than, 'Herber, I am killed,' a few moans being the only sign from him. I felt his pulse, which was fluttering and then searched for his wound. He was shot through his breast with a bullet, which left a small red spot, but which shed no blood." At the 1903 dedication, Irish's sister, Sarah Hartwell, unveiled the monument. (Courtesy of the Western Maryland Room, Washington County Free Library.)

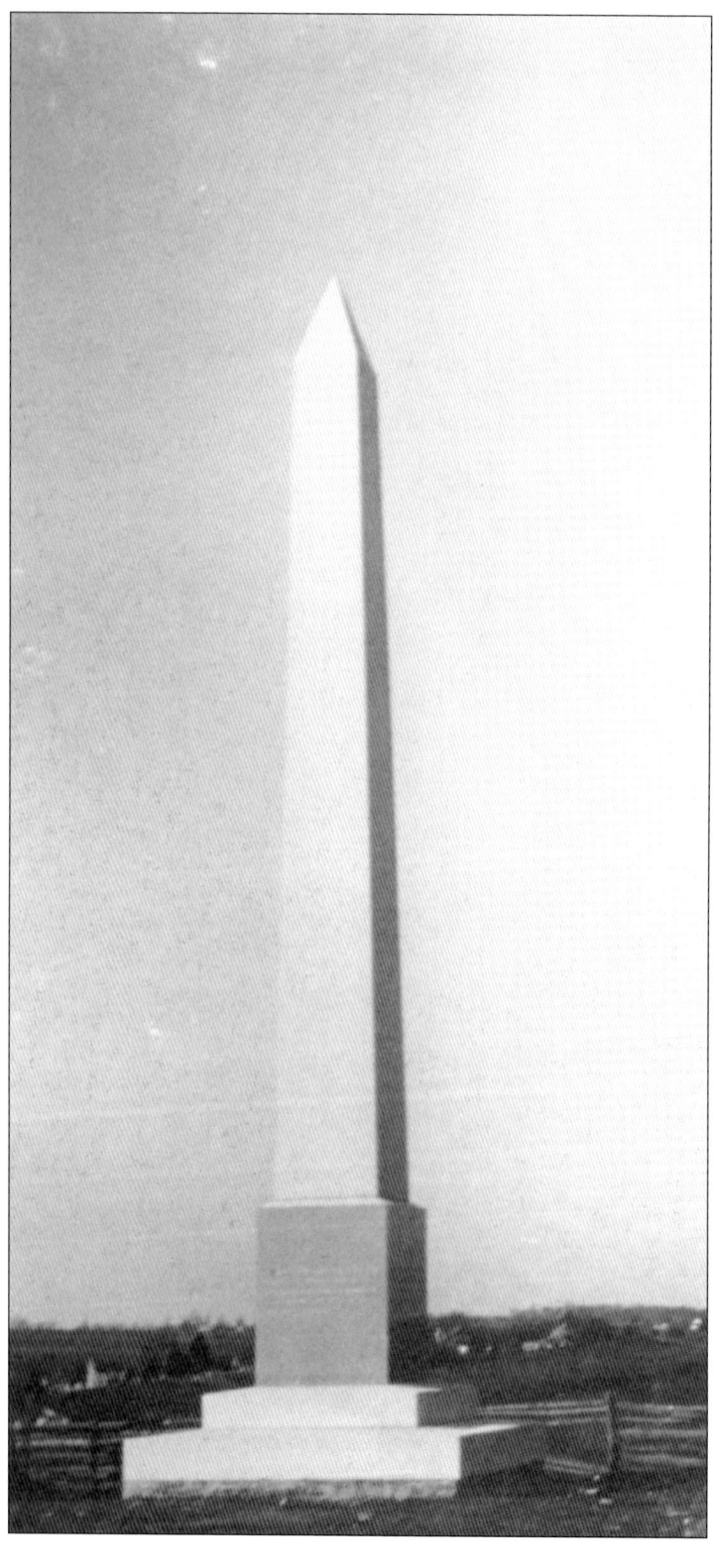

The monument to the men of the 9th New York Infantry, or Hawkins' Zouaves, stands 52 feet tall atop a prominent ridge south of town. This regiment engaged in intense and close quarters fighting with the enemy there. A total of 373 New Yorkers charged toward the location of the monument; the unit lost 240 of those soldiers. Their monument was built in 1897. Rush Hawkins, the original commander and namesake of the 9th New York, personally purchased the land on which the monument stands. David Thompson, a veteran of the unit, wrote this after the war about the experience of battle: "When bullets are whacking against tree trunks and solid shot are cracking skulls like egg shells, the consuming passion in the breast of the average man is to get out of the way. Between the physical fear of going forward, and the moral fear of going back, there is a predicament of exceptional awkwardness from which a hidden hole in the ground would be a wonderfully welcome outlet." (Courtesy of the Western Maryland Room, Washington County Free Library.)

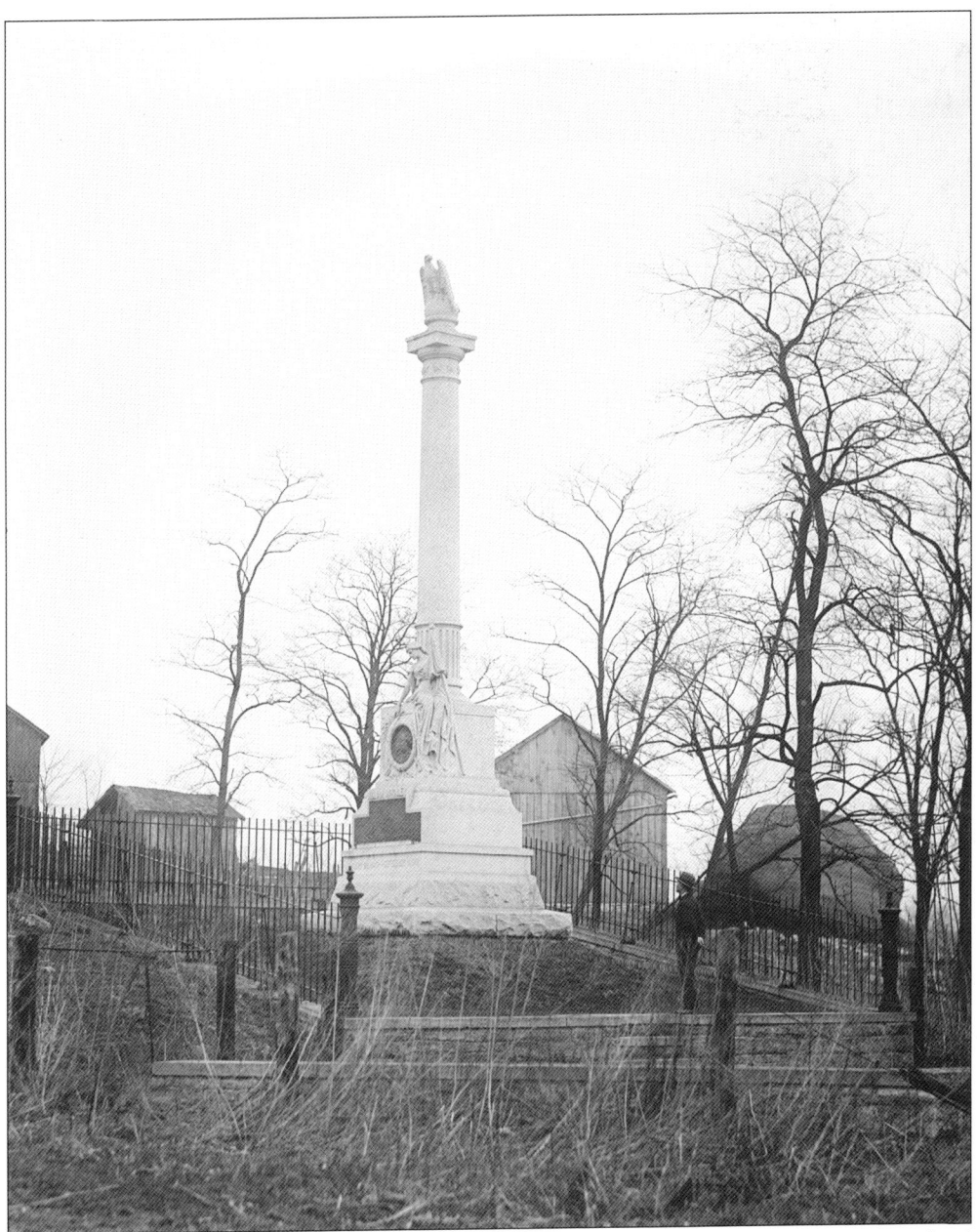

William McKinley, 23rd Ohio Infantry, was the unit's commissary sergeant in the Maryland Campaign. On September 17, McKinley rushed a wagon of coffee and food across the Burnside Bridge to his fellow Ohioans and served them on the battlefield. "God bless the lad!" shouted one Ohioan during the episode. McKinley later said that those words "were the highest reward that he could possibly have received" for his act. Shortly after Antietam, he was promoted to second lieutenant for his actions there. McKinley later became president of the United States and died by assassination on September 14, 1901, the 39th anniversary of the Battle of South Mountain. He was the last Civil War veteran to serve as president. This monument, dedicated on October 13, 1903, to the memory of his public service to his country, stands near the Burnside Bridge. (Courtesy of the Library of Congress.)

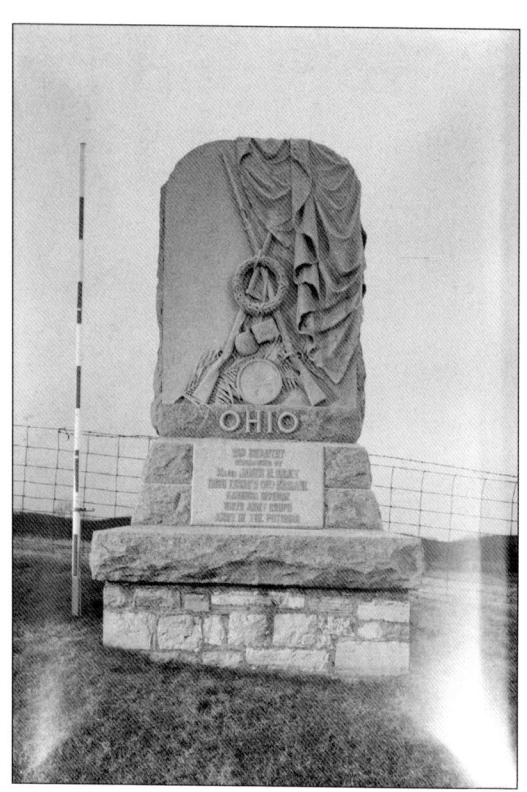

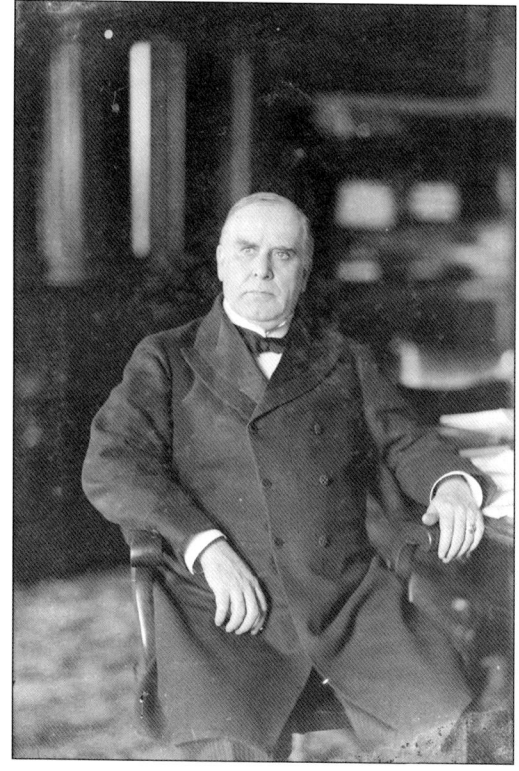

William McKinley (below) was the only future president of the United States to fight at Antietam, but he was not the only future president who served within the ranks of the 23rd Ohio, whose monument can be found along Branch Avenue on the southern end of the battlefield. Lt. Col. Rutherford B. Hayes commanded the regiment during the campaign but a wound he received at the Battle of South Mountain three days prior prevented him from participating in the battle at Antietam. All told, this storied regiment produced two presidents, two Ohio governors and two lieutenant governors, four congressmen, a Supreme Court justice, and a senator. (Both, courtesy of the Library of Congress.)

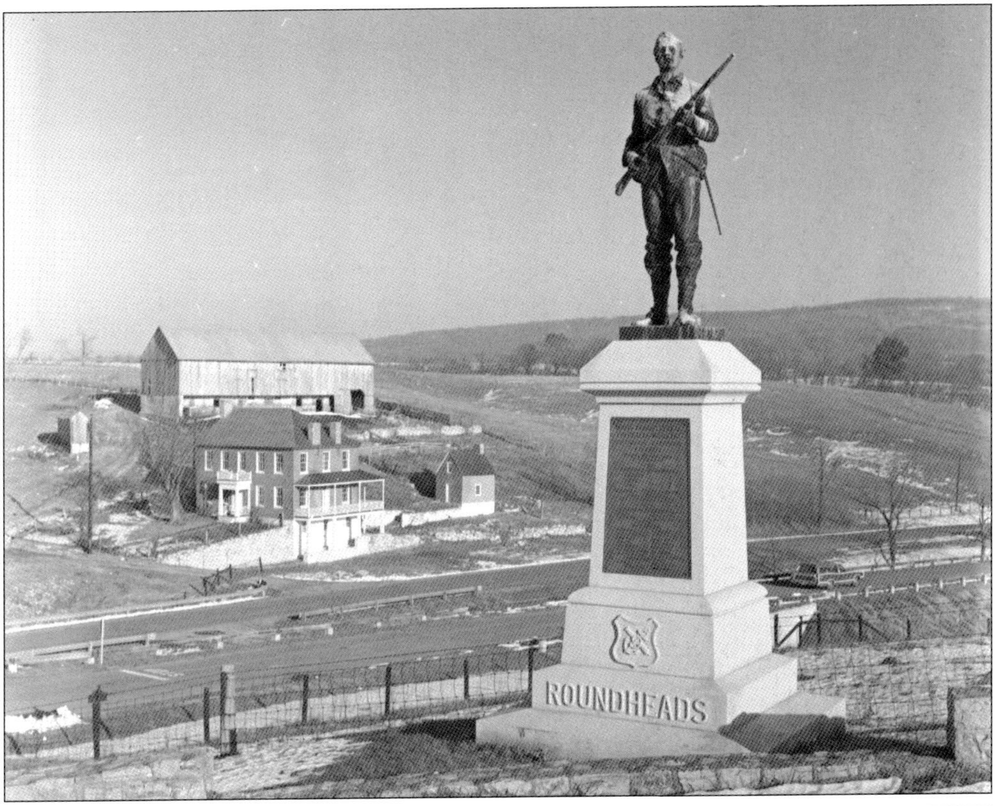

Pennsylvania erected the monument to the 100th Pennsylvania Infantry on Antietam Pennsylvania Day, September 17, 1904. The sculpture atop the monument is titled *Challenge*, and depicts a soldier on picket duty. W.H. Underwood gave the dedication speech. He believed the monument was "a just tribute to the true hearted soldiers of the rank and file" as well as to their commanders. (Courtesy of the National Park Service.)

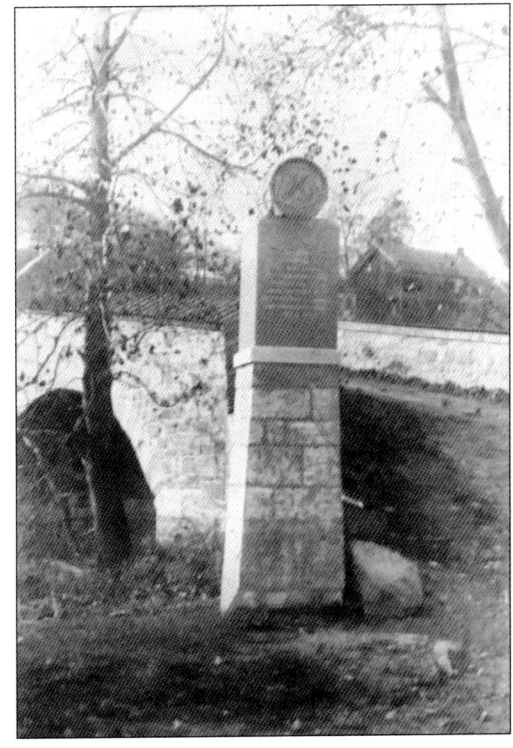

The 51st Pennsylvania Infantry has two monuments on the Antietam battlefield. The first was dedicated along with a number of other Pennsylvania monuments on September 17, 1904. This second and smaller marker was erected in 1906 on a corner of the Burnside Bridge, where the 51st Pennsylvania, alongside the 51st New York, played a crucial role in capturing the bridge. (Courtesy of the Western Maryland Room, Washington County Free Library.)

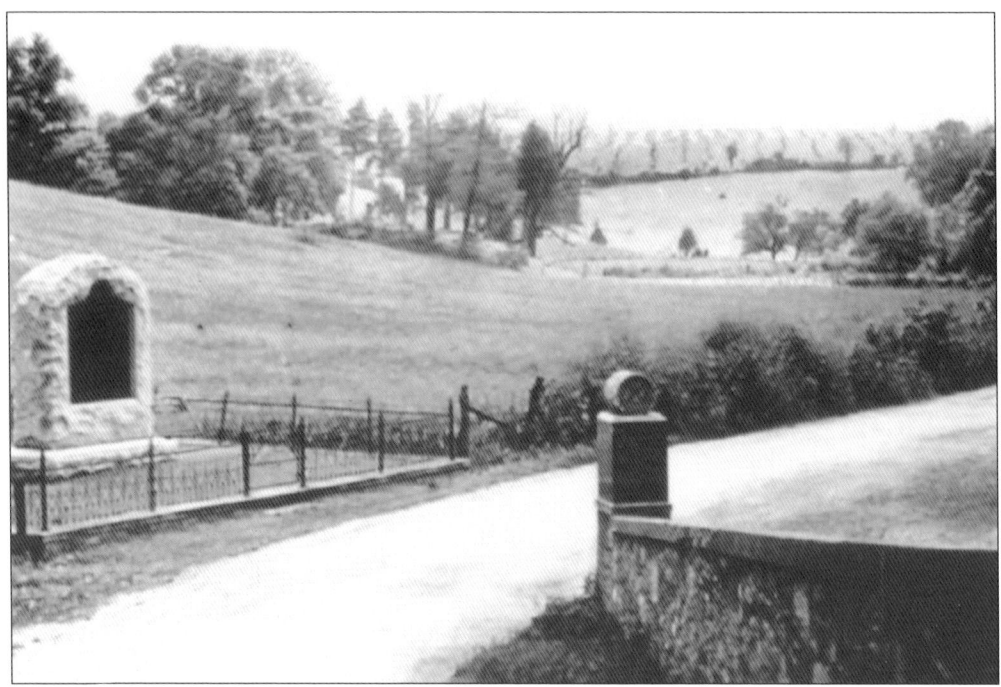

Veterans of the 51st New York Infantry dedicated their monument, left, in 1908. The fence surrounding the monument no longer stands, though the concrete curbing on which the fence stood still survives. While the 51st Pennsylvania utilized a stone fence for cover during the action at the Burnside Bridge, the New Yorkers had to take a position behind a post and rail fence. (Courtesy of the National Park Service.)

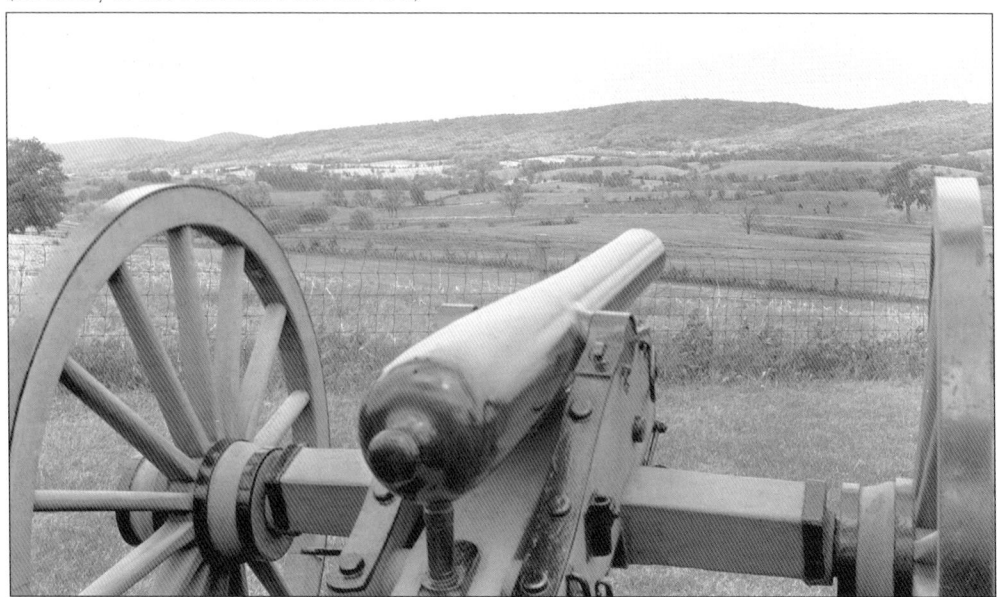

Civil War–era cannon positioned at the intersection of Harpers Ferry Road and Branch Avenue mark the approximate location of William Pegram's Virginia artillery battery. This undated view looks east across the fields over which 8,000 Union soldiers attacked on the afternoon of September 17. (Courtesy of the National Park Service.)

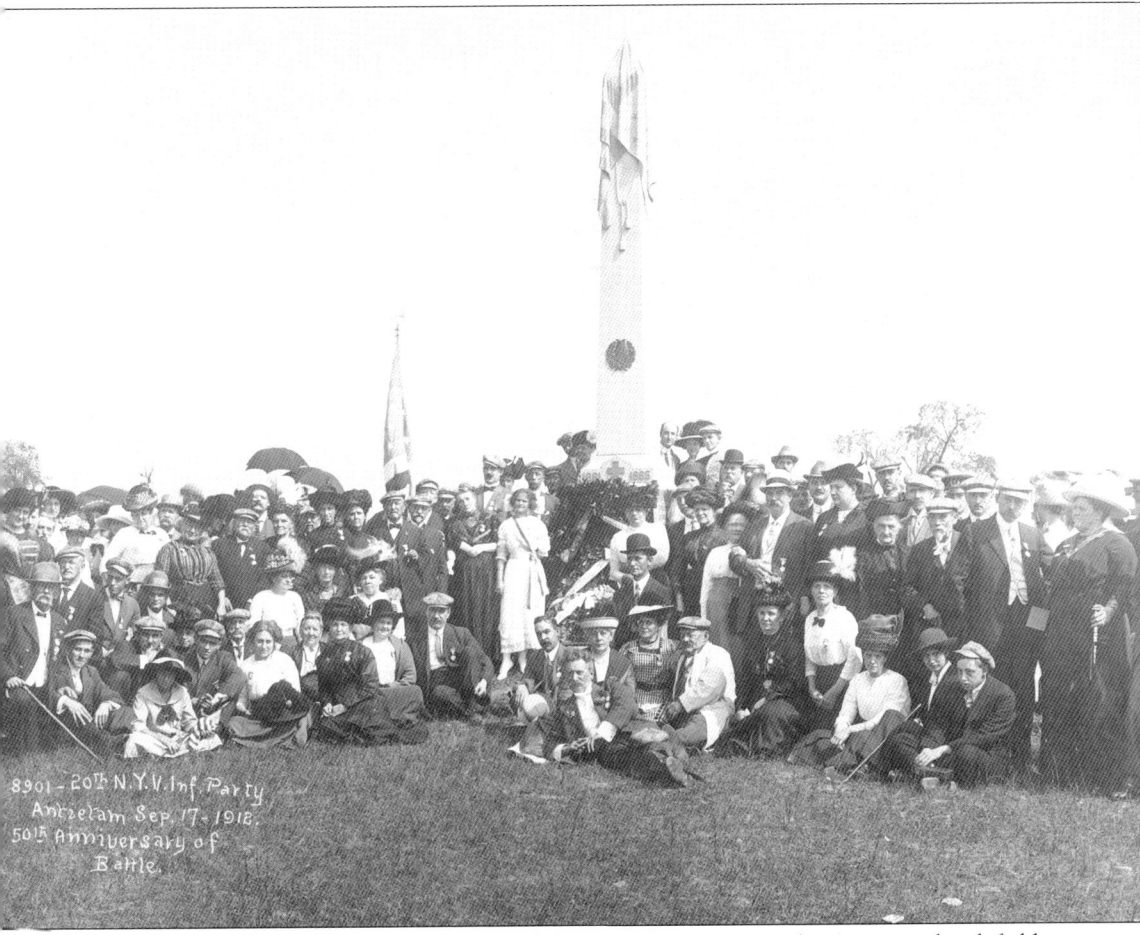

The 20th New York was the first regiment to dedicate a monument on the Antietam battlefield. Their first monument, erected in 1887, sits in the National Cemetery. There is both German and English text inscribed on the monument. The 1912 dedication of the 20th New York's second monument, seen here, created a political commotion. Placed on their firing line during the battle, the owl that appears halfway up the monument's shaft caused the uproar. It symbolized the German Turner Society, which provided a large number of its men to the 20th New York's ranks. However, monument regulations "prohibit the insignia of civic organizations whose membership is not restricted to persons having military or naval service." The New York City Germans wrangled President Taft into the controversy. Fortunately, Antietam superintendent Charles W. Adams found other exceptions to the rule and the dedication proceeded as planned on the battle's 50th anniversary. (Courtesy of the National Park Service.)

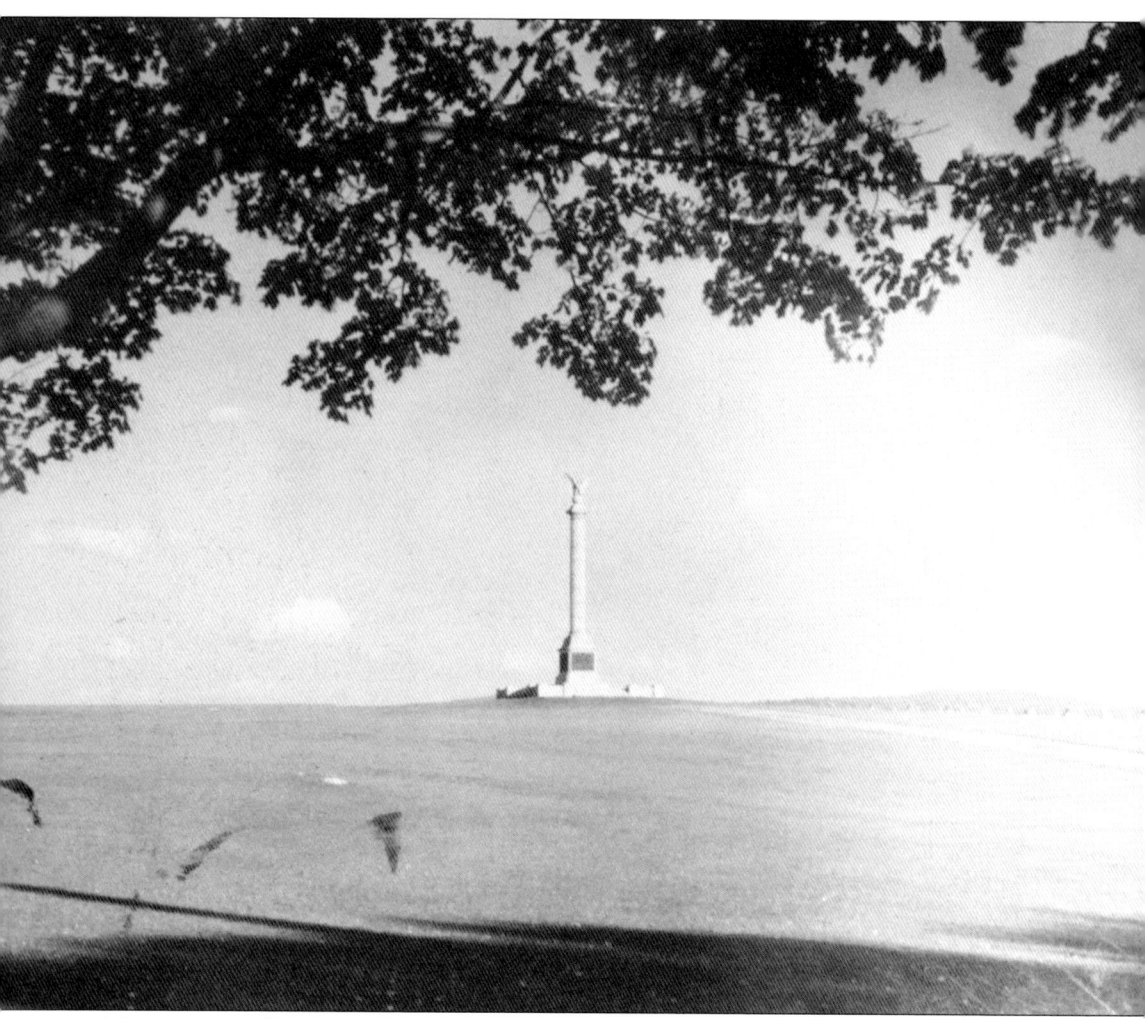

Most states made organized efforts to place their monuments on the Antietam battlefield. The New York Monuments Commission instead only assisted individual veterans' organizations that wanted to place monuments on various battlefields. The commission explored putting a state monument at Antietam beginning in 1906, and the state purchased a 7.01-acre plot of land on the Dunker Church Plateau for $1,402 in 1907 for the purpose of erecting a state monument in the future. Cement posts and iron railings denoted the boundaries by 1916. The state dedicated its monument, which cost $29,022.06, on September 17, 1920, with nearly 250 veterans in attendance. The final report of the commissioners succinctly described the monument and its location as "standing on an eminence, and centered in what were the most hotly contested arenas of battle, this memorial, the most majestic on the field, is entirely worthy of representing the Empire State at Antietam." Park historian Susan Trail wrote, "Perhaps fittingly, it was to be the last monument placed on the field by Civil War veterans." (Courtesy of the Western Maryland Room, Washington County Free Library.)

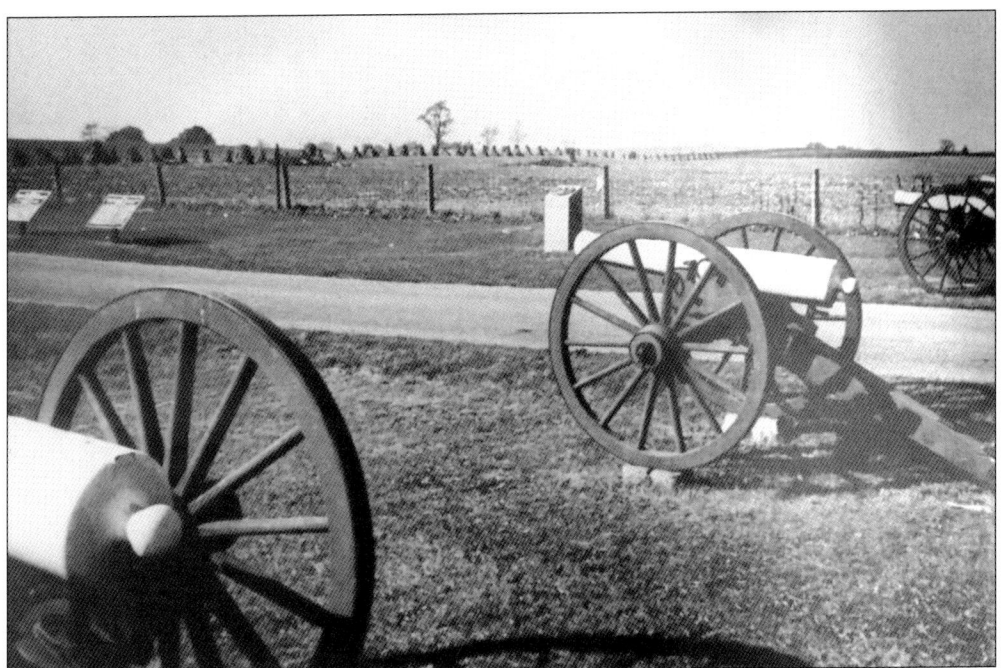

The Antietam Battlefield Board sought to mark the positions of prominent artillery batteries on the battlefield as early as 1894. As many as eight cannons dotted the park by 1937; that number increased to ten by 1953, including these four guns seen facing west along Cornfield Avenue. To date, there are 34 mounted cannons within Antietam National Battlefield. Each set of guns marks the position of a prominent battery that saw action during the battle. Altogether, the 542 guns at Antietam fired roughly 50,000 rounds of artillery ammunition during the battle. One Confederate artillerist, Stephen D. Lee, referred to Antietam as "artillery hell." (Both, courtesy of the Western Maryland Room, Washington County Free Library.)

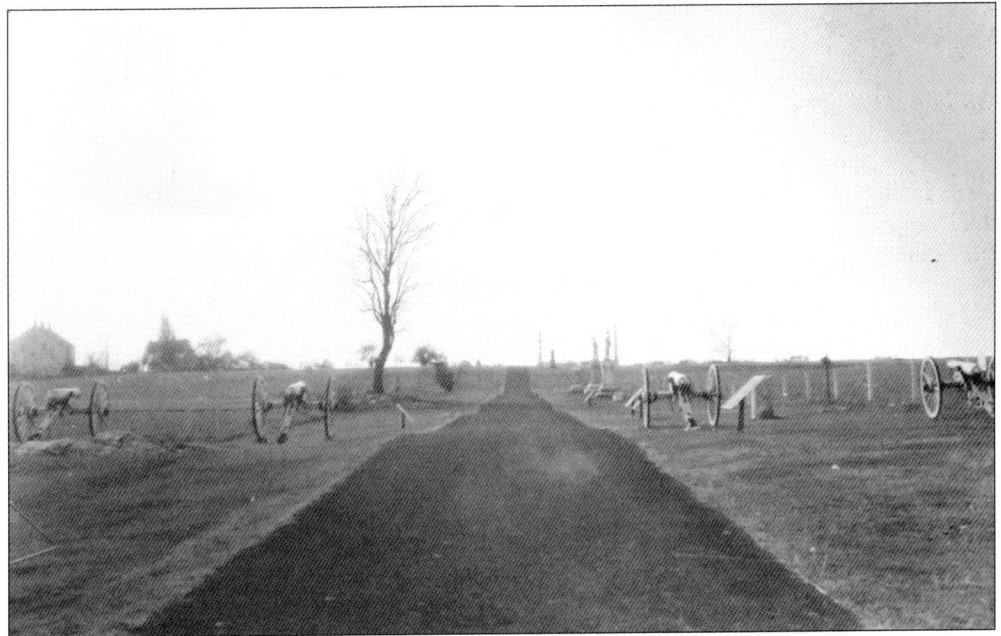

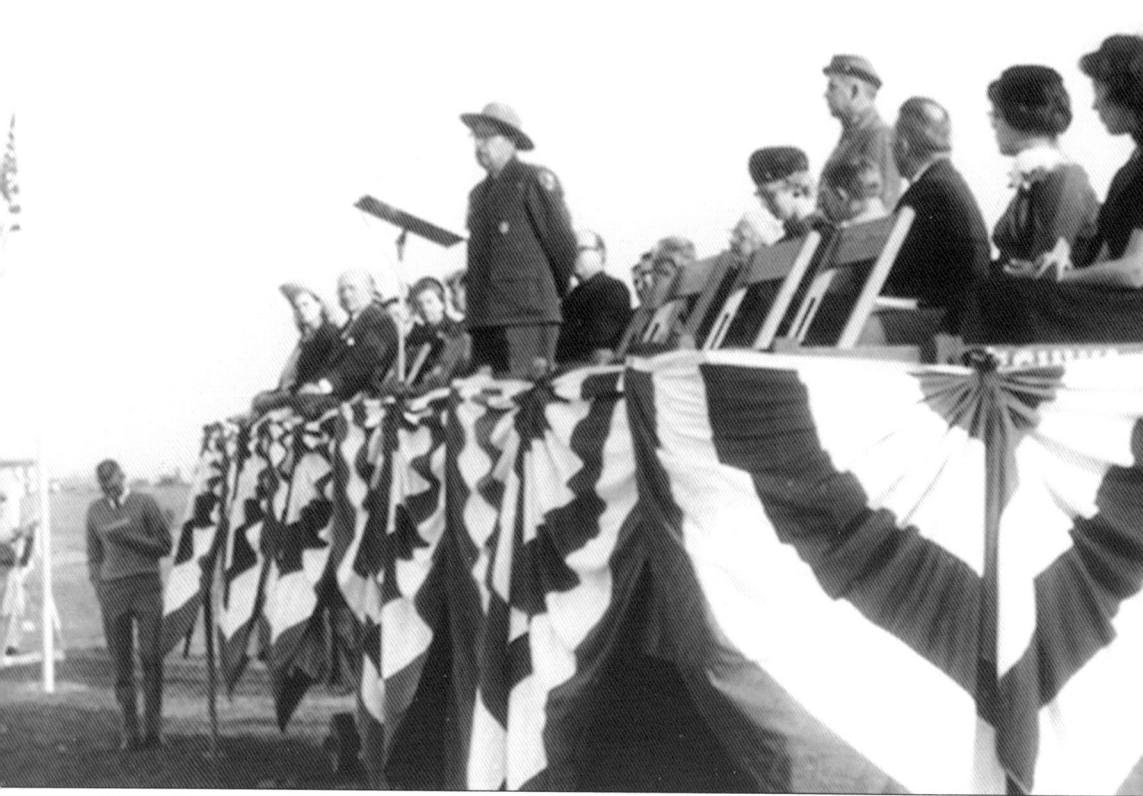

Three Texas regiments fought at the Battle of Antietam, including the 1st Texas Infantry, which lost approximately 82 percent of its men in the action. These Texans were some of the best fighters in the Army of Northern Virginia. On November 11, 1964, the state dedicated a monument to the memory of the Texans who fought around Miller's Cornfield in the morning's battle north of Sharpsburg. Cooper Ragan, a Houston attorney, gave the keynote address. Sharon Keesecker, a South Hagerstown High School student, performed "America, The Beautiful" on a fife recovered from the battlefield. Donna McCauley, 1964's Miss Maryland, unveiled the monument. Here, National Park Service director George Hartzog Jr. accepts the monument on behalf of his agency. The creators of the monument used pink granite, a type of stone native to Texas. The Texas State Capitol in Austin is likewise made from pink granite. (Courtesy of the National Park Service.)

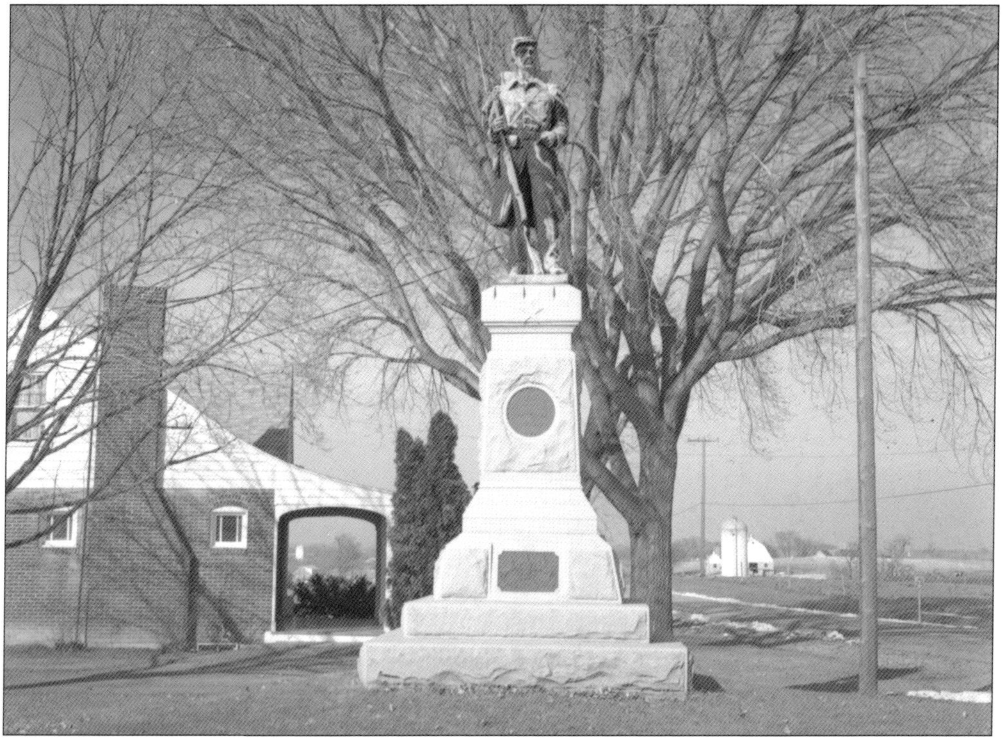

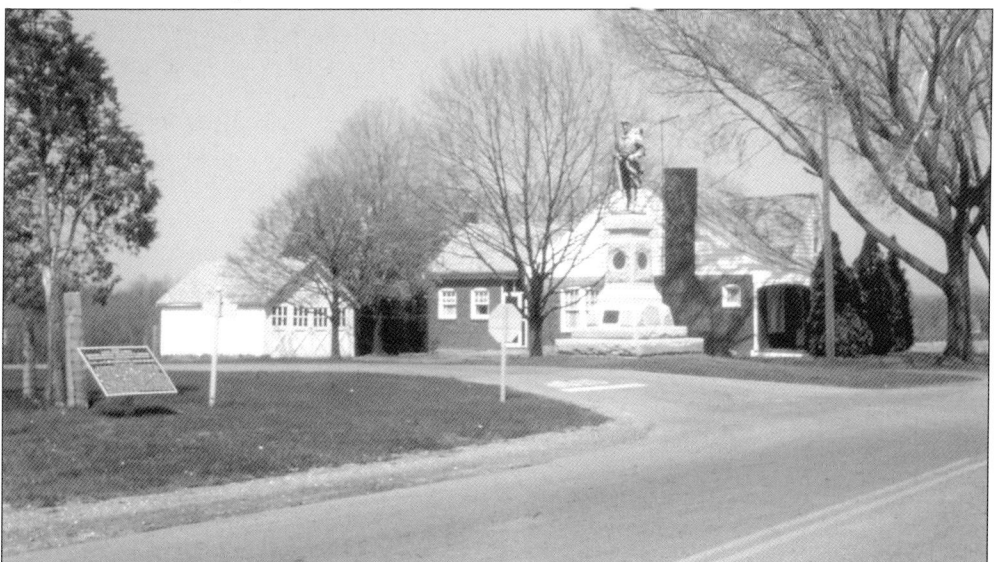

The 124th Pennsylvania was mustered into the US Army one month before their baptism by fire at Antietam. Five men of the regiment were killed, 42 were wounded, and another 17 were declared missing or captured. The regiment's colonel, Joseph Hawley, suffered a wound during the battle but helped unveil the monument at its dedication. Veterans of the 124th Pennsylvania Infantry first attempted to purchase property upon which to erect a monument in 1888. Their bids received no reply. Finally, the veterans succeeded in erecting their monument along Starke Avenue. They dedicated it on September 17, 1904. The chief ranger's house seen in the background no longer stands. (Both, courtesy of the National Park Service.)

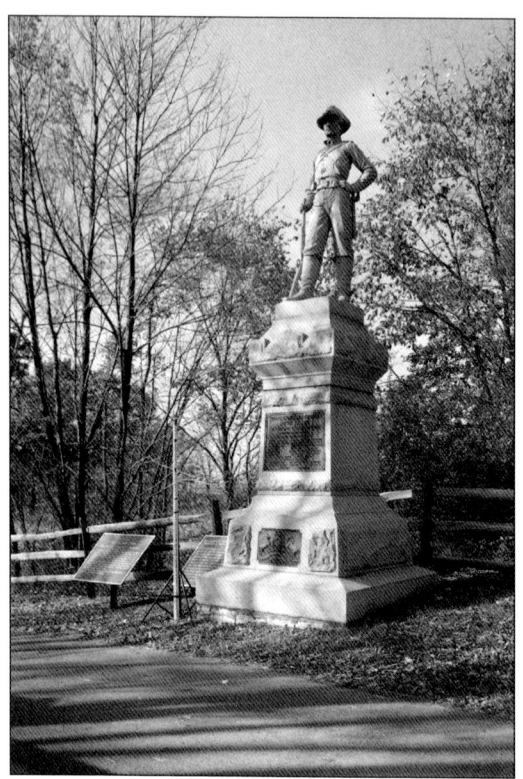

This monument to the 12th Pennsylvania Cavalry is the only one at Antietam depicting a cavalryman. They held a position on the right end of the Federal line. Union cavalry was scattered around the battlefield, though most of it maintained positions in the center of the field. (Courtesy of the Library of Congress.)

The veterans of Durell's Pennsylvania Light Artillery, Independent Battery D erected this monument on Branch Avenue on September 17, 1904. It is the only monument of an artilleryman on the battlefield, this one in his shirt sleeves peering into the sun, tracking the path of a shell. (Courtesy of the Library of Congress.)

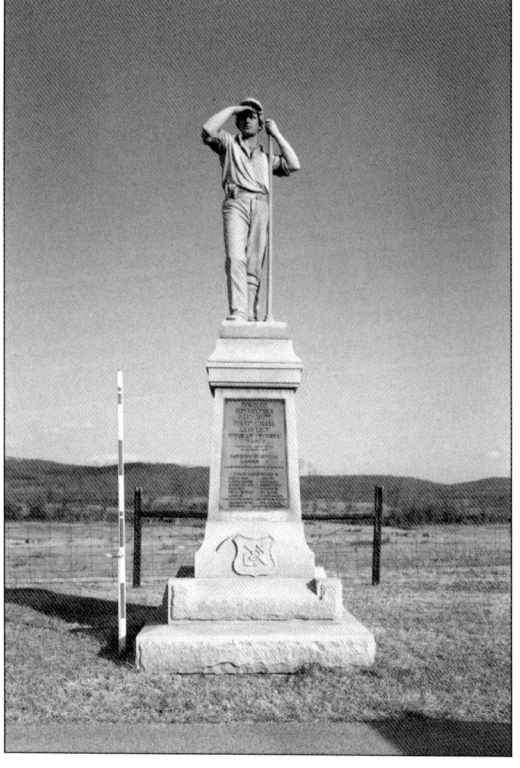

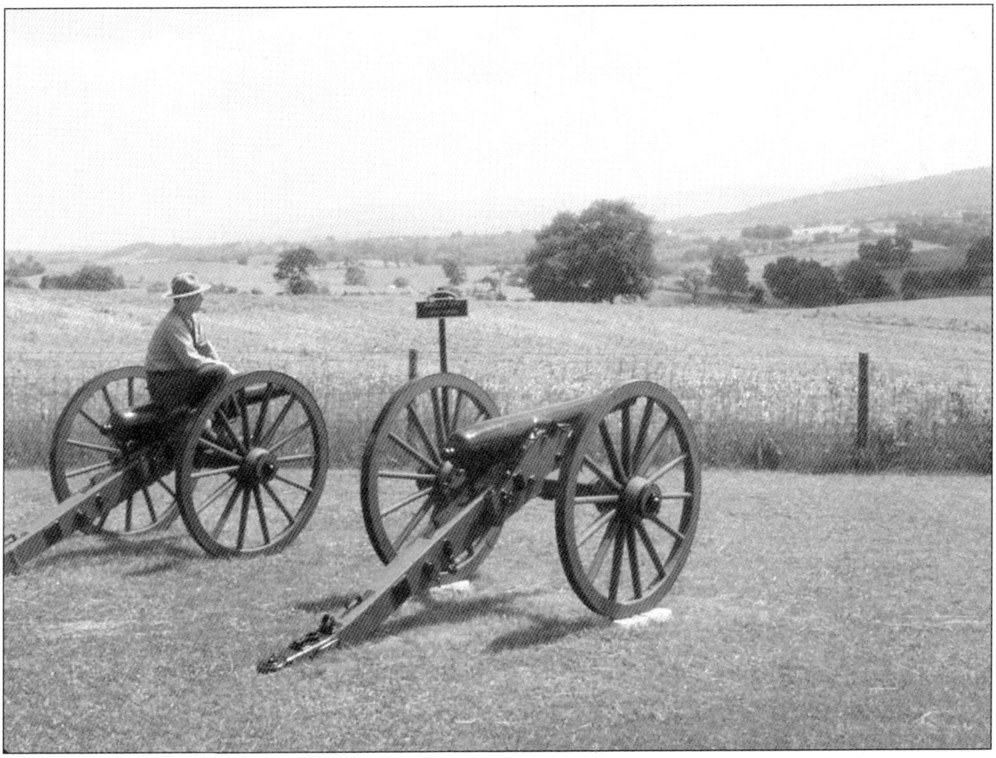

A park ranger sits atop a gun representing Capt. William Pegram's battery. Pegram survived the battle, though a Federal shell exploded nearby, and a piece of shrapnel struck him on the head, injuring him. The battery lost one man killed, 13 wounded, and 10 horses killed at Antietam. (Courtesy of the National Park Service.)

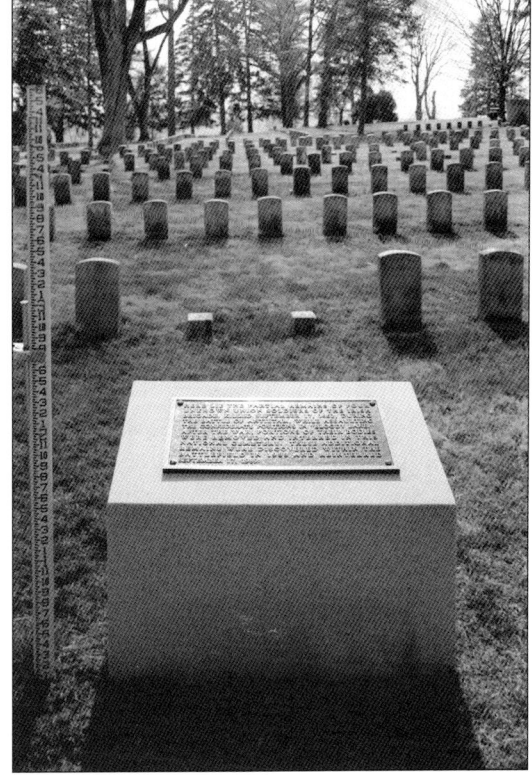

Before the land was owned by the National Park Service, relic hunters near the Sunken Road discovered several sets of remains in 1988 that were deemed to be those of Irish Brigade soldiers. They were reinterred in the National Cemetery under this marker near the New York section. (Courtesy of the Library of Congress.)

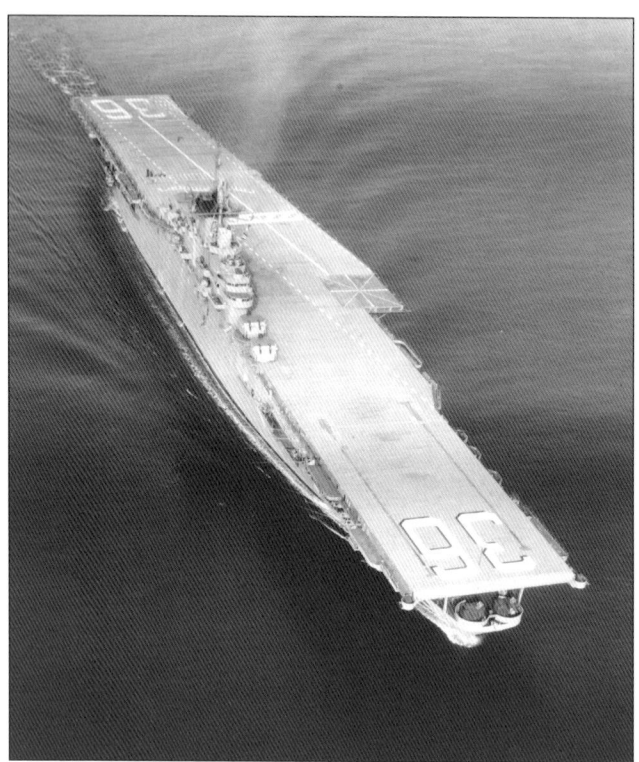

The USS *Antietam* (CV-36, left) was an Essex-class aircraft carrier that served in the US Navy from 1945 to 1949 and again from 1951 to 1963. It barely missed seeing action in the Pacific during World War II but instead served in an occupation role in Japan. The carrier earned two battle stars during the Korean War. The ship was scrapped in 1974. Her bell currently resides in a permanent exhibit outside of the Antietam National Battlefield Visitor Center and was rung during the sesquicentennial commemoration events on September 17, 2012. Below is the guided missile cruiser USS *Antietam* (CG-54), the third and most recent ship to bear the name. (Both, courtesy of the National Archives and Records Administration.)

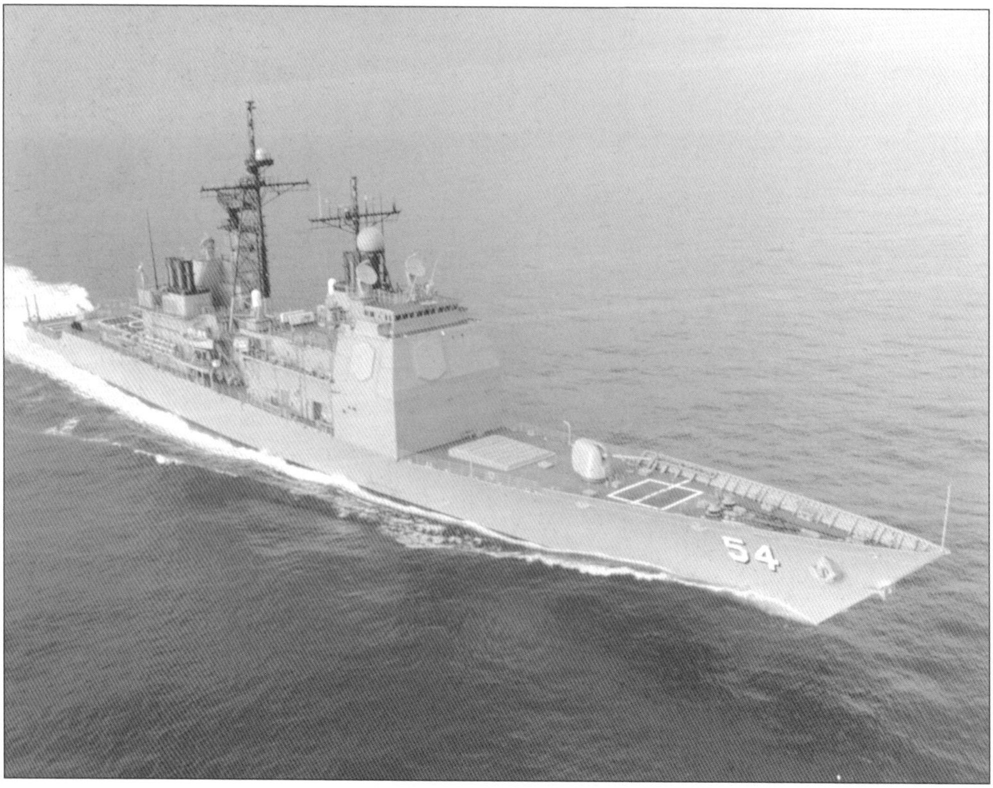

Commissioned in 1987, the USS *Antietam* (CG-54) is still on active service today. Seen within its coat of arms is the famous Burnside Bridge as well as two Parrott cannon tubes crossed at the top. The current USS *Antietam* has served across the world, including in Operation Iraqi Freedom as part of the War on Terror. (Courtesy of the National Archives and Records Administration.)

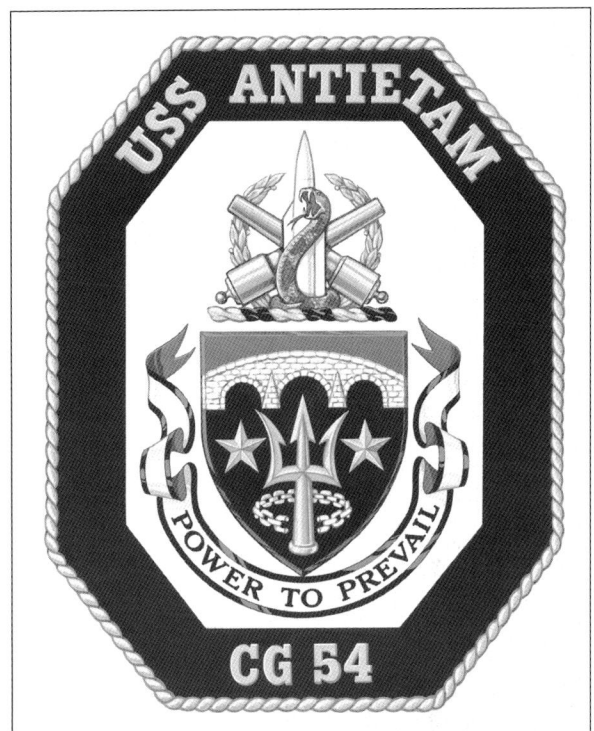

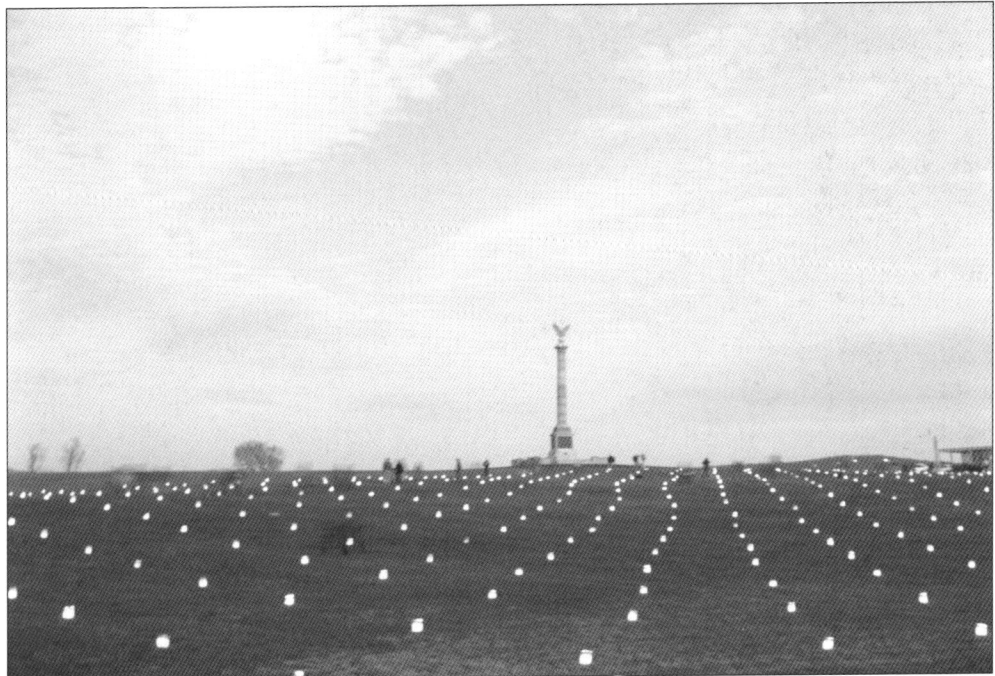

Antietam National Battlefield's annual memorial illumination has been held every December since 1988. Thousands of visitors drive through the battlefield lit by 23,110 candles. Each candle represents a casualty of the battle. It is the largest memorial illumination in North America. (Courtesy of the National Archives and Records Administration.)

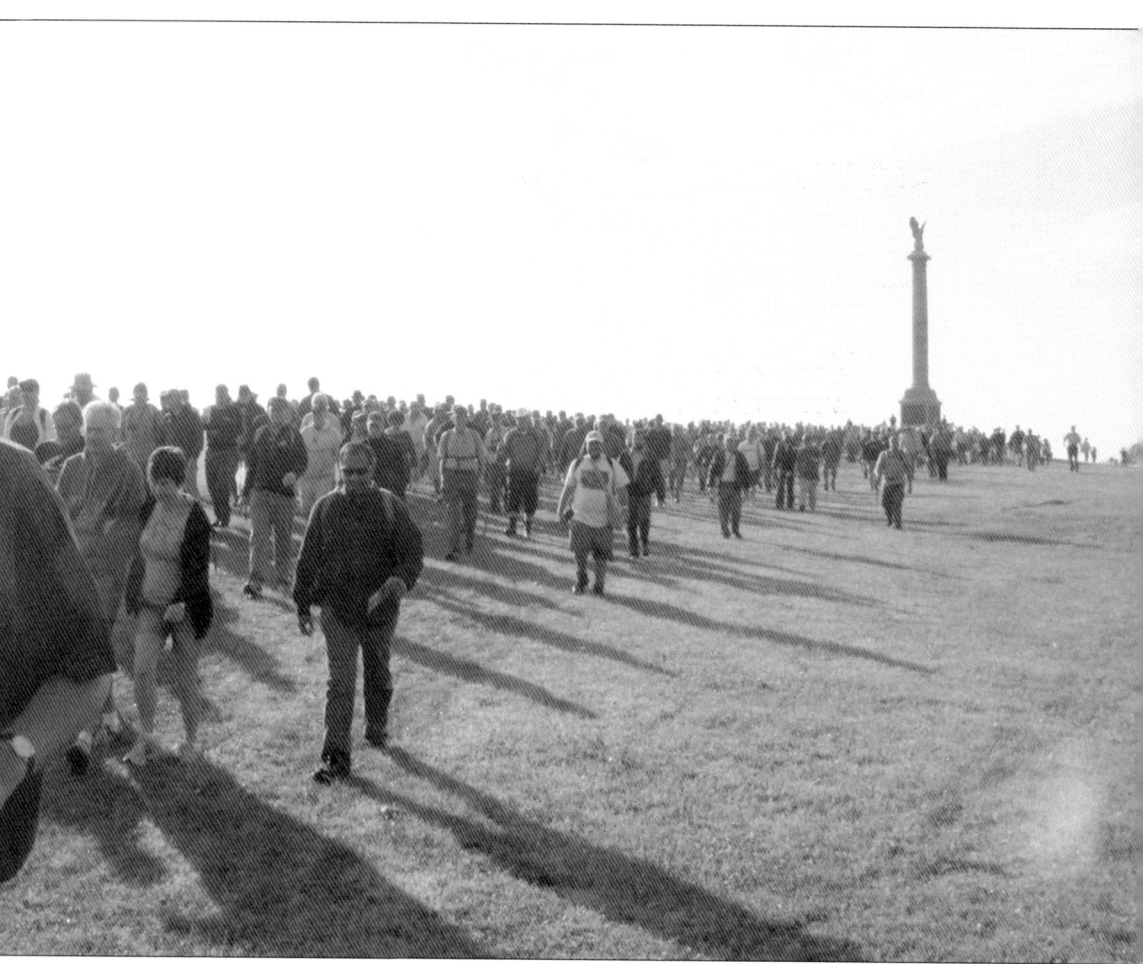

The National Park Service commemorated the 150th anniversary of the Battle of Antietam from September 14–17, 2012, followed by a remembrance program of Abraham Lincoln's announcement of the preliminary Emancipation Proclamation the following weekend. The battlefield, aided by partner organizations, hosted tens of thousands of visitors from across the country during the commemoration. Visitors could enjoy any of the nearly 300 special programs offered during the anniversary, including hikes (such as the all-day September 17 hike seen here), talks, living history programs, a family and youth tent, and more. The commemoration of the battle began with a real-time program in the morning fog at the Cornfield. Other detailed programs continued throughout the day. The park annually attracts about 370,000 visitors, though, for the sesquicentennial month of September 2012, approximately 75,000 people attended just these special events, demonstrating Antietam's continued relevance today. (Author's collection.)

BIBLIOGRAPHY

Adams, Charles S. *The Monuments at Antietam: Sharpsburg's Silent Sentinels.* Shepherdstown, WV: Charles S. Adams, 2000.

Frassanito, William A. *Antietam: The Photographic Legacy of America's Bloodiest Day.* Gettysburg, PA: Thomas Publications, 1978.

Recker, Stephen J. *Rare Images of Antietam and the Photographers Who Took Them.* Sharpsburg, MD: Another Software Miracle LLC, 2012.

Snell, Charles W., and Sharon Brown. *Antietam National Battlefield and National Cemetery: An Administrative History.* Washington, DC: United States Department of the Interior, 1986.

Trail, Susan. "Remembering Antietam: Commemoration and Preservation of a Civil War Battlefield." PhD dissertation, University of Maryland, College Park, 2005.

Discover Thousands of Local History Books Featuring Millions of Vintage Images

Arcadia Publishing, the leading local history publisher in the United States, is committed to making history accessible and meaningful through publishing books that celebrate and preserve the heritage of America's people and places.

Find more books like this at
www.arcadiapublishing.com

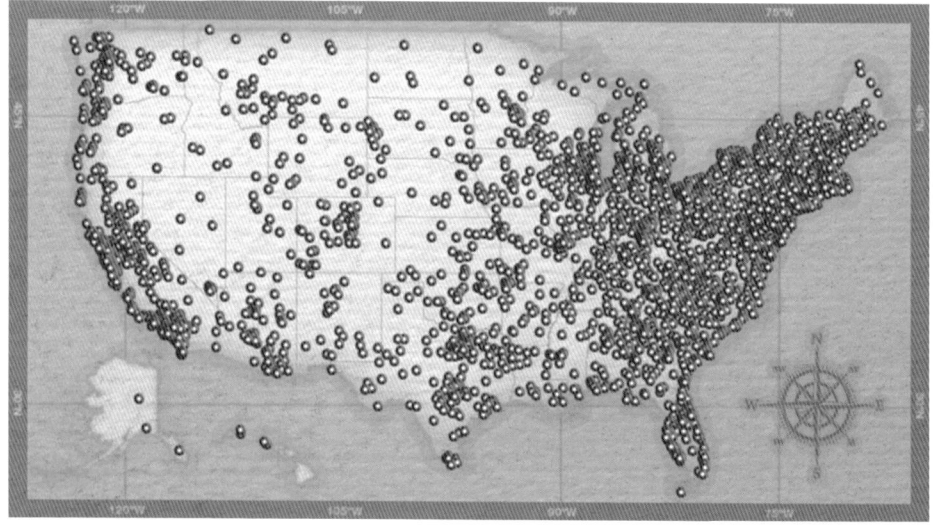

Search for your hometown history, your old stomping grounds, and even your favorite sports team.

Consistent with our mission to preserve history on a local level, this book was printed in South Carolina on American-made paper and manufactured entirely in the United States. Products carrying the accredited Forest Stewardship Council (FSC) label are printed on 100 percent FSC-certified paper.

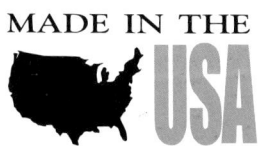